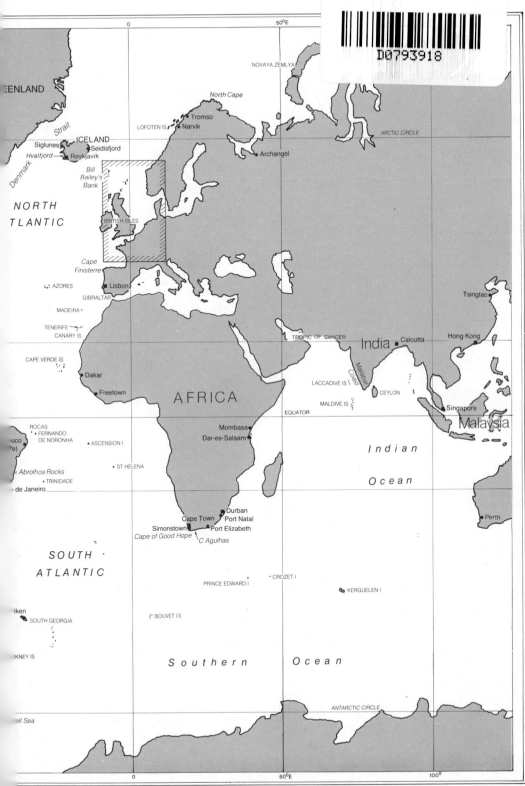

EENLAND

NORTH
ATLANTIC

Denmark Strait

Siglunes
Hvalfjord
ICELAND
Reykjavik
Seidisfjord

Bill
Bailey's
Bank

BRITISH ISLES

Cape
Finisterre

Lisbon
GIBRALTAR

AZORES

MADEIRA

TENERIFE
CANARY IS

CAPE VERDE IS

Dakar

Freetown

AFRICA

ROCAS
FERNANDO
DE NORONHA
uco
e)

Abrolhos Rocks
TRINIDADE
de Janeiro

ASCENSION I

ST HELENA

SOUTH
ATLANTIC

Cape Town
Simonstown
Cape of Good Hope
Durban
Port Natal
Port Elizabeth
C Agulhas

iken
SOUTH GEORGIA

KNEY IS

ell Sea

North Cape

Tromso
LOFOTEN IS
Narvik

Archangel

NOVAYA ZEMLYA

ARCTIC CIRCLE

TROPIC OF CANCER

India
Calcutta

Malabar Coast

LACCADIVE IS

MALDIVE IS

EQUATOR

CEYLON

Mombasa
Dar-es-Salaam

Indian

Ocean

PRINCE EDWARD I

CROZET I

BOUVET IS

KERGUELEN I

Southern   Ocean

ANTARCTIC CIRCLE

Tsingtao

Hong Kong

Singapore
Malaysia

Perth

0   50°E

0   50°E   100°

ARMED MERCHANT CRUISERS

ARMED MERCHANT CRUISERS

Kenneth Poolman

LEO COOPER
in association with
SECKER & WARBURG

First published in Great Britain in 1985 by
Leo Cooper in association with Secker & Warburg Limited,
54 Poland Street, London W1V 3DF

ISBN: 0–436–37706–3

Printed by Redwood Burn Limited,
Trowbridge, Wiltshire

To the memory of my father
Sub-Lieutenant (E) B. Poolman RNR,
late of HM Armed Merchant Cruiser *Salopian*

Contents

Acknowledgements

I wish to thank Mr Geoff Jones for making available to me notes and material on Armed Merchant Cruisers gathered during the writing of his book *Under Three Flags*, and Mr Ludovic Kennedy for permission to use extracts from letters written by his father, Captain Edward Kennedy RN, to his family, previously quoted in Mr Kennedy's book *Sub-Lieutenant*.

I am grateful for help and guidance to: Bibby Bros. Ltd; the Canadian Pacific Company; Cunard Shipping Services Ltd; the Fleet Air Arm Officers' Association; the Furness Withy Group; the Imperial War Museum; the Lamport & Holt Line; *Lloyds' Register* Library; the Mercantile Marine Service Association; the Historical Section and Home Division, Ministry of Defence (Navy); *Navy News*; the Public Records Office; *Sea Breezes* Magazine; T. H. I. Group Services Ltd and the Union Castle Line.

I also wish to thank: Lieutenant-Commander A. G. S. Arnot RN; Mr Brian Barlow; Ms Penelope Bloom; Mr Alan Brown; Mr David Brown; Mr T. D. Bentley; Mr Oscar Baker; Mr W. R. Barlow; Captain A. Beharrel MN; Captain E. D. Brand MN; Mr R. Bruce; Mr C. E. Collyer; Mr T. Davison; Mr J. E. Duckett; Mr Doug Elliott; Mr E. J. K. Gibbs; Mr G. A. Gibson; Mr Bill Haynes;

ACKNOWLEDGEMENTS

Mr A. J. Henderson; Captain H. J. Holdrup MN; Lieutenant H. Howe RN; Mr Rodney James; Lieutenant-Commander W. R. H. Jeffery RD RNR; the late Mrs Rose Kennedy; Mr Ludovic Kennedy; Mrs Anne Lance; Commander J. D. E. Lewis RD RNR; Mr J. E. Lingwood; Mr E. S. Lunnon; Mr Malcolm MacSween; Commander H. D. McMaster OBE RNR; Mr Ray Menadue; Mr George Musk; Mr W. B. Nisbet; Captain H. B. Peate MN; Mr D. W. Pennick; Mr G. W. Penny; Lieutenant-Commander Alistair Peter RD RNR; Mr J. B. Pizer; the late Mr B. Poolman; Mr Richard Pryde; Mr Arthur F. Reed; Mr George Richardson OBE; Mr Ken Sims; Mr S. P. Smith; Mr T. S. Smith; Mr A. N. Williamson.

KENNETH POOLMAN

1 "A magnificent fleet..."

"There is a magnificent fleet of British Merchant Ships, possessing the most valuable elements of warlike efficiency, viz, high speed, coal endurance, strength of structure and seaworthiness."

This glowing testimonial was included in a report which reached the in-trays of selected officers and officials of the British Admiralty on 28 March, 1876.

The report went on: "The introduction of torpedoes into offensive warfare has given, to the weakest of these ships, the power of inflicting swiftly and secretly, fatal blows upon Ships of War, clothed with armour, and defended by powerful guns."

With a growing public and professional unease that the Royal Navy, upon whose ships and shellbacks the Pax Britannica depended, was understrength, particularly in cruisers to police the trade routes of the world, discussion had begun the year before in the Admiralty "as to the desirability of reverting to the former practice in the Navy of partially fitting Mail Steamers for war purposes".

Royal Mail steamers were the obvious first choices for armed merchant cruisers, being Treasury-subsidised already, and the fastest mercantile ships afloat. The committee dusted off a contract of 29 January, 1852, with the African Mail Steam Ship Company for "A sufficient number (not less than three) of good substantial and efficient steam vessels ... fitted with a screw propeller and supplied with first rate appropriate steam engines ... and to be of such construction and strength and her equipments so arranged as to be fit and able to carry and fire such an armament as the Commissioners shall decide to be suitable and requisite." Eight more ships, some iron, some wooden, of the Pacific & Oriental and the Royal West India Mail Packet Companies had also been earmarked in 1852 for possible use, to be equipped to RN standard of armament with 8-inch guns and 32-pounders, but a report compiled by two Royal Navy captains, a colonel of Marines and an assistant master shipwright had found "that they would not make efficient substitutes for regular men of war", but might be suitable "for armed packets and armed troop ships", and a Treasury committee, grumbling about the "enormous cost of the Mail Packet service" and the "prospect of a reserve of ships of war" to be drawn from it, regarded them as not "likely to be of any great service in an engagement".

Even the rampage of the Confederate armed steamer *Alabama* in the American Civil War of 1860–64 does not seem to have disturbed the complacency of the Victorian Naval establishment. This wooden, unarmoured ship had actually been built illegally in England for the tiny Confederate Navy under the nose of the British Government as a "screw despatch vessel". Armed in the Azores, she had done serious damage to Federal US merchant shipping, leading five regular cruisers and the armed liner *Vanderbilt* a two-year dance until sunk by the more heavily armed, armoured regular cruiser USS *Kearsage* right in the English Channel. The two Prussian Naval observers who had joined the *Alabama* at Cape Town took back a detailed report to Bismarck.

By 1875 all references to the armament or fitness for war service of Royal Mail packets had disappeared from British shipping contracts. All that remained, in contracts with four companies, was a clause allowing the Admiralty to charter ships in cases of "great public emergency".

The 1875 Director of Naval Construction, Mr Barnaby, at first thought that, "As the modern Mail Steamer is so strongly built structurally as to be capable of receiving an armament upon its decks without distress, it might be found possible to regard it as an auxiliary to the unarmoured fleet."

But on detailed study of plans and drawings, and on inspection of the vessels, he became "afraid it would not be wise to employ such ships as men-of-war".

These ships lacked the extra protection of even "unarmoured" warships, which had thick wooden planking over their iron skins. Their engines rose too high above the waterline and would be very vulnerable to shellfire.

These weaknesses could be expected, of course. No merchant ship was in any way strengthened for war. She was built to carry as much freight or as many passengers as fast or as far as possible. But further examination revealed a common feature which, even in merchant ships, was positively scandalous. Drawing after drawing showed no proper subdivision into compartments in the hull, and even such divisional bulkheads as did exist were not carried up high enough for safety. Too many hulls were virtually nothing more than one vast hold – frail, unstiffened shells which any small rock or pinnacle of ice, let alone an armour-piercing projectile, could rip apart in seconds, and in this event narrowness of beam, incorporated for speed, would increase instability. These were simply unsound, unsafe ships for any purpose.

High speed and good coal endurance could make some of the more properly constructed ships useful, perhaps, to carry mails, war cargoes and military passengers, with "light swivel guns" for defensive purposes only, but not as warships.

To the compilers of the 1876 report DNC's views appeared over-cautious.

The vulnerability of propulsion machinery located above the waterline could be overcome "by the erection of solid screens of iron, of fuel, or of stores between decks".

The shoddy hulls were more serious. The committee allowed that their "swift and strong Merchant Ships are very frequently so imperfectly divided by bulkheads that a single shot-hole under water in any one compartment between the foremost collision bulkhead and the stern bulkhead would, in most cases, cause the ship to founder." Such a ship could only be improved by "the employment of a considerable number of men for some weeks" to strengthen existing bulkheads and fit new ones. They expressed the hope that by calling attention to these weaknesses owners who had been so careless of safety might be persuaded to demand changes in construction. This would reduce profits initially but would lower insurance rates, and they would receive an annual Government subsidy.

However, an efficient subdivision into compartments did exist in some ships, and it was decided that those approaching closest to Admiralty standards would be taken over first, the main requirements being that they should be "capable of steaming for at least twelve hours at not less than $11\frac{3}{4}$, say 12, knots" and be "so divided by bulkheads that with a hole of any size, in any one compartment, they should continue to float in smooth water."

This debate on the best formula for an auxiliary cruiser was basic and fundamental to the establishment of the breed in steamships. The ideal cruiser was the custom-built regular version, but even Victorian capitalism could not afford to maintain a permanent force big enough to cover all commitments immediately on the outbreak of a major war. It was thought that armed merchantmen could not be stiffened sufficiently to carry heavy guns, or armoured for proper protection in the short time which would be available for the work. Besides, armour plate would reduce their main asset, which was speed, linked with as powerful an armament as their decks could bear. A slow auxiliary cruiser was next to useless. As a raider she could not catch fast enemy merchantmen or auxiliary cruisers, and could neither fight nor elude an enemy regular cruiser. Of course, for the protection of Empire trade, range could not be sacrificed to high speed, and fast liners gobbled coal. Even the best auxiliary cruiser would always be a makeshift.

The merchant cruiser lobby in the Admiralty had its way. On 20 May, 1878, a list of thirty-six steamers reserved for use as auxiliary cruisers in the event of war was circulated.

Money had also been allocated in the 1877/78 Naval Estimates for a practical experiment. The Admiralty bought the SS *British Crown*, a sail/screw merchantman of 6,400 tons, length 391½ feet, beam 39 feet, with a top speed of 12 knots. At Harland & Wolff's Yard in Belfast she was equipped with five muzzle-loading guns 3 or 3½ tons in weight and firing a 64-pound shell, and one newer breech-loading 40-pounder, located so as to give either broadside or bow and stern fire. Captain Singer RN commissioned her on 7

March, 1878, as HMS *Hecla*, the first British armed merchant steamer to go to sea as an auxiliary cruiser.

Identical batteries were set aside for the other ships, most of them in the Atlantic trade, on the auxiliary cruiser list, together with magazines, at Portsmouth, Chatham, Sheerness and Devonport.

"My object," announced the Director of Naval Transport, "is to secure a certain number of fast Cruisers which would be capable of meeting and of disposing of similar vessels equipped by the enemy in order to prey on our commerce, and there is some evidence that this would be attempted."

"The enemy" was most likely to be Imperialist Russia, with her large fleet, or one of her allies—Austria or Bismarck's Prussia. In fact HMS *Hecla* just missed a possible real trial by war. Russia had declared war on Turkey in April, 1877, ostensibly to protect Turkish Christians from persecution, and had swept through the Balkans until, in January, 1878, their armies reached Constantinople. A British fleet steamed through the Dardanelles and the Sea of Marmora to the Bosphorus; at home Army reserves were called up, and Indian troops were moved to the Mediterranean. But some complicated horse trading at the Congress of Berlin in June brought what Disraeli called a "peace with honour" between the major powers.

The new auxiliary cruiser had to make do with a practice cruise. On 6 December Captain Singer, helped by Admiral Boys, who had also been on board, drew up a report on the operation of his battery. "The strength and convenience of these guns," he said, "were thoroughly tested by firing a large number of rounds from each gun, under various conditions of service, and the results were very satisfactory, as the fittings did not complain in the slightest degree, and every duty connected with the working of the guns was readily performed.

"Taking into consideration the duties which armed merchant steamers would be required to perform, and the character of the crew with which they would probably be manned, I am of the opinion that the nature of the armament of this ship ... is well adapted for that class of vessel; the guns, being light and powerful, and mounted in an effective and, at the same time in a very simple manner, do not require highly trained men for their efficient working."

As a result of the *Hecla* trials, twenty-four complete sets of armament similar to hers, each including seventy rifles and ten revolvers for boarding, were sent to foreign stations for local fitting to merchant ships on the ocean trade routes.

By August, 1881, there were no fewer than 207 ships on the Admiralty auxiliary cruiser list, and another seventy on the stocks, twenty-four of the latter designed for top speeds of 14–17½ knots. Nearly all these ships were of the conventional single-screw type, but there was one twin-screw 4,000-tonner, and two more building. Twin screws were now preferred for more agile manoeuvering and for making way with one engine disabled. All first class ships in build complied with Admiralty design requirements. More bulkheads were fitted, and beam was increased for greater stability. There was a total of 120 of the 64-pounder guns approved for armed merchantmen in readiness, and armament sets were being prepared for every fast, 17-knot ship coming on to the Admiralty list. Wartime crews would be drawn from the Royal Naval Reserve or the Colonial Naval Reserve. The ideal auxiliary cruiser was now a moderate-sized ship like the new 15-knot Union vessel, 360 feet in length, or the new Castle boat, 420 feet long, top speed 16–17 knots.

The *Hecla* was retained on strength, and in 1883 Captain A. K. Wilson took her to sea.

Tug Wilson did not like the ship's armament at all. To begin with, there was too wide a variety of guns. The four broadside 64-pounder muzzle-loaders used 8-pound charges, the poop gun a 10-pound charge, and the bow gun was a 40-pounder breech-loader. This meant that there were three different kinds of ammunition for just six guns, which could mean confusion in battle and in supply.

And they were all too light, especially the bow and stern guns. Armed merchant cruisers were not expected to lie in line of battle. Most of their fighting was likely to be while chasing or being chased by their own kind or by weaker types of unarmoured men-of-war, and their fore and aft guns were therefore of primary importance. The *Hecla*'s 64-pounders weighed from 3 to 3½ tons, but Wilson thought that auxiliary cruisers could comfortably carry 12-ton, 9-inch calibre guns, though with the existing slides nothing heavier than a 7-inch, 6½-tonner was feasible – "a poor makeshift". Wilson had been very impressed with the way in which the little *Angamos* had used an 11½-ton gun effectively in the Chile-Peruvian war. The gun had been fitted before the mainmast, but large British merchantmen were quite strong enough to carry "many times that weight on their bows and sterns. It is with them only a question of strengthening the deck." With 12-ton guns at her extremities an auxiliary cruiser would be more powerful in the chase than all but a 1st Class regular cruiser, and an enemy's merchantmen would find it difficult to defend their engines against them. Coal armour could protect against 64-pounders, even 7-inch, but not against 9-inch 12-tonners – and there would be plenty of these guns available as regular men-of-war were rearmed with new breech-loaders.

About the only things Wilson liked about the *Hecla*'s armament were the six 1-inch calibre Nordenfelt quick-firing cannon she now carried. These could keep an enemy's small arms fire down and hit his crew within 1,000 yards range, while the 12-tonners destroyed his machinery. Of course, a larger calibre would be even better – something which could punch holes at a fast rate in a ship's side – and there should be more of them, say a dozen per ship. Broadside guns could then be dispensed with, except in large liners, where space might allow the luxury of some 7-inch on the main deck.

As for the ship's Whitehead torpedo armament, which it had been hoped would give the weak auxiliary cruisers "the power of inflicting swiftly and secretly fatal blows upon Ships of War clothed with armour," it was too elaborate, with its tubes, portable engine, pumps and reservoirs, for swift fitting in ordinary merchant ships. A revised version should be developed so that all that was needed before fitting was to cut holes in a ship's side.

With her large coal capacity, the *Hecla* could keep the sea for three months, but the capability to maintain a long chase at extended range would not mean much if she ran out of ammunition trying for a lucky shot. The ship had been given a portable magazine, which seemed like a good idea as it was comparatively easy to deliver and quick to fit. This was big enough to contain the eighty rounds per gun which *Hecla* had been allocated, but this amount could easily be used up in a three-hour action. Wilson wanted at least six times as much in the ship, and for that amount the portable magazine would not be large enough. He suggested dividing off one of the holds by wooden bulkheads for proper magazines and shell rooms.

He evaluated the ship as suitable for a "torpedo depot" to be attached to the Fleet, dependent on its ironclads for protection, but "did not look on her as in any way a satisfactory example of an armed cruiser".

He also proposed that annually a ship from the auxiliary cruiser list be armed and exercised, coupled with use as a transport, selected from a different shipping line each time and with a different crew, to build up a pool of experience in the operating of merchant cruisers.

Wilson's criticisms and recommendations made unwelcome waves in the Admiralty. The Director of Naval Ordnance said that 12-ton guns at bow and stern, with the extra stiffening, would add too much weight, and Admiral Sir A. C. Kay thought that the fitting would take too long. Wilson's suggestion for *Hecla*'s change of role was, however, taken up, and she became a depot ship.*

His other recommendations were not implemented. Two years later, in March, 1885, there was another war scare. Russia, taking advantage of Britain's preoccupation with the Sudan, where General Gordon had been killed in January, activated her constant threat to India by invading Afghanistan in force.

The Admiralty chartered the Cunard liners *Oregon* and *Umbria* for six months as auxiliary cruisers, and bespoke the services of their *Etruria, Umbria*'s sister ship, if required.

The *Oregon* was well known on the North Atlantic run, and had regained the Blue Riband for Cunard in the previous June by crossing to New York in six days, nine hours and forty-eight minutes. An iron ship, propelled by screw and sail, she had been built by John Elder & Company of Fairfield on the Clyde for the Guion Line, but had been bought by Cunard after she had shown her paces at sea. Of 7,375 tons, 501 feet in length and a comfortable fifty-four feet in the beam, she had been equipped with compound, direct-acting, inverted steam engines which developed 13,500 indicated horsepower, giving a fast maximum speed of 18 knots.

The *Umbria* (8,128 tons) and *Etruria* (8,120 tons) were updated

---

* She had a long life. She was rebuilt in 1912 as a 5,600-ton ship with an armament of four 4-inch guns, and sold in 1926.

copies in steel of the *Oregon*, ordered from the same builder, 501 feet long, slightly broader in the beam. Their sweating firemen shovelled 320 tons of coal a day into the furnaces of nine boilers, which generated steam for their triple, three-crank compound engines to drive them at 18½ knots via a single screw, and their three steel masts were fully barque-rigged in the Cunard style, with an extensive spread of canvas.

As luxury passenger liners these ships were very popular, with spacious decks, saloons and staterooms well lit and ventilated, and they had both been built on Admiralty guidelines for auxiliary cruisers. There were ten watertight compartments, with most of the bulkheads carried up to the upper deck and fitted with waterproof/fireproof doors with access to all parts of the ship. The latest steam steering gear was fitted, and powerful backup hand steering gear with three steering wheels in the after wheelhouse – a feature which could be vital in battle, as later merchant cruisers were to find. There were powerful steam windlasses under the long turtleback which covered the wheelhouse and sick bays, with a big capstan on the foc'sle for working anchors and manoeuvering the ship in harbour. Five big steam winches were fitted at the hatchways, with strong derricks on the masts for prompt handling of cargo and the shipping of guns and war stores.

The *Oregon* and *Umbria* were specially strengthened, equipped with 5-inch guns and completely fitted up under the supervision of Admiralty officers, but Wilson's recommendations for the annual training of ships and crews had not been taken aboard. Lack of experience in rapid fitting out, and uncertainty over equipment, caused long delays, and the *Oregon* was the only auxiliary cruiser ready to sail before the emergency was over, when the Tsar accepted arbitration on the disputed frontiers.

In July the *Oregon* was chosen to accompany Admiral Sir Geoffrey Hornby's Evolutionary Squadron. As the only auxiliary cruiser with the Fleet she attracted the attention of the Squadron's officers. Hornby thought she would be "invaluable in time of war ... And not only as a scout to accompany a fleet, but as an independent cruiser, or armed transport ... for she is as remarkable for her economy in fuel when steaming under 11 knots per hour, as for her wonderful speed when driven at full power." The *Oregon* could steam at 7.5 knots for 107 days, or at 10 knots for

54½ days, and reached 18 knots at full revs. The only criticism was that her size made her a rather big target.

Influential brass hats like Admiral Sir Edward Seymour and Vice-Admiral Fitzgerald went for a cruise in her and watched her fire her guns frequently "without any indication of strain on the structure of the vessel," as Fitzgerald said later in committee. "Although not required for the purposes for which they were chartered," Hornby reported, "the opinion has been generally expressed by competent authorities that if occasion had arisen to tell their capabilities, the *Umbria* and *Oregon* would have shown themselves to be powerful auxiliaries to our ironclad navy."

Following this encouraging example, an agreement was signed in the following year, 1886, which gave the Admiralty an option for five years on the use of Cunard's five fastest ships as auxiliary cruisers, with a total subsidy of approximately £20,000 per ship being paid annually for *Umbria*, *Etruria* and *Aurania* as part of the deal. Half of each crew were to be Royal Naval Reservists. Platforms for four guns were to be fitted on poop and foc'sle right away. The owners were to store and maintain mountings for these and eight other guns per ship, and to guarantee to fit them out as auxiliary cruisers in one week at short notice. *Servia* (7,392 tons) and *Gallia* (4,809 tons) were the other Cunard ships, and White Star's *Adriatic*, *Britannic*, *Celtic* and *Germanic* were also reserved.

In 1888 ten ships of the P & O Line, four of the Inman Company's new "City" liners and White Star's new *Majestic* (9,820 tons) and her sister *Teutonic*, among others, were added, making a total of twenty-seven ships on the AMC list, drawn from eight different lines. The newer ships were allocated new 4.7-inch quick-firers and the 1-inch, four-barrelled Nordenfelt machine-cannon which Wilson of the *Hecla* had liked so much. Other ships would have to make do with the older 5-inch.

The addition to the auxiliary register of these fast ships was part of a wind of change which produced the Naval Defence Act of 1889, sweeping away the Royal Navy's collection of obsolete warships, built in twos and threes and mainly experimental, and replacing them with more definitely defined categories of ships, a new armada of battleships, protected cruisers, light cruisers and torpedo boats.

In the Spanish-American War of 1898 the liners *St Louis*, *St*

Paul, New York and *Paris* were taken up as auxiliary cruisers by the United States Navy, each fitted with four 5-inch QFs and eight 6-pounders, and topped up with 4,457 tons of coal, 2,000 tons above normal bunkering, permitting them sixty-eight days' steaming at 10 knots. Manoeuvering together as a squadron, they could go to 20 knots in twelve minutes.

In 1902 the German Norddeutscher-Lloyd Company launched the 19,360-ton *Kaiser Wilhelm II*, designed to carry guns in wartime at a top speed of 24 knots. The *Deutschland, Kronprinz Wilhelm* and *Kaiser Wilhelm der Grosse* had also been stiffened, and were only a fraction of a knot slower. There were thirty-five other German merchantmen known to have been earmarked for war service as cruisers. Some of these, like the Hamburg-Amerika Line's 6,000-ton *Prinz Adalbert* and *Prinz Oskar*, were only 12½-knot ships, but with a good radius of action.

None of the British subsidised ships could match the fast Germans for speed, and many of them were now effectively owned by foreign companies.

My Lords decided that in future only the fastest ships would do for auxiliary cruisers, and that these ships must at all costs remain under the Red Ensign. The costs would be high.

If the *Kaiser Wilhelm* could make 24 knots, her British counterpart must achieve 25–26. The *Lucania*, the fastest British stiffened liner, had made 22 knots on 25,500 horsepower, and had cost £470,000. The extra knots would demand another 40,000 horsepower, and add some £750,000 to the building cost of a ship which would probably lose money. The fast German Atlantic liners, unsubsidized by their government, were uneconomical to run, but these losses were made up from the big emigration and freight business and the unspectacular but lucrative runs to the West Indies, South America and the Far East.

The British Government made a loan to Cunard of £2,400,000 at 2¾% interest to provide two new 25 – 26-knot liners, ultimately to be the RMS *Lusitania* and *Mauretania*, stiffened to carry 6-inch guns, with an annual operating subsidy of £75,000 per ship in addition to a Royal Mail subsidy. Security for the loan included Cunard's whole fleet, which was to be held at the disposal of the Government. Cunard was one of the very few British trans-Atlantic lines which had not joined the American financier John

Pierpont Morgan's International Mercantile Marine cartel, and by the terms of the new loan they were also bound never to allow either the management or the shares of the Company to fall into foreign hands. The British Government stopped the transfer of any of the cartel's newly acquired ships from British registry, and proposed blocking future transfer of flags by owning not less than 33/64ths of any subsidized ship.

Launched on 7 June, 1906, the *Lusitania* went into service in September, 1907, and immediately recaptured the Blue Riband from Germany with a speed of 25.88 knots. Two months later the *Mauretania* sailed on her maiden voyage to New York and recorded 26 knots. *Lusitania* had only another eight years of life, but her sister was to hold on to the Riband for twenty-two of the twenty-eight years of her service.

2 Rendezvous at Trinidade

On 28 July, 1914, Winston Churchill, the young First Lord of the Admiralty, warned the Superintendent of Contract Work to make preliminary arrangements for fitting out the new Cunard Liner *Aquitania* at Liverpool as an auxiliary cruiser.

She and the *Mauretania* and *Lusitania* were to be taken up immediately if war broke out. There was a "short list" of fifteen 19-knot ships, with two 22½-knotters and two 20-knotters building, and forty-five other possibles of various, ages, ranges and speeds plying their trade in different parts of the world.

On 31 July secret advance notices were sent to various ship-owners that certain ships from the Armed Merchant Cruiser register might be required for war service.

The Admiralty feared that roving German cruisers, including auxiliaries, would do great damage to the British Merchant Marine on the outbreak of war, and there were plans to arm a first batch of a dozen fast British liners, give them the simplest modifications necessary to make them fit to fight, and get them to sea as soon as possible.

On 1 August work on the *Aquitania* was begun, and the first of her twelve 6-inch guns were taken out of storage. Cunard's *Caronia* was also taken up at Liverpool, the P & O's *Macedonia* and *Marmora* at Tilbury, and next day the White Star *Olympic*, the Cunard *Mauretania* and *Lusitania*, followed two days later by the *Carmania* (Cunard) *Kinfauns Castle* (Union Castle) *Empress of Britain* (Canadian Pacific), *Alsatian* and *Victorian* (Allan Line), *Otranto* (Orient) and *Mantua* (P & O).

The *Aquitania, Lusitania* and *Mauretania* had been fitted with stiffening and packing rings for their guns during their original construction. In the others, positions for guns, magazines and other equipment had been previously selected and recorded in books of instructions for fitting out. Gun mountings were fitted on teak beds covered by steel plates; protection for engines, boilers and steering gear was improvised with roughly secured steel plates and by coal.

In the Orient Line's *Otranto* the owners did the work at Tilbury. Decks under the gun platforms were strengthened and shored up, packing rings were fitted, and the guns themselves secured in place – eight 4.7s, four with shields, four older ones without. Bollards and fairleads were cut away to give a good arc of fire. A rangefinder was fitted on the bridge, magazines and shell rooms built in the fore and aft holds, with flooding arrangements. Steel plate half an inch thick was installed round the steering engine house, bagged coal was stowed abreast the engine cylinder tops. Cabin bulkheads, glass ventilators and furniture were removed to make space for messdecks, a large sick bay with cots was fitted up in the old smoking room, and an operating theatre set up amidships, the most stable part of the ship at sea. The work was begun on 4 August and finished in nine days.

The 19,524-ton Cunard turbine liner *Carmania*, in service since 1905, was three days out of New York on the night of 5 August with eight hundred passengers for Liverpool and ten million dollars' worth of bullion in her strongroom, when the blacked-out shape of the light cruiser HMS *Bristol* came up out of the darkness and flashed,

"War is declared. Darken ship. Maintain wireless silence."

Captain James Barr, known as "Smokey" because he was always complaining about soot from the funnels, though it could have been "Shorty" because he was only five foot four, went below to his safe and opened sealed orders which instructed him to make all speed for home and hand his ship over to the Navy.

At Liverpool landing stage, where the *Carmania* arrived at 8 am on 7 August, the Navy was waiting in the person of Captain Noel Grant RN. Grant, aged forty-five, had worked his way up from boy seaman. A rather cold and humourless man, he was an expert navigator and a thorough professional, like Smokey Barr, but he had just come from a sanatorium in the Alps and was suffering from advanced tuberculosis, which the Navy preferred to call asthma so that it would not be liable for paid leave to the sufferer. With him he brought the offer of Royal Naval Reserve Commander's rank for Jim Barr, provided the latter agreed to serve under him as his navigator and "adviser". Barr swallowed his pride and instant dislike, and accepted, mainly because he felt he could not trust his tricky old ship to Grant, who, he discovered from the Navy List, had never commanded anything really comparable in size to the *Carmania*, unless you counted his few weeks in the old battleship *Irresistible* just before he was invalided ashore.

With Grant, as his First Lieutenant and Gunnery Officer, came Eric Lockyer, a retired RN lieutenant-commander of nearly seventy. *Carmania*'s Chief Officer Murchie was also to remain aboard, as Lieutenant RNR, because of his special knowledge of the ship, as were Surgeon Maynard, the Chief Steward, about fifty Cunard ratings as cooks, stewards and officers' servants, and the carpenter, who was retained as a Chief Petty Officer and given six CPO mates, including cooper, blacksmith, plumber and painter. All the Cunard engine room staff agreed to stay in the ship and were specially enrolled for six months in the RNR.

First and Second Class passengers were hurried ashore, while police checked the Third Class passengers carefully for Germans. *Carmania* left the landing stage at noon and immediately docked at Sandon, where the underprivileged Third Class passengers landed, after further officious delays. The *Caronia* was fitting out in *Carmania*'s proper berth. When completed, *Carmania* and *Caronia* had been called "the pretty sisters", and they were identical except that *Carmania* had been given the new turbines, *Caronia* conventional steam engines. After one season on the Atlantic run it had been calculated that *Carmania* could produce one more knot for the same coal consumption. *Caronia* and the almost completed *Aquitania* were using all the available manpower, so *Carmania* could not discharge her cargo or bunker right away. But the painters had finished with the two other AMCs and were switched to the *Carmania*, to cover her familiar red and black funnels and her black hull and white upperworks with battleship grey.

The *Aquitania* sailed on North Atlantic patrol next day, Saturday, 8 August, and Captain Shirley-Litchfield RN commissioned the *Caronia*. A gang of shipwrights started to cut away *Carmania*'s bulwarks fore and aft on B Deck, to allow for the training of the guns. Cunard stewards began to clear out the passenger accommodation, joiners stripped out woodwork. On Sunday the ship's new midshipmen arrived.

On Monday, 10 August the *Caronia* sailed for duty in the North Atlantic, based on Halifax, Nova Scotia, and *Carmania* took her berth, discharged her cargo and took on coal.

Steel plating, bags of coal or sand were positioned to cover vulnerable machinery, two holds were fitted with platforms, and wooden magazines were built on them. Eight 4.7-inch guns, with a maximum range of 9,300 yards, were fitted, two in the bows and two in the stern, to port and starboard, and two on either side of the upper deck. A six-foot Barr & Stroud rangefinder, two semaphore machines and two searchlights were mounted on slightly raised platforms in the wings of the bridge.

By Wednesday, 12 August all bunkers were full, and Captain Grant went off to London to get married. At 5 a.m. next morning a mixed party of Fleet Reserve seamen, mainly fishermen from the Scottish herring fleets, and Royal Marine gunners arrived from Portsmouth.

On Thursday, 14 August, just one week after entering harbour as an Atlantic luxury liner, RMS had become HMS, the *Carmania* an armed merchant cruiser of the Royal Navy. Grant was away on his very brief honeymoon, which was probably just as well, as Barr, who knew how ornery the ship could be to handle in a confined waterway, with her three screws, two turning one way, one the other, had the tricky job of easing her out of her berth and into the Mersey, where he anchored and waited for the bridegroom to return. Grant rejoined later in the day, and the *Carmania* sailed on the morning tide.

In crossing the Atlantic one way the ship normally burned about ninety percent of her coal, and with her high freeboard it would be impossible to refuel from a collier at sea. *Carmania* was at first employed in home waters within comparatively easy range of port, to patrol an area of a hundred square miles across the main east-west Atlantic shipping lanes to the north-west of Ireland, watching for enemy warships breaking out into the wide ocean, or merchant-men, German or neutral, heading for Europe.

Shakedown troubles were to be expected with a mishmash of Merchant and Royal Navy men, Scottish fishermen and Marines. The Scots, used to small sailing smacks, were uncomfortable in a big liner, and resented Naval discipline, but they made first-class boats' crews. The Marines were the men who would fight the guns in battle, and looked down on mere seamen. But under Barr's influence the bootnecks took their turn in the boats, the seamen at the guns and in ammunition supply parties, and the mixture began to smooth out.

Lockyer had his problems too. Standing at his rangefinder high on the bridge, the wind drowned his orders, which were by word of mouth via a human chain to the guns or through field telephones, one to each pair of 4.7s. An order to fire a broadside issued at one point in a roll by the ship, for example, would not be carried out until she was at quite the wrong angle for accuracy. He worked out that if he gave an order when the ship was on an even keel, there was a fair chance of it being carried out the *next* time she was straight and upright.

Carmania had been fitted out in such a hurry that there had been no time to convert to Navy victualling, and Cunard had replenished the ship's pantries and wine cellar as for a normal peacetime Atlantic voyage. There was little or no rum, but the Scottish traw-lermen were delighted to be given the alternative of fine Scottish malt whisky. There was Scotch salmon, best beef, Dover sole, eggs, butter and cream in abundance. Officers were served from silver salvers, the stokers had a special ration of four pounds of prime steak per day, which they needed. Throwing a shovel with the Black Gang was strength-sapping in the hot August weather.

Grant and Barr were interrupted in the middle of their port and fragrant Havanas on Wednesday 19 August by an urgent wireless message from the Admiralty. Decoded, the signal read "Leave patrol station immediately. Proceed Bermuda soonest."

The Royal Navy was still the world's biggest, but Germany had a very powerful fleet. Britain had sixty-nine battleships and battle-cruisers, twenty-nine of them the new all-big-gun Dreadnoughts; Germany had forty capital ships, but half of them were Dreadnoughts. Britain had more cruisers available in 1914 (80 to Germany's 50) but the average age was higher.

Scattered round the world were forty-two listed German armed merchant cruisers. The 23-knot, 14,349-ton (22,700-ton displacement) Norddeutscher-Lloyd *Kaiser Wilhelm der Grosse* had sailed, fully armed, on 4 August for commerce raiding, the 23-knot, 14,908-ton *Kronprinz Wilhelm* was at New York, the *Prinz Eitel Friedrich* at Tsingtao, the new *Cap Trafalgar* at Buenos Aires. There were fourteen ships in German ports awaiting guns, and the rest were in neutral ports watching for their chance to slip out.

Rear-Admiral Sir Christopher Cradock's 4th and 5th Cruiser Squadrons, old 6-inch armoured ships and more modern light cruisers, based in the West Indies, faced the task of patrolling the routes to and from South and Central American ports. Added to his problems was Admiral Graf von Spee's East Asia Squadron of two fast armoured cruisers armed with 20-centimetre (8.1-inch) guns, and three modern light cruisers, believed to be heading for the South Atlantic from the Pacific. Two more enemy light cruisers were known to be out in the Atlantic.

As soon as he had received the telegram announcing the outbreak of war, Sir Edwin Grey, HM Consul General at Buenos Aires, had sent the Argentine Minister for Foreign Affairs, Dr José Luis Murature, an urgent note reminding him of the international law forbidding the arming of belligerent warships in neutral ports – with particular reference to the *Cap Trafalgar*, lying menacingly at the wharf, quoting evidence that a gun had been seen aboard her. On 6 August Dr Murature told Grey that a search had been made revealing no arms or ammunition in the *Cap Trafalgar*, and her Captain, Kommandant Langerhannsz, had sworn an oath to that effect, though there *were* platforms for guns.

On 7 August Grey was told that British ships had been selling coal to the German Coal Company which was immediately sent to the *Cap Trafalgar*. This trade was stopped at once, but ten days later the Consulate had to admit to the Minister that the "evidence" of guns in the *Cap Trafalgar* could not be substantiated. He suggested that they were hidden in the ship's double bottom. Later the same day Mr Mitchell Innes, Britain's man in Montevideo across the river, received the urgent telegram from Grey "German Mail Steamer *Cap Trafalgar* sailed at 5 pm for roadstead with large quantity of timber baulks which in opinion of naval officer can only be used for gun mountings." Next morning Grey telegraphed "Urgent desire knowledge if *Cap Trafalgar* which has taken 3,000 tons of coal is at Montevideo and whether danger threatening."

Other German merchantmen in Buenos Aires had also been loading coal. The *Santa Isabel* took on so much that the surplus had to be stored in the holds, which also contained sandbags, shovels and live bullocks. The *Pontos* also loaded 350 casks of oil and large baulks of timber. They and the *Gotha, Santa Clara* and *Grenada* then left, ostensibly for the roadstead, but in reality for the high seas.

The Admiralty certainly thought "danger threatening". They had almost caught the *Kronprinz Wilhelm*, which had slipped out of New York. On 16 August Cradock surprised her as she was being armed by the regular light cruiser *Karlsruhe*. Both ships escaped, after the AMC had embarked two 10.5-centimetre (4.1-inch) guns.

On 19 August HMS *Carmania*, shaking down in the North Atlantic, received her urgent orders for Bermuda. Cradock, ordered on the one hand to search for five possible commerce-raiding cruisers in the South Atlantic and on the other not to split up his squadron in case von Spee appeared, was short of ships.

On 21 August Grey telegraphed Mitchell Innes: "I am informed that *Cap Trafalgar* which took 3,500 tons of coal here is taking more at Montevideo." A Uruguayan Government naval architect examined the *Cap Trafalgar*, looking for hidden compartments, and reported no arms, ammunition or timber, and only 2,100 tons of coal in bunkers with a capacity for 4,000 tons. When the official had left, the ship took on 1,600 more tons and some baulks of timber. Mitchell Innes reported this to Grey, presuming that she "proposes to supply coal to a German cruiser".

On the evening of 22 August one of Cradock's ships intercepted a signal addressed to the German Consulate at Rio and transmitted from a position off the Brazilian coast with a call sign known to be that of the German gunboat *Eber*, normally stationed in West African waters.

The Admiralty at once suspected a concerted move against South Atlantic shipping routes by a German raiding squadron. Cradock was sent off to West Africa in his flagship, the old armoured cruiser *Good Hope*. *Carmania*, now nearing Bermuda, was ordered to coal as fast as possible there and join in hunting regular cruisers a thousand miles to the south.

At midnight that night the *Cap Trafalgar* quietly cast off from the quayside at Montevideo and slipped down river towards the sea.

She was a new ship, the proud flagship of the Hamburg-Sud-Amerika Line. Kommandant Fritz Langerhannsz was the Senior Captain of the line. Tall and handsome, he was every lady passenger's idea of what a captain should be. A yachtsman of international class, he had risen to seagoing command via naval architecture, which he had studied in England, and was an Anglophile, with a keen knowledge of and admiration for Horatio Nelson and his battles.

One of the many *ipsissima verba* of his hero which he could quote was Nelson's "I have again to deeply regret my want of frigates". Now Langerhannsz's beloved ship was to makeshift for Gross-Admiral von Ingenohl's want of cruisers.

The *Cap Trafalgar* was heading for a rendezvous at Trinidade Island, 1,750 miles to the north-east off the Brazilian coast, a mid-ocean haven for ancient mariners previously known as Trinidada and sometimes called Trinidad Rocks, not to be confused with the better known Trinidad in the West Indies.

In that remote anchorage the ship, like others long before her, would take on fresh water and refuel from the *Pontos* and *Santa Isabel* – and get her armament, the eight modern 15cm (5.9-inch) guns reserved for her.

Meanwhile, as the big ship creamed along at her full 18 knots, Langerhannsz did all he could to disguise her for the run through the British blockade.

Her three-funnel silhouette would give her away immediately to a British cruiser. He had discussed the problem with Korvettenkapitän Muller, who had brought him his orders in the collier *Berwind* at Buenos Aires. Muller had recently taken passage across the Atlantic in the two-funnelled British RMS *Carmania*, and there was on board the *Cap Trafalgar* a veterinary, Dr Braunholz, who had also been in the British liner. Braunholz had come out with a superior strain of German master pigs for the Argentine, but the health authorities had refused to let him in. He had press cuttings describing his work in tending some human burns cases from another ship while in the *Carmania*, with pictures of the latter. There were a number of other two-funnelled British Atlantic liners as well.

The *Cap Trafalgar*'s third funnel was not connected to the boilers and was virtually a dummy, providing fresh air for the galley and passenger decks and containing a condenser serving the reciprocal steam engine for the ship's central propeller shaft. They would remove the third funnel.

To do this at sea was quite a challenge, but nothing that German ingenuity could not overcome. With much sweat, the mild steel plating of the huge funnel was cut by oxy-acetylene torch into narrow vertical strips, which were carefully removed like the peel from a banana. Then the condenser was dismantled, and the *Cap Trafalgar* became a two-funnelled ship.

Unfortunately, the loss of the condenser meant that two boilers had to be shut down, and the ship's top speed was reduced from 18 to 16 knots. It was a vital loss.

The *Carmania* also had wings to her bridge, unlike the *Cap Trafalgar*. Sailing in the ship, and working their passage by assisting in the stokehold, were the members of a travelling German light opera company. False bridge wings were knocked up from their backcloths and scenery. Tenors and baritones willingly came up like Don Giovanni from the dramatic hell of the shut-down boiler room and handled a paint brush to paint the two remaining funnels in the red and black Cunard colours and daub over with white the magnificent glass superstructure of the Winter Garden aft. Deck rails were covered with canvas to increase the apparent height of the hull.

Most of the work had been completed by 26 August. On that day the *Kaiser Wilhelm der Grosse*, having stopped eleven Allied merchantmen, sunk three of them and destroyed the cargoes of some of the others, was intercepted and sunk by the British regular cruiser HMS *Highflyer*.

There was only one good anchorage off Trinidade Island, in the southwestern part. As the *Cap Trafalgar* approached on the evening of 28 August a signal lamp blinked in the bay, where Langerhannsz could just make out a huddle of ships against the rocky backdrop.

What he had hoped to find was the *Karlsruhe* with his guns. What he got were the rusty little *Eber* and the five colliers *Eleanore Wouvermans, Berwind, Pontos, Santa Isabel* and *Santa Lucia*.

A boat came over from the *Eber*, and her commander, young Korvettenkapitän Julius Wirth, came aboard up the liner's long ladder.

Wirth said, "I am taking over command of your ship. Where is your armament?"

Langerhannsz said, "I was hoping *you'd* be able to tell *me* that."

The *Carmania* had spent six days in Bermuda coaling. The ship's Gunner, Harry Middleton, also persuaded Captain Grant to add some extra protection against the lethal splinters which could fly off from all woodwork still left aboard in a battle. Shields made from old steel anti-torpedo nets and interwoven 4-inch rope hawsers were hung from the derricks. Some of the thick rope was also passed round the bridge, sandbags added to the superstructure and round the tiller and engine controls, surplus sand poured into the empty swimming pool ready for dousing fires.

When they were given their final orders it all seemed a waste of time. Cradock's cruisers were now operating at extreme range all the way down the South Atlantic, and the *Carmania* was going south as their collier.

And Barr and the Surgeon were worried about the Captain's health. Grant was obviously ill. The fiery coal dust had not helped his "asthma". He coughed badly, and had several times brought up blood. The elderly Lockyer was also far from fit, and had had to rest ashore from the heat.

Carmania squeezed her bulk back down the narrow, shallow channel from the coaling station. It was even trickier than going in, but Grant knew the Bermudan waters well, and she made it with just six inches clearance under her keel.

Three thousand miles to the south, off Trinidade Island, a line of buckets on a moving cable slung from the *Cap Trafalgar*'s for'ard derrick was emptying the coal from the *Eleanore Wouvermans*, made fast alongside to port, into the big ship's bunkers. It was hard work in the swell, and the *Berwind*, lying to starboard, was having trouble getting the coal up over the liner's sheer side, frequently crashing against her.

But this was not the biggest problem. The *Eber*'s main armament of two old 10.5cm (4.1-inch) and six 3.7cm (1.4-inch) heavy machine-guns was to be transferred to the *Cap Trafalgar*. Wirth then intended to try to capture a British armed merchantman and take her guns and stores. The liner's derricks would not lift one of the *Eber*'s four-ton 10.5s all in one piece, so the stern gun was partially dismantled and swung across in bits, with the gunboat heaving about on the swell. And *Cap Trafalgar*'s four gun rings, two for'ard, two aft, had been drilled for the new 15cm (5.9-inch) guns still in Hamburg – the bolt holes did not match those on the base of the 10.5s. Bigger holes were drilled, by relays of sweating men using bits that were too small for the job. It took from 4 a.m. till noon. The guns were then lowered into position on *Cap Trafalgar*'s port for'ard ring and after starboard quarter ring.

With only two old guns as her main armament, Wirth would need special tactics if he met a British AMC. "'No Captain can do very wrong if he places his ship alongside that of the enemy,'" quoted Langerhannsz the Nelsonian to Wirth.

All but twenty-five of *Cap Trafalgar*'s crew of 279 volunteered to stay with her for active service, and 177 of the most useful of these were accepted. They were joined by 113 ratings from the *Eber* and all the gunboat's officers and petty officers.

Fritz Langerhannsz did not believe that a ship should have two captains, and opted to leave. Wirth put him in charge of all the colliers and the small depot on the island. Langerhannsz busied himself with the installing of an old brass cannon which he had found on the island in the bows of the *Eleanore Wouvermans*. A supply of shot was made from lead, scrap metal and tarred rope soaked in oil and coal dust.

Wirth went aboard the *Cap Trafalgar*, bringing with him a brand-new battle ensign and orders to destroy British shipping heading north from the Plate, with an initial cruise north to check out Rocas Island, between the coast of Brazil and Fernando de Noronha, as a possible raider's rendezvous. He packed off the empty *Santa Isabel* and *Santa Lucia* to Rio for more coal, the *Eber* to Bahia Blanca, and sailed for Rocas.

British Naval Intelligence had picked up signals from German colliers indicating that they were making trips of some twelve days, leaving one port loaded and entering another one empty. With the heavy swell running they could not be transferring coal at sea. It must be in some sheltered anchorage. Cradock was ordered to search all likely bays and islands. The Vaz Rocks looked like a good bet, Trinidade Island, thirty miles further west, even more promising.

On 7 September the *Cap Trafalgar* was approaching Rocas from the south in mist when the *Carmania*, heading east to top up the heavy cruiser *Cornwall* off Fernando de Noronha, crossed her bows within firing distance, but neither ship sighted the other.

Cornwall diverted *Carmania* south-west to watch for the German collier *Patagonia* which seemed about to leave Pernambuco. Wirth heard the British signals loud and clear and stopped engines, lying to in the fog. The *Carmania* passed by three miles away.

Wirth circled Rocas, noted a good anchorage, then turned south for the long haul down the Brazilian Basin to Trinidade Island to rendezvous with the *Kronprinz Wilhelm* on the 14th. The *Carmania* and *Cornwall* almost fired on each other in the mist. It was impossible to transfer coal in the swell, and the AMC was ordered south to refuel the light cruiser HMS *Glasgow* off the Plate.

Two hundred miles east of her the *Cap Trafalgar* was steaming on a parallel course south for Trinidade Island. Wirth was picking up signals from British cruisers all round him and was regretting his reduced maximum speed. Everyone knew that if they were sighted they could not get away. They rigged hoses, filled baths with water, slung cargo nets and rolled-up carpets for boarders.

The *Eber* arrived at Bahia on 11 September. The British Consul noticed her at once and informed the Admiralty. The gunboat could well have come from a rendezvous with some of the German cruisers. At 10 am the *Carmania* was diverted from her southward course to search the Vaz Rocks via Trinidade Island.

The *Cap Trafalgar* anchored near the *Eleanore Wouvermans* in the Trinidade Island anchorage at 5 pm on Saturday, 12 September. On Sunday evening Wirth, brought up as a strict Lutheran,

held Evensong. The wireless log showed that the last signal intercepted had come from a British ship fifty miles to the north.

In the *Carmania*'s charthouse Smokey Barr made a neat pen-
cilled cross, took his dividers and measured off the same distance,
which he reported to Grant as they sat down to a birthday dinner
for the Captain. Grant decided to slow down during the night and
arrive off Trinidade Island at dawn. The ship now had a third
funnel, a dummy of wood and canvas run up by the carpenter to
alter the *Carmania*'s silhouette, which was too easily recognizable
as non-German

At 4 am, as soon as there was light in the sky, Wirth started
coaling, anxious to get away south out of the net of British cruisers,
towards Von Spee's ocean. It was the eighteenth anniversary of his
commission, a date particularly precious to Wirth as he, like
Grant, had risen from the lower deck. Langerhannsz gave him his
cherished copy of Southey's *Life of Nelson*. Wirth sent the
Eleanore Wouvermans out to steam within signalling distance to
the south-west, doubled the lookout on the hill.

At 9.30 am the *Carmania*'s masthead lookout sighted the hilltop
on which Wirth's lookouts were posted, two points on the starboard bow. Grant and Barr wondered what lay behind the hill.
Was it *Karlsruhe*, or *Dresden*, or both? A single enemy ship, a
squadron? If they sighted masts it was not their job to engage,
merely to report and shadow. At 10.45 am the whole island came
into view. *Carmania* went to action stations.

In the south-eastern anchorage hidden from Grant the *Cap Trafalgar*'s hook was clanging home in the hawsepipe and she was
gathering way. She headed to sea, followed by the *Pontos* and
Berwind. It was a bright, clear day, with a gentle breeze out of the
north-east.

At 11.04 *Carmania*'s lookout sighted three sets of masts behind
the westernmost headland of the island. "We've got company,"
said Barr.

The two tallest masts and a big two-funnelled ship emerged from
the rocks, followed by two smaller ones. Their derricks were still
topped, and they looked as if they had been working cargo recently.

Grant said, "Who is she?" The *Karlsruhe* had four funnels, the
Dresden three, and this ship was too bulky for a light cruiser. *Kronprinz Wilhelm* also had four funnels, the *Konig Wilhelm* only one.

Barr said, "From her funnels she ought to be one of ours – she's painted like a Union Castle boat."

Grant said, "Not in this area."

"She could be the *Berlin*. Seventeen-knotter."

"I don't like it. It could be a trap. He might have more friends hiding behing the island."

"Well, we shall soon know."

The *Cap Trafalgar*'s lookout reported the stranger coming in from the north. Wirth and Feddersen raised their binoculars.

The former Chief Officer said, "Three funnels. She looks like the *Cap Finisterre* – like *us*."

"Let's find out," said Wirth. "Flash her."

In *Carmania* Grant said, "Signal 'What ship? Where bound?' Hoist the White Ensign."

The two signals, one by signal lamp, one by wireless, overlapped one another. As if in answer to Wirth's challenge the British flag went up in the other ship.

The *Cap Trafalgar* held to her south-westerly course, away from the *Carmania*. Wirth was trying to draw the other ship between him and the island, to limit her freedom of manoeuvre. Grant saw the two smaller ships break away, one to the south-east, the other to the north-west. He altered course slightly to starboard to give himself sea room.

The two big ships were some 15,000 yards apart, with the slightly faster *Carmania* closing. Then the other ship turned to starboard as if to intercept the *Carmania*.

The gap shrank rapidly. At 8,500 yards Lockyer sang out, "In range, sir!"

Grant said, "Fire a shot across her bows."

"Aye-aye, sir." Lockyer lifted the telephone to Number 1 Gun on the port side for'ard.

The solid shell whistled through the clear blue sky and sent up a fountain of white water a hundred yards ahead and some fifty yards to starboard of the *Cap Trafalgar*.

Wirth shouted, "Hoist the battle ensign!" Then he waited tensely for the range to shorten enough for the *Eber*'s old 10.5cms to open up.

As the range came down to 7,000 yards the *Cap Trafalgar* opened fire.

It was 4.7 against 4.1-inch. *Cap Trafalgar* had only two main guns to *Carmania*'s eight, and as yet could only use her after starboard gun. The British AMC was able to fire with three forward port side guns.

Cap Trafalgar's first round went over, *Carmania*'s fell short.

Cap Trafalgar's second shell brought down *Carmania*'s signal halliards and wireless mast, cutting her off from Cradock's cruisers. The third disabled one of her guns, killing the gunlayer and sight-setter and wounding all the others in the gun's crew.

Then two shells from *Carmania* shattered the Winter Garden. Knife-edged shards of glass and wood flew round the decks, killing men, severing steam pipes. But the range was closing fast and in a few minutes *Cap Trafalgar* would be able to use her three forward heavy 3.7cm pom-pom type machine-guns. Then another shell burst near the bridge. Splinters killed the quartermaster, the wheel spun and the ship yawed to port. Wirth and Leutnant Rettberg heaved at the wheel but with steam and hydraulic lines cut it was almost impossible to move it. The mock bridge wings were burning, a pall of smoke and flame and hissing steam hid the *Carmania*, away to starboard. She had now brought two more guns into action.

But the crew of the German's after 4.1 could see the enemy, and opened a rapid fire on her. In minutes the *Carmania*'s bridge was on fire. Then *Cap Trafalgar* slowly came back on course. The smoke was being blown to starboard, masking her guns. Wirth shouted down to the for'ard gun's crew, "Fire at the gun flashes!" A shell from *Carmania* burst on the foc'sle 10.5, jamming it solid. The crew were badly wounded and a sharp splinter decapitated the officer of the quarters.

Suddenly the wind dropped. Wirth saw the enemy clearly on his starboard bow, about a mile away. Now was the time. He ran to the bridge rail, shouted to his three starboard machine-guns to open fire, ran back to the wheel and lent his weight to try to turn the *Cap Trafalgar* towards the British AMC.

Carmania's bridge was already almost consumed with flames, and the hail of pom-pom shells stopped all fire control efforts. One just missed Lockyer but smashed the rangefinder. He leapt down on to the bridge. "Sir," he shouted to Grant, "Open the range and get clear of the machine-guns!"

Grant ran down the comparatively sheltered starboard upper-deck to the after control position while Barr ordered "Full ahead port, full astern starboard!'

Carmania swung to starboard. The north-east wind blew the raging flames over her bows. The after port guns were still firing. The *Cap Trafalgar*'s guns were also firing, hitting *Carmania*'s masts, boats, ventilators and derricks and keeping heads down on deck. As *Carmania* continued her turn, her starboard guns came to bear. Lockyer ran along the upper deck shouting "Individual fire! Aim for her waterline!"

Grant watched the enemy turn on her heel to starboard to follow him. The range was only about 1,000 yards as it was. *"My God, he's trying to board us!"*

The shells from five of his guns hit *Cap Trafalgar*'s waterline. Round after round punched through the thin plating. One burst in a bunker, another right on the junction of the boiler room bulkhead and the side. The bulkhead collapsed and the sea poured in. Another exploded in a for'ard reserve bunker. The stokehold was flooded in seconds. Wirth chose that moment to screw his turn to starboard tighter, with the result that the water rushed in through the holes even faster. Fourth Engineer Riech ran to the voicepipe and screamed to him to turn back to port or all the bulkheads would give way. *Cap Trafalgar* turned slowly back to her original heading.

The *Carmania* also turned a full 180° back on to a south-westerly course. At 12.30 a.m. the *Cap Trafalgar* was about 5,500 yards on her starboard bow, taking water fast and badly on fire below.

But Grant also had his problems. A shell from the enemy's after gun had shot away his after emergency steering controls, and orders had to be passed down to the engine room and tiller flat through open hatchways. And he had no wireless, and no compass to con the ship with. Worse still, with all the water mains severed, an almost uncontrollable fire was raging below in the main dining room and some of the cabins. Grant sent Barr below with spare hands to tackle the fire, and young Midshipmen Colson and Dickens recovered the compass from the burning navigating bridge at the cost of badly burned faces and hands.

Grant reduced speed so that his guns just outranged the enemy's.

He had not noticed the small ship coming up from the south-west. Then suddenly there she was, steaming for the gap between the two heavyweights, on an opposite course. It was the *Eleanore Wouvermans*, loaded brass cannon on her bows, Langerhannsz with lighted cigar at the touch-hole. She seemed to be heading for the *Cap Trafalgar*.

Barr seemed to have got the fire below in hand, though the flames from the bridge were still shooting skywards, so Grant turned to starboard into the wind towards the *Cap Trafalgar*, which was now lying stopped. The water had almost reached her boilers, and the fire in the foc'sle was out of control.

But so was the inferno below decks in the *Carmania*. What had looked to Grant like a damping down of the fire there was merely Barr closing down the ventilation to starve it of oxygen. The wind now blew through the ship and fanned the flames.

Grant opened fire. The shells fell all round the *Eleanore Wouvermans*. The *Cap Trafalgar*'s after 10.5 opened up again, wrecking Grant's cabin and destroying the *Carmania*'s after winch.

Smokey Barr, blackened and singed, came up from the fires of hell. "What the blazes are you doing?"

Grant pointed to the *Eleanore Wouvermans*. "I'm going to take that ship."

The little collier had turned 180° and was coming back. With *Carmania* on her port bow Langerhannsz fired the cannon. From the *Carmania* the burst of flame and dense black smoke looked like a hit from one of her shells.

Barr said, "You're going to lose *this* ship if you continue on this course."

Grant looked at the stricken enemy AMC and her little comic-opera champion, which was now closing her.

He coughed harshly. "All right," he said wearily, "let's put the fire out."

The *Cap Trafalgar* was listing badly to starboard now. Men were jumping into the sea, and the few boats left seaworthy were being lowered. The collier was lowering her own boats. Sharks took three of the swimmers. The *Carmania* ceased fire and turned back downwind to help keep the flames down, while her men fought the blaze with buckets of water and stokehold shovels.

On the steeply canting bridge of the *Cap Trafalgar* Wirth was dying from a deep splinter wound in his armpit. He asked the burly Leutnant Steffan to shout for three cheers for the Kaiser. The cheering from the boats turned into singing. The *Cap Trafalgar* began slowly to right herself, then settled gently by the bow. Suddenly she lifted her stern high in the air and plunged below. It was 1.50 pm, one hour and forty-six minutes from the firing of the first shot.

Men in the *Carmania* cheered. Then there came a scare. Just before sinking, the enemy had been heard broadcasting on W/T to some ship nearby. Now smoke was reported on the northern horizon. A signalman thought he could make out four funnels. If this was an enemy cruiser, the *Carmania* was in no condition to fight her. Grant increased speed and shaped course to the south-west, steering by the sun and wind. The stranger was the *Kronprinz Wilhelm*, but on receipt of *Cap Trafalgar*'s last message she sheered off.

The *Carmania* ran blazing before the wind. Water mains were repaired, and by nightfall the fires were out. The W/T staff got another aerial rigged, and help was requested. At dusk she altered course for Abrolhos Rocks, where she was to rendezvous with HMS *Cornwall*. At 4.30 a.m. next morning the light cruiser *Bristol* joined her and escorted her until relieved by *Cornwall*. After the hard fight the AMC was unseaworthy. She had been hit by seventy-nine shells, and there were 304 holes in her hull and superstructure. It could have been worse. Her coal protection saved one shell from penetrating the top of the engine room, and the steel plating round the top of the boiler room stopped another. Her deck was a ruin of smashed machinery, winches, ventilators, boats and derricks, her bridge was wrecked and much of her accommodation below was gutted.

She had lost nine men (killed), with four badly wounded. *Carmania* and *Cornwall* reached Abrolhos at 8 am next morning. There temporary repairs were made, with the help of *Cornwall*'s engineers, and the worst of the holes patched, then the AMC HMS *Macedonia* came in to escort *Carmania* to Gibraltar for proper repairs. She was in dockyard hands there for eight weeks, then went on patrol off Lisbon. Grant was awarded a CB, then found unfit for sea service not long afterwards. Promoted to Rear-Admiral, he died of tuberculosis in 1920. Smokey Barr, also given a

CB, was invalided home, then commanded the troopships *Maure-tania, Saxonia* and *Carpathia*. He retired as Senior Commodore of the Cunard Line in 1916 and died in 1937. Lockyer, who received the DSO, served briefly in *Carmania* off Lisbon, then returned to retirement. The *Carmania* returned to Company service in May, 1916, and was broken up in 1925.

Neither Grant nor the Argentinian and Uruguayan authorities would believe that the *Cap Trafalgar* had carried only the *Eber*'s two old 10.5cm guns. When Grant found out at Gibraltar what ship he had been fighting he gave her eight 4.1-inch guns in his report, in addition to the pom-poms, and a speed of 18 knots. When the *Eleanore Wouvermans*, having eluded the British blockade, arrived in the Plate with 286 survivors from the *Cap Tra-falgar*, Langerhannsz was accused of breaking his word that she had been unarmed before she had left there. He was put on trial in Montevideo but acquitted. He and the others from the *Cap Trafal-gar* were interned for the duration of the war on the island of Martin Barcia in the Plate estuary.

The ex-Orient liner *Otranto* was also in the southern oceans, part of Cradock's far-flung force.

In late October Cradock, his power weakened by division, was searching for Von Spee's squadron up the Chilean coast when, on the morning of the 31st, the *Otranto* located the call sign of the *Leipzig*, one of Von Spee's light cruisers, near the port of Coronel. Cradock began a sweep up the coast towards her with his two old armoured cruisers *Good Hope* and *Monmouth* and the light cruiser *Glasgow*, and on the following day his four ships ran into Von Spee with the armoured cruisers *Scharnhorst* and *Gneisenau* and the light cruisers *Nurnberg, Leipzig* and *Dresden*.

The German ships had been two years together and were crack ships. Most of Cradock's men were recently mobilized reservists, and through the Admiralty's fear of wasting ammunition had not fired a shot since the opening of hostilities. *Scharnhorst* and *Gneis-enau* were faster and better armed than *Good Hope* and *Monmouth*, and their modern 8.2-inch guns much more efficient than the old British 9.2s and 6-inch, which could not penetrate the German armour.

The result was practically a foregone conclusion, but Cradock formed a battle line, *Good Hope* leading *Monmouth*, *Glasgow* and

31

Otranto, and steered for the enemy. Then he concluded that the armed liner could help him very little, and he ordered her to turn back.

Within minutes *Good Hope*'s forward turret had been knocked out and *Monmouth* was on fire. Captain Edwards of the *Otranto*, in direct disobedience of orders, turned round and zigzagged towards the German ships, hoping to buy time for Cradock. Almost nonchalantly the *Gneisenau* swivelled her turrets away from the *Monmouth* long enough to bracket the frail AMC with two salvoes. Edwards took the hint and, to save his ship from complete annihilation, retired. Von Spee completed the destruction of *Good Hope* and *Monmouth*. The *Glasgow* and *Otranto* escaped.

On 8 December the tables were turned when the two British battle-cruisers *Invincible* and *Inflexible* with 12-inch guns, the armoured cruisers *Kent, Cornwall* and *Carnarvon*, and the *Glasgow* fought Von Spee off the Falklands. *Scharnhorst* and *Gneisenau* were sunk by the battlecruisers' big guns, and in a hot chase the British cruisers sank the *Nurnberg* and *Leipzig*. The *Dresden* got away and hid from the hunting cruisers for three months in the channels of Tierra del Fuego, then tried to escape into the Pacific but was bottled up in Cumberland Bay, Juan Fernandez Island. Ordered to leave by the Chilean authorities, she was shelled by HMS *Kent, Glasgow* and the auxiliary cruiser *Orama*, ex-Orient Line. The crew got clear under a white flag, and demolition charges sank her.

The *Kronprinz Wilhelm*, with the two 10.5cm guns which she had managed to get from *Karlsruhe*, captured or sank thirteen Allied ships without causing any loss of life, then her boilers broke down and she interned herself in Newport News, Virginia. The *Prinz Eitel Friedrich* had a similar history, and she too interned herself with mechanical troubles and a dwindling coal supply.

In March, 1916, Captain Grant won, on behalf of everyone aboard the *Carmania* in the fight with the *Cap Trafalgar*, the "prize bounty of a sum calculated at the rate of £5 for each of the persons on board the enemy's ship at the beginning of an engagement" which the Naval Distribution Prize Agency Act of 1864 could authorize to be awarded "to the officers and crew of any of His Majesty's ships of war who were actually present at the taking or destroying of any armed ship of an enemy". The President of the

Prize Court generously based the award on a crew of 423, which the Consul-General at Buenos Aires calculated were aboard the *Cap Trafalgar* when she sailed on 7 August, though some men had in fact left the ship by then, and the amount was therefore assessed as £2,115.

3 "Stop engines!"

In the last hours of peace a great grey ship crept north through Norwegian territorial waters, her lookouts watching with their new Zeiss binoculars for Norwegian patrol boats ahead and for British warships to seaward.

In the great anchorage of Scapa Flow in the Orkneys hovered the biggest battle fleet in the world, and the British Commander-in-Chief had his Dreadnoughts out policing the gaps from Scapa up to Shetland and across to Stavanger.

Armed and commissioned in the Elbe, the 22,700-ton *Kaiser Wilhelm der Grosse*, ex-Norddeutscher-Lloyd Line, was bound for the high seas and the shipping lanes along which the mighty British Merchant Marine plied. In the summer haze she sighted smoke on the western horizon, and at one point in her dangerous voyage was only forty miles from scouting cruisers of the Grand Fleet. But she was not spotted, steamed on northwards, crossed the Arctic Circle, went westabout round Iceland and through the cold Denmark Strait into the Atlantic, where in her heyday she had won the Blue Riband. There she sank 10,400 tons of British shipping in three weeks, then met her end before the guns of HMS *Highflyer* off West Africa.

Admiral Jellicoe expected heavy two-way traffic between the North Atlantic and the "German Sea" after war began at midnight on 4 August – more armed raiders coming out, German merchantmen running for home with war stores, neutrals with copper, rubber, lead, coal and cotton for the German war effort, food and clothing for a blockaded people. He could spare some ships for patrols, but his main job was in the North Sea, watching the movements of the German High Seas Fleet, poised in the Elbe, the Kiel Canal and the Heligoland Bight.

The Admiralty first took eight of their oldest armoured cruisers of the *Crescent* and *Edgar* classes, children of the Naval Defence Act of 1889, HMS *Crescent* and *Royal Arthur, Edgar, Endymion, Gibraltar, Grafton, Hawke* and *Theseus*, 7,700 tons, middle-aged now, like the reservists who manned half the Fleet, but refitted and rearmed with the same mix of 9.2s and 6-inch as the doomed *Good Hope* and *Monmouth*. Their coal-burning boilers could raise steam for 17 knots, though they would then be writing their signatures on the sky for the enemy to read. They were called, first, Cruiser Force B, then the 10th Cruiser Squadron, forming the Northern Patrol Force, and their job was to patrol Scotland – Shetlands - Norway, looking for German warships breaking out and contrabanders slipping in. As soon as they were ready, armed merchant cruisers would be joining them.

With many German ships likely to be heading home from foreign parts, these blockaders could not come on station too soon, especially when the U15, one of the ten new German submarines out looking for the British Fleet, missed the Dreadnought HMS *Monarch* with a torpedo off the Orkneys on 8 August and sent the Grand Fleet scuttling back into the Flow. Then the cruiser *Amphion* was sunk by a mine thought to have been laid by a disguised merchantman.

Two days after the *Monarch* incident the old cruisers of the 10th took up their stations on the Scotland – Norway barrier, under Rear-Admiral Dudley de Chair.

One week later, on 18 August, HMS *Alsatian*, 16,000 gross tons, formerly of the Allan Line, built in 1913, came up to patrol off the Shetlands. A fast, strong ship, she met all the requirements for an Armed Merchant Cruiser, with ten stout bulkheads, built-in stiffening for her guns, her steering lines and her six turbines all well below the waterline. She could make 22 knots, and big rudders gave her a quick response to the helm. With her coal capacity doubled from a normal 3,500 tons to 7,000 by filling nearly all the cargo space in her lower holds, she could steam 11,500 miles. On 24 August she was joined by HMS *Mantua*, ex- P & O, and three days later by the armed White Star Atlantic liner *Oceanic*, built in 1899 and famous for her steadiness and luxury ever since.

Two ships which would not after all be commissioning as Armed Merchant Cruisers were the Atlantic record breakers *Lusitania* and *Mauretania*. These huge vessels, built from scratch and heavily subsidized by the Government as potential warships fast enough to catch the *Kaiser Wilhelm II*, consumed 1,200 tons of coal a day, and were uneconomical as cruisers. Unfortunately they continued to be listed in *Jane's Fighting Ships* and *The Naval Annual 1914* as auxiliary cruisers, which Kapitänleutnant Walter Schwieger of U20 consulted when he sighted *Lusitania* through his periscope on 7 May, 1915 off the Old Head of Kinsale, and fired the torpedo which killed 1,198 men, women and children, and helped to bring America into the war.

Another ship dropped from the list was the *Aquitania*. On 22 August, after a fortnight's war service as an AMC, she collided with the Leyland liner *Canadian*, and returned for repairs. By the time she was ready again it had been realized that smaller, more economical ships were better for cruiser service, and she became a trooper and hospital ship.

The *Oceanic*, 17,274 tons, fifteen years old, with unprotected steering gear and only 2,830 tons coal capacity, had originally been a dubious contender, but with 1,800 tons in the holds and another 1,470 tons of coal "armour", which could be burned, she could range 6,250 miles and make 20½ knots if pushed, her narrow hull vibrating anxiously. On 8 September she was leaving what had been a temporary detachment to the Northern Patrol when she ran aground near Foula Island, twenty-four miles west of Shetland, and was wrecked.

As she was written off, an even older vessel, the White Star *Teutonic*, 9,984 tons, built in 1889, joined the Northern Patrol. She had the distinction of being the first British merchant ship custom-built to be an auxiliary cruiser in wartime. At the time of

her launch her name was acceptable by virtue of Royal Family con-
nections, and she did in fact appear at the Spithead Naval Review
of 1889 as an "armed merchantman" in honour of Kaiser Wilhelm
II, who inspected her and took the idea home to Von Tirpitz. The
decision to arm her in 1914 had been marginal as she was considered almost worn out, though she could still manage 19 knots in
good conditions. Her sister ship *Majestic* had been rejected. Originally designed to carry twelve 5-inch guns, the standard main auxiliary cruiser armament of the day, and twelve 3-pounders, she was
now equipped with eight 6-inch. In smooth water she lived up to
her nickname of "The Greyhound", but in rough seas she took it
green, and her for'ard guns were washed out.

The 17,000-ton, 17½-knot AMC *Prinz Friedrich Wilhelm* was
lurking in Tromso, but the 10th Cruiser Squadron was not picking
up any German ships, either eastward or westward bound. AMCs
in German ports were still waiting for their guns, German merchantmen abroad were laid up in neutral ports, nervous of the
blockade.

On 15 October Kapitänleutnant Otto Weddigen's *U9* was lying
submerged at periscope depth east of Aberdeen when three of the
old *Edgars* were sighted, zigzagging fast, converging on a point
near the submarine. One of the ships slowed down and lowered a
cutter to pull to the other cruisers. Weddigen's torpedo struck her,
and within minutes all that was left of HMS *Hawke* was the cutter
and forty-nine men from her ship's company of five hundred. It
was only three weeks since the same U-boat and commander had
sunk the three "live bait" cruisers *Aboukir*, *Hogue* and *Cressy* on
patrol off the Dutch coast.

Jellicoe withdrew the Grand Fleet from the North Sea and used
some of the battleships and cruisers of the Fleet to help the old con-
temptibles and AMCs of the 10th CS to try to plug the Orkneys-
Faeroes gaps. *Alsatian* and *Mantua* took the northern flank of the
line up near the Faeroes.

Some ships got away from them and went round north of the
Faeroes. Disguised as a British ship, the 17,000-ton
Norddeutscher-Lloyd liner *Berlin* got out with a clutch of mines,
one of which sank the battleship HMS *Audacious* off north-
western Ireland. Five ships of the 10th CS, with the 3rd Cruiser
Squadron stretched on their northern flank, took station north-

east of Muckle Flugga, the northernmost point of the Shetlands. The *Berlin* escaped by going north of Iceland through the Denmark Strait, but was interned when she tried to sneak home through Norwegian territorial waters.

The hunt cooled down, Jellicoe's cruisers returned to Scapa, the old *Edgars* began to break down under the strain of continuous hard seatime, and for a short period after the *Berlin* affair AMCs *Alsatian* and *Mantua* found themselves the only ships of the Northern Patrol on station, shivering in the icy seas south of Iceland. Their coal would only stretch for eleven days, which included a long haul to and from Liverpool.

Jellicoe, who had asked for more auxiliary cruisers to fill the blockade line, now doubted the value of the Northern Patrol. Of twenty-five ships boarded, sometimes in heavy weather and at great risk to boarding parties, since the beginning of October, only one had been detained, and one other forced to land part of her cargo. One reason for this was that Britain was treading carefully among the international laws of contraband, and neutral ships, especially American, were getting the benefit of the doubt. Until the end of September such items as copper, rubber, lead and iron ore were on the Free List and could not be seized at all. Then they were shifted to the Conditional List, and could be seized if the ship's orders showed her to be calling at an enemy port or fleet, or if the goods on her manifest had been consigned to an enemy government or an enemy agent in a neutral port (the doctrine of the "continuous voyage") or to a fortified base in hostile territory – or if the ship were caught suspiciously off course. Many ships sailed smugly through the legal loopholes to the Baltic or Holland with copper, grain, petrol, sulphur or coal, much of it obviously meant for Germany. When the German Government was alleged to have taken control of all foodstuffs, these were added to the Conditional List, but the report turned out to have been false, and ships sent in for examination on these grounds had to be released. Angry shippers went to law. On 29 October another Order in Council placed such items as copper, rubber and lead on the Absolute Con- traband List, along with arms, munitions and gun cotton, which were seized if the ship was shown to be merely calling at an enemy port or was off course for her stated neutral destination.

The Admiralty's reply to Jellicoe's criticism was that the

blockade had caused shipowners to think twice about running contraband or made it impossible to insure, and many had sworn guarantees of non-co-operation with Germany. To increase the efficiency of the Northern Patrol, seventeen more merchantmen, of 4,000–6,000 tons and speeds of 14–17 knots, were to be taken up as auxiliary cruisers, ranging from the old *Viking* (to be renamed *Viknor*), built in 1888, to the five 6,000-ton Elder & Fyffe banana boats *Bayano*, *Changuinola*, *Motagua*, *Patia* and *Patnea*, built 1912–1913, the last two being 16-knotters.

These ships were to be manned by the crews of the old *Edgars*, which were to be paid off, and by RNR men. On 20 November the old cruisers were ordered to return to their home ports. On 3 December Rear-Admiral de Chair hauled down his flag in HMS *Crescent*, and on the following day hoisted it again in HMS *Alsatian*, which was, however, due to leave to have her 4.7s replaced by 6-inch. Since he had taken command, the Northern Patrol had boarded over three hundred ships, often in the most atrocious conditions of heavy seas, ice and freezing fog that the cruel northern seas could produce.

Between the departure of the *Edgars* and the arrival of the new AMCs the Northern Patrol virtually ceased to exist. At the end of November the old *Teutonic* was the only ship on patrol, steaming west of the Hebrides; then she was joined in early December by the *Otway*. In this period the German collier *Rio Negro* slipped through, carrying survivors from the cruiser *Karlsruhe* which, after sinking 76,000 tons of British shipping, had been trapped off Venezuela and had blown herself up.

By Boxing Day, 1915, twelve AMCs held the blockade barrier. *Teutonic*, *Cedric* (ex-White Star), *Columbella* (Anchor Line), *Mantua* (P & O) and *Virginian* (Allan Line) patrolled from Iceland to the Faeroes and east to the coast of Norway. *Otway*, *Oropesa* (Pacific Steam Navigation Company) and *Hilary* (Booth Line) covered the approached east-west either side of the Faeroes. *Hildebrand* (Booth), *Patuca* (Elder & Fyffe), *Calyx* (ex-*Calypso*, Thomas Wilson of Hull) and *Ambrose* (Booth) stretched out into the Atlantic from just north of St Kilda's Island off the Outer Hebrides.

The flagship *Alsatian*, re-armed with 6-inch guns, rejoined on the 26th along with the ex-Clan Line's 5,000-ton *Clan McNaught-*

on, which took station on the Hebridean patrol just in time to face a fierce south-westerly gale which cost her her wireless aerials and forced the ships on Patrol Line D to lie to west of the Hebrides. By early January there were fourteen auxiliary cruisers on station with the Northern Patrol. Five were coaling in Liverpool, though the long supply line would be reduced when Loch Ewe in western Scotland had its boom in place, and Busta Voe and Olna Firth in the Shetlands were also to be used as advanced coaling bases.

Too many *Rio Negros* were slipping through the blockade. Jellicoe now expected de Chair, with nearly twenty armed merchant cruisers, to do something about it. The Grand Fleet, leery of U-boats sneaking up out of the North Sea, was exercising west of the Orkneys and Shetlands when a report came in that the homeward bound Norwegian-American Line's *Bergensfjord* had gone missing somewhere in the area. Intelligence suspected that some German reservists had joined her in the USA with fake neutral passports provided by their embassy in New York, in which case her Captain, who must be aware of their presence, was not going to risk being sent into Kirkwall.

Gunboats patrolling the mouth of The Minch between the Butt of Lewis and Cape Wrath were alerted in case he was thinking of a daring dash through the whirlpools of the Pentland Firth. Further north two cruisers were sent to patrol north-east of Sule Skerry to cover the Fair Isle Channel between the Orkneys and Shetland. In the deep field were de Chair's AMCs. He realigned them to form an arc from Kristiansand through the Faeroes round the west of Ireland, to trap the crafty *Bergensfjord* and hopefully the Danish *Mjolnar* as well.

In the forenoon of 10 January faint W/T signals were intercepted and identified as the *Bergensfjord* talking to her head office in Bergen. She was going to make a dash for home. The nearest cruisers were ordered to intercept.

The *Viknor*, 5,300 tons, was the oldest of the auxiliary cruisers. Built as the *Viking*, flagship of the Viking Cruising Company, she had been renamed HMS *Viknor* to avoid confusion with the F (Tribal) class destroyer HMS *Viking*. She could make 17 knots if asked nicely, and had some life in her old bones yet.

Early in the misty forenoon of 11 January *Viknor*'s "man in the barrel" up the foremast sighted a ship. *Viknor* altered course to head her off. As the old AMC, straining her rivets, came up with the stranger, she began to look more and more like the *Bergensfjord*. Her funnel was yellow, with the red, white and blue stripes of the Norwegian-American Line.

In clear weather a red flag hoisted at the yard meant "Stop engines!" In murky conditions or at night the orders were to fire a rocket or a blank from one of the guns to produce the same effect.

Viknor fired a rocket, so as to keep all her guns, loaded with live rounds, at the ready in case of trouble. The red flare burst above the bows of the white-hulled vessel. If this failed, the next move was a live shot across her bows.

The rocket did the trick. *Viknor* beat to windward and lowered a boat with a boarding party. They found that the stranger was indeed the elusive Norwegian. *Viknor* reported the news, and *Alsatian*, *Patia* and *Teutonic* converged at full speed on the position.

Meanwhile the Norwegian Captain tried to bluff it out. "Why should I go into Kirkwall – and add many days to my voyage? What will my owners say?"

The boarding officers suspected that he had a more pressing reason for avoiding inspection. They checked the ship's papers with the Captain, while the men of their party chatted to the crew to see what information they could pick up. A thorough search of the ship revealed six stowaways, all German, some hiding in the lifeboats, and an interrogation of the passengers uncovered the suspected reservists with their forged passports. Pick of the bunch and a bonus for Admiralty Intelligence was the poorly disguised Baron von Wedell of the Imperial Secret Service.

The *Viknor*, low on coal after the chase, continued southwards en route for Liverpool. At 4 p.m. on 13 January she called up with a position north of Tory Island, off north-western Ireland, as she steered for the North Channel and home. She was never heard from again. Five days later bodies of some of her ship's company and wreckage were washed ashore near Portrush off the mouth of Lough Foyle. No mention of a sinking in her area was ever found in any U-boat's logbook, and she could well have been a victim of one of the mines laid by the *Berlin* which had sunk the *Audacious* in the same area. The *Viknor* was the first of the conscript cruisers to go.

In the month 24 December, 1914, to 24 January, 1915, a total of

122 merchantmen were intercepted by the 10th Cruiser Squadron. Boarding parties learned to look for contraband in double bottoms, above dummy deckheads, behind false bulkheads, even inside hollow steel masts, which could be filled with copper, rubber or gun cotton.

On 25 January Korvettenkapitän Hersing in *U21* surfaced in Morecambe Bay, Lancashire. On 5 September, 1914, Hersing had destroyed the small light cruiser HMS *Pathfinder* in a few minutes off the Firth of Forth and had thus become the first submarine commander to score in this war, *U21* the first submarine to sink a ship since the crude Confederate submersible *Hunley* had sunk the USS *Housatonic* in 1863.

This time Hersing had threaded the minefields in the English Channel, avoided the fast destroyers of the Dover Patrol, crept round Land's End and into the Irish Sea. Naval experts at Vickers' shipyard on Walney Island were examining the submarine casually through their binoculars when they saw a flash from her gun, and shells began to fall on the airship sheds. Hersing went on to stop and sink the collier *Ben Cruachan*, loaded with coal for the Grand Fleet, north of the Bay, then in quick succession the freighters *Linda Blanche*, *Kilcowan* and *Estacha*, the latter eighteen miles north-west of the Bar Lightship off Liverpool.

He gave north-western England its biggest scare since John Paul Jones had burned a ship in Whitehaven harbour in 1778 and spiked the guns of the fort. Six AMCs, including the flagship *Alsatian*, coaling in Liverpool, were bottled up there for a week, under orders not to sail until the full moon had waned, then put to sea and dodged mines off the Hebrides. Other 10th CS ships refuelled in Loch Ewe or the Clyde. Destroyers and patrol boats hunted what the Admiralty was convinced was a whole flotilla of U-boats, but Hersing was gone, to climax his career by sinking two battleships off the Dardanelles.

After the *U21*'s arrogant penetration of intimate coastal waters, further sorties into the 10th Cruiser Squadron's manor were expected. Patrol lines were changed, the interval between ships doubled to twenty miles, cruising speed raised to 13 knots. and zigzag the order of the day, every day. Bad light and dirty weather hampered hunter and hunted alike, and on 2 February the most savage gale for many years howled out of the north-west. When at last it had blown itself out, the AMC *Clan McNaughton* was not answering signals. The *Hildebrand, Patuca* and *Digby* searched her patrol line for a week, sighted some unidentifiable wreckage but no *Clan McNaughton*. Heavy weather or floating mine, or perhaps a combination of both, there was no way of telling, but the armed merchant fleet had suffered its second casualty.

From the totality of the destruction, de Chair thought a freak giant wave or the overwhelming by huge seas of a vessel already mortally hit by a mine to be the most likely cause of the end of *Clan McNaughton*, and reported his older ships, *Teutonic, Oropesa, Calyx, Columbella* and others, unfit for the strain of operations in the nothern seas.

In response the Admiralty took up six former cruise liners, the Royal Mail's *Alcantara* 15,300 tons), *Andes* (15,620 tons) and *Arlanza* (15,044 tons); the Pacific Steam Navigation Company's *Orcoma* (11,500 tons) and *Ebro* (8,470 tons); and the P & O's *India* (7,940 tons), all of which could stay at sea for thirty days, more than double the stamina of most of de Chair's other ships.

On 4 February, soon after the Northern Patrol's run of successful interceptions, the German Government declared the waters round Great Britain and Ireland a military area. Neutral ships were warned to steer clear of it and pass north of the Shetlands – or risk being sunk. They were given a fortnight's grace. But Britain had already warned neutral skippers of similar danger on that northern route. Life for a neutral skipper was very hard.

It did not get easier for the storm-tossed auxiliary cruisers of the 10th CS, which now had to cover all the gaps up as far as Iceland. The Germans started the ploy of re-registering their ships under the US flag, which sometimes guaranteed them less probing examination by the Northern Patrol.

On 2 February a reluctant Kaiser finally gave his consent to unrestricted submarine warfare against Allied merchant shipping. Merchantmen could now be sunk on sight. Stoss' *U8*, an old kerosene-burning boat, ushered in the new campaign by sinking five ships without warning off Beachy Head.

It needed a star U-boat skipper to penetrate the North Channel, with its anti-submarine nets. Such a man was Wegener of the *U27*. He had already sunk the British submarine *E3* and the seaplane carrier HMS *Hermes*, a converted cruiser, early in the war. The

AMC *Bayano*, former Elder & Fyffe banana boat, had left the Clyde and was idling along at 8 knots waiting for daylight, to leave the North Channel. Wegener caught her north of Stranraer at dawn, and she sank with more than half her crew.

Wegener then withdrew from the North Channel. Between Rathlin Island and Islay he fired two torpedoes at the AMC *Ambrose*. The twelve year old ex-Booth liner was making 14 knots and dodged the torpedoes. When the *U27* surfaced for an attack with gunfire she herself was hit by a shell from one of the AMC's guns and crash-dived.

The 10th CS had now lost three of its auxiliary cruisers. With the White Star *Cedric* returned to trade because she was too big, and Thomas Wilson's *Eskimo* because she was too small, there were now eighteen AMCs left for the Northern Patrol, with some of their ship's companies seriously reduced by boarding parties and armed guards.

On 11th March a new British Order in Council decreed that no neutral ship must sail to German ports, on pain of future seizure by Britain, but must discharge all goods consigned to Germany in a British port, while all goods loaded in a German port for export would, if discovered, be confiscated. In effect this meant that every ship intercepted had to be thoroughly searched. More hard seatime for the 10th CS, more crews depleted.

On 7 May the *U20* sank the *Lusitania*. Schwieger's reference books had told him she was an armed merchant cruiser, and in fact almost all her cargo was contraband, including copper, brass, cases of shrapnel shells and ammunition, and a mysterious consignment marked on the manifest as "325 bales of furs", thought later to have been gun cotton. Schwieger was appalled when his periscope's eye revealed the carnage he had caused to innocent civilians, ninety-seven of whom had been American citizens, and one of them a Vanderbilt.

In mid-June Captain Webster's HMS *Motagua*, ex-banana boat, caught *U33* as she was attacking the Norwegian SS *Daranger*, and the submarine crash-dived before the AMC's fire. She came up again next day off the Butt of Lewis and was put down again by HMS *Orotava* before she could recharge her batteries or ventilate the boat.

By July, 1915, no neutral shipowners would accept German

cargoes, though some dubious neutral ships with cargoes of meat, grain and wool were released after interception by British warships, to cultivate neutral, especially American, opinion.

In the long summer days de Chair needed more ships on the Northern Patrol. He rearranged his patrol lines to try to cope.

Captain Randell's old 10,700-ton *Victorian* and her sister ship HMS *Virginian* had once been famous as the world's first turbine liners. In a sunny haze in July *Victorian*'s masthead lookout sighted the white sails of a fully rigged ship. She turned out to be the 1,571-ton American *Pass of Balmaha*, one of the last of the clipper ships, built in 1888. Her papers said she was heading for Archangel with her cargo of southern cotton, but Randell was suspicious and put an armed guard in her to take her into port for inspection. They had not been long aboard when the *U36* surfaced and stopped the big sailing vessel. By international law armed boarding parties were not at that time allowed to fight unless attacked. *Victorian*'s punctilious boarding officer thought the best thing to do was for his men to remain out of sight below. The U-boat escorted the *Pass of Balmaha* to Cuxhaven, where the British sailors emerged to find themselves prisoners of war. After this incident the Germans threatened to sink any neutral ship with a British armed guard aboard, and British boarding parties were given permission to defend their charges.

The *Victorian* sank the *Friedrich Asp*, which was creeping down the Norwegian coast with a cargo of iron ore from Sweden via Narvik, and captured a Swedish ship with 7,000 tons of it, again obviously intended for the German war effort. Then Captain William Kennedy's HMS *India*, ex-P & O, recently commissioned for the Northern Patrol, replaced *Victorian* when she went off to refuel at the new coaling base of Swarbacks Min, a good, deep anchorage in the Shetlands with room for seven ships.

Kapitänleutnant Hoppé in the *U22* had been sent especially to deal with the aggressive British AMC on the Norwegian patrol. On 8 August he torpedoed the *India* in the Vestfjord and she sank in five minutes with heavy loss of life. Of the twenty-two officers and 119 men saved, some were rescued by HM trawler *Saxon*, others by the SS *Gotaland*. The *Gotaland* landed four dead, including the pathetic body of seventeen-year-old Boy Seaman Sam Harding. The SS *Andanaes* brought in three bodies, the Norwegian naval vessel *Juarez* the body of a young cook with a purse containing 9s 3½d in it. The *Saxon* landed seven dead, comprising an assistant paymaster, a young sub-lieutenant, a warrant telegraphist, a writer, a leading seaman, an able seaman and a fireman. Bodies of the dead were driven through the town of Narvik to the Chapel, the coffins covered with flags and flowers from the ladies of the town and large wreaths contributed by Vice-Consul Aagaard on behalf of the British Minister and Legation. The dead were accorded military honours at the funeral, which was attended by Norwegian Army and Navy representatives and by some of the *India*'s survivors interned at Bjerkvik. Captain Kennedy asked Vice-Consul Aagaard for "some indoor games to amuse the men such as draughts, dominoes, chess, also pipe tobacco, cigarette tobacco, papers and cigarettes." Norwegians did not roll their own, and could not supply cigarette papers, but all the rest was sent to the camp. Eighty-one men saved by neutral ships outside territorial waters were released to make their way home.

Unrestricted U-boat warfare was growing more savage all the time. On 24 July, just after she had taken the *Pass of Balmaha* and *Victorian*'s armed guard, the *U36* stopped a coaster off the Orkneys and had just surfaced when the U-boat captain saw another small merchant ship approaching. Eager to bag her as well, he turned his attention to the newcomer and fired a shell across her bows. She stopped at once and lowered boats. Still firing, the U-boat closed her. When the *U36* was six hundred yards off the stranger suddenly unmasked two 6-pounder and two 3-pounder guns and returned the fire. Her broadside sank the U-boat, leaving her captain and fourteen crewmen in the water.

The unlucky U-boat had run into a Q-ship, or Special Service Vessel, the *Prince Charles*, commanded by Lieutenant Mark-Wardlaw. These armed merchantmen with hidden guns had been operating since the beginning of the war. Often called "mystery ships", they looked like ordinary coasters or small freighters but carried naval crews. Trailing their coats in known U-boat hunting grounds, if stopped by a German submarine they sent away a "panic party" in the boats, with guns' crews left in the ship ready to unmask the armament, hidden behind hinged panels, false bulwarks or deckhouses.

4 Hidden Guns

Did the books of 10th CS balance? Credit – 200,000 square miles of ocean patrolled in the year 1915 in all weathers, with submarines present, 3,098 merchantmen intercepted. Debit – four ships lost, with the lives of 863 officers and men out of a total of 9,000.

A sad incident at the beginning of 1916 added to these statistics. HMS *Ebro*, one of the latest ships to join the Northern Patrol, intercepted the Norwegian barque *Olivia* on 14 January. Her intended movements were suspect, and an armed guard was put aboard her to take her in, consisting of Lieutenant Austen Bennett in charge of Leading Seaman Alf Pottinger, Able Seamen George Moore, Albert Nears and Newfoundlander Anderson.

Nothing more was heard from the *Olivia* or the armed guard. On 15 February a boat from the *Olivia* was picked up near Floro, and the barque was posted missing by the Norwegian authorities. On 20 April Mrs Annie Moore wrote to the Admiralty "to ask you if you can give me any information regarding my husband G. H. Moore, AB, (Chatham Division) who was last heard of January 2nd of this year 1916 on His Majesty's Ship *Ebro*. Would you be so kind as to make enquiries to see if he is still alive for I am very anxious to know." All that the reply, from the Accountant General of the Navy, could tell her was that "enquiries are still proceeding and that the result will be communicated to you as early as possible".

In her little house in Barking Alice Nears went on studying the Admiralty Lists of prisoners of war in Germany, but her husband was never on one. In a letter of 9 June she confided in My Lords: "I feel that only my worst fears are to be confirmed but that would be even better than this long suspense. It is now five months since I last heard from him." She went on hoping, but none of the five men was ever seen again.

As a result of American protests over the *Lusitania* and *Arabic*, U-boats had been forbidden to sink any merchant ships west of Great Britain and the English Channel without first giving adequate warning and providing proper safety arrangements for crews and passengers. The heavy British merchant ship losses immediately fell. The U-boat initiative was blunted for the time being, but there was a fresh attempt to get armed merchant raiders to sea to prey on Allied shipping on the far flung trade routes.

On 6 January the pre-Dreadnought battleship HMS *King Edward VII* hit a mine and sank west of the Orkneys. Next day the Swedish freighter SS *Bonheur* went the same way off Sule Skerry. There was a raider loose.

The SS *Pungo*, 4,789 gross tons, was a typical small refrigerated fruit vessel with capacity for a few passengers, rather like the British Elder & Fyffe banana boats. Like them she had graceful lines, with a rakish flare to her foc'sle, long low midships deckhouse for accommodation, single raking funnel. She was built for the West Indies trade and could make 14 knots comfortably. Armed with four 15-centimetre (5.9-inch) guns, one 10cm (4.1-inch) gun, four 50cm (19.7-inch) torpedo tubes and three hundred mines—all concealed behind false bulwarks and dummy superstructure, or camouflaged as deck cargo – and renamed SMS *Möwe* (Seagull), she left the Elbe on 29 December, 1915, Swedish colours painted on her sides, under the command of Fregattenkapitän Graf zu Dohna-Schlodien. Penetrating the blockade unchallenged, she laid her mines west of the Orkneys, steamed south still unchecked, swung east into the Bay of Biscay and sowed another field off the Ile d'Oléron and the mouth of the Gironde River, and returned to the broad Atlantic, all prepared to alter her appearance from time to time by rigging a second, dummy, funnel or changing the height of the real one, which was telescopic, like her masts.

On 11 January 180 miles west-nor'-west of Cape Finisterre *Möwe* captured and sank her first victim, the British freighter *Farringford*, and later the same day the Seagull swooped on the *Corbridge*, a loaded collier, which the raider kept with her for the time being. Three more freighters, the *Author, Trader* and *Dromonby*, followed on 13 January. These ships were sunk by bombs placed on board and their crews taken aboard *Möwe*.

On 15 January Elder Dempster's refrigerated fruit carrier *Appam*, which traded with West Africa, was four days out of Dakar, bound for Plymouth. At 2.30 in the afternoon a strange steamer crossed her course, hoisted the signal "MN" meaning "Stop immediately" and ran up the German Naval ensign.

The *Appam* manned her small 3-pounder gun. The German immediately opened fire with a gun previously concealed on her poop, its breech covered to look like a wheel box, a dummy wheel stuck on the muzzle with a dummy compass just for'ard of it. Three shells hit the after part of *Appam*'s wheelhouse and she stopped. A boarding party removed bullion worth £36,000, and a German prize crew took over the *Appam*, which also remained in company with the raider.

Möwe also took the steamer *Ariadne* on the 15th, and further east in the Bay that evening her mines claimed their first victim. Captain Luzarraga of the SS *Belgica* was a good seaman who had saved the crews of three wrecked ships in the past. At 7 p.m. he was on the bridge enjoying a quiet pipe when there was a tremendous detonation under the bows and he lost his beloved ship, which he had commanded for twelve years. The British Vice-Consul at La Rochelle sent back a report of "a fast steamer of 2,000 to 3,000 tons register, large and long superstructure, two sloping funnels, hull apparently convex (as seen broadside on), straight stem". The Lisbon-bound freighter *Demerara* reported sighting off the Azores a ship apparently painted "grey with a painted bow wave" and grey funnel. When the ship turned away her other side was black, her funnel buff with a black top.

On the evening of 16 January Dohna intercepted the Clan Line's *Clan MacTavish*. This braw ship fought back and *Möwe* destroyed her with gunfire. Some of her crew were taken on board the raider, others joined the crowded *Appam*, where they found the crews of the *Author, Dromonby, Trader, Corbridge, Farringford* and *Ariadne*.

The raider appeared to be a new ship. She had come up with the *Clan MacTavish* like something out of a nightmare, painted all black, or like a steam-age Flying Dutchman, and her tall, dark, aristocratic Captain fitted the picture, a remote, mysterious figure always on his bridge, binoculars raised to the horizon. The black paint was fresh, and had been laid on over white, as one of the prisoners noticed when he brushed against it coming up over the side. The only relief in this sombre coat were the Swedish flags painted on the sides, abreast the fore hatches, and on the 17th men started painting the upper part of the poop white. She had a low bridge, which made the unusually tall raking masts appear even loftier. Suspended high up from truck to truck to get the best possible conditions for transmission and reception were the wireless aerials. A very conspicuous feature was the 30-foot tall ventilating derrick post just for'ard of the poop. There was a lookout position high up the foremast, and a lookout chair which could be hoisted up the mainmast. The prisoners were not allowed to get near the armament, but some of them were able to make out two guns in hidden positions on the foc'sle, two bigger ones either side of the fore hatch, and mine rails amidships hidden by hinged metal plates raised to look like bulwarks. A brass plate on the bridge, which one captain managed to get a quick look at, identified her as vessel Number 258 built by Tecklenborg of Swinemunde and Bremerhaven in 1914.

On 20 January the *Möwe* caught and sank the sailing vessel *Edinburgh* thirty-five miles east-nor'-east of Fernando de Noronha. On 29 January *Möwe, Corbridge* and *Appam* arrived off the mouth of the Amazon. The raider spent three days coaling from the *Corbridge*, which was taken out to sea and sunk on 2 February. On 4 February *Möwe* was back in action when she sank the Belgian *Luxembourg*. The British ship *Flamenco*, intercepted on 6 February, was foolhardy enough to send out an SOS and was shelled into a blazing, sinking wreck.

The Sunderland steamer *Westburn* was captured on 8 February and retained in company; the SS *Horace* was taken and sunk next day.

By this time *Möwe*'s stores and fuel were running low, and Dohna could not count on continual replenishment from captured ships. Ship and men were in need of overhaul and replenishment. Besides, the prisoners, who were eating up the rations, were overflowing all the spare spaces on board. The crews of the *Clan Mac-Tavish, Flamenco, Corbridge, Horace, Luxembourg* and *Edinburgh*, including any officers who gave their word not to engage in further hostilities against Germany, were transferred to the *Westburn* under a German prize crew. On the 22nd the overloaded *Westburn* arrived at Santa Cruz in the West Indies. Dohna set course for home, capturing the SS *Saxon Princess* on the way.

In the Imperial Dockyard at Kiel in February there was some speculation and idle rumour about the new 4,493-tonner *Guben*, originally ordered for the Hansa Line. She had been fitted, supposedly in secret though everyone knew about it, with guns – four 15-centimetre and one 10cm – and two torpedo tubes in her fore hold. In particular the men from the merchantmen *Rown* and *Schwaben* who had been drafted to her goggled at the armament. "What is she, then?" "What are we in for?" "Where are we bound?" Every morning it was "What's the buzz, then?"

Then they got caught up in the feverish slog to prepare the ship for sea. It was obvious from the amount of coal and stores they shifted aboard that this was to be no fortnight's pleasure trip. The holds were mostly full of coal, or compressed cork for buoyancy. Their destination remained veiled in mystery until news began to come through of the *Möwe*'s adventures in the Atlantic, where she was capturing Allied ships. It dawned on the crew of the *Guben*, otherwise *Auxiliary G*, that they were meant for a similar mission. The ship's Exec, Kapitänleutnant Nebresky, spread the word that she had a job to do in the Baltic, but no one believed him.

Whatever it was must be important, because on 24 February the Kaiser himself came aboard and made them a stirring speech, having brought officers from other ships to hear it.

On 25 February the ship entered the Kiel Canal, and bets laid on the Atlantic got few takers. On her arrival in the Elbe final preparations were made. She was re-christened SMS *Greif*, though for the purposes of her mission she was to bear the name of the Norwegian steamer *Rena* of Tonsberg. Norwegian colours were painted on her hull, the two blue rings of *Rena*'s company on her funnel. Then everything was finally squared off and secured for sea, boats turned in and lashed down, ladders stowed, oilskins issued. After a few other alterations she got under way towards evening on Saturday 26 February and anchored off the lightship *Elbe I*.

Fregettenkapitän Tietze cleared lower deck and gave them the final word on their mission. In her Swedish disguise, with her armament masked, the *Greif* was to ease her way through the British blockade for a raiding cruise, going north of Iceland to work her way down well south of the Cape of Good Hope and not to begin raiding until they were off Dar-es-Salaam, Tanganyika, in the Indian Ocean. They were provisioned for a year, and would stay at sea until the war was over, if necessary.

"Men," said Tietze, "I congratulate you on being selected for this important mission and hope it will be crowned with success. Now – three cheers for the Kaiser!" The men aboard the lightship heard the hearty cheering as it rang across the water, and turned back to their humdrum, safe duties.

On the 27th *Greif* stood out to sea, steering for Norway. There were some three hundred and sixty men aboard the raider, a very large crew for an innocent merchantman, and the order was passed to keep below out of sight as much as possible.

The AMCs HMS *Columbella* and *Patia* were about to leave their patrol lines off the Faroes to return to port for coal when they were ordered to join a force of light cruisers and destroyers searching for "a German merchant auxiliary, fitted as a decoy" reported as having left the Kattegat.

The *Greif* steered north between Norway and the Shetlands, double lookouts peering to westward through their binoculars. It was the right sort of weather for running the gauntlet – fog and snowstorms.

About 5 a.m. on the 29th they had reached the latitude of the Shetlands when through the murk a lookout sighted a ship about a mile away. Even through the mist there was no mistaking the silhouette of a British cruiser. Tietze stopped engines, doused all lights, and hove to. The cruiser disappeared into the darkness. The guns were manned, but they had been told that the seas had been cleared of British ships. *If* a British cruiser was sighted they would run from her in the interests of their mission. Tietze got up speed again and altered course away from the enemy cruiser's patrol line.

The day dawned clear. Captains Young and Wardle in the AMCs HMS *Andes* and *Alcantara* blessed the change as the two ships were due to rendezvous north-east of the Shetlands at 9 a.m. to transfer secret papers. In *Greif* Tietze cursed it. Now they had only their lucky star to get them through the blockade.

As *Andes* and *Alcantara* approached their rendezvous both ships received a wireless signal from Admiral Tupper, who had taken over 10th Cruiser Squadron from de Chair, ordering them not to leave the meeting point until further orders. "Armed disguised auxiliary from south may pass patrol line today," he added.

After dawn a lookout in the *Greif* reported a cloud of smoke ahead to starboard, approaching them rapidly. It was an enemy blockading cruiser. Everyone waited tensely, like actors poised in the wings for their big performance. The sea was calm, the weather clear, though with a slight overcast. There was no chance of avoiding a confrontation. They would just have to be convincing.

At about 8.30 a.m. the *Andes* was about 100 miles north-east of the Shetlands when she sighted smoke bearing south-west. At 8.35 Young altered course towards the smoke. Fifteen minutes later masts and funnel came up over the horizon. He thought she must be the *Alcantara*, but by 8.55 she could be made out to be a steamer painted black with a black funnel relieved by two blue bands, and two masts, of distinctly Germanic appearance, steering north-by-east, with Norwegian flags painted on her sides and the name *Rena* in white letters on her bow. Young ordered the W/T office to send an urgent sighting report, and turned *Andes* on to the same course as the stranger, keeping ahead of her.

In *Alcantara*, coming up from the south, Wardle had also sighted the smoke, on his port beam, bearing North 75° West. Almost at once Chief Yeoman of Signals Frank Coombes handed him the pink signal pad page with the message from *Andes*, "Enemy vessel in sight steering north-east at 15 knots." Young gave his own position and a short description of the other ship, which Wardle read as stating that she had two funnels.

Alcantara was ready for action. On receipt of Tupper's previous signal the guns had been readied for instant action. Four boats each side were swung out on a level with E Deck, in addition to the seaboats abreast the Boat Deck and one boat each side swung out in line with the old Second Class Promenade Deck.

Wardle increased to full speed and altered course, steering for the smoke and bringing it three points on his port bow. Almost at once more smoke was reported bearing about due north. Wardle signalled to *Andes*: "Have you both in sight" and ordered HMS *Patia* by wireless to close them, giving his position.

Andes was hull down to the north, steering north-east. Wardle did not consider the first smoke sighted on his port bow, which he had made out to be a steamer with *one* funnel and two masts, to be the enemy referred to by *Andes*. He thought that Young was chasing the enemy, his own duty being to investigate his steamer first before helping *Andes*.

When *Alcantara* was about three miles from the stranger Wardle hoisted the "MN" and fired two rounds of blank. The other ship at once stopped and signalled "RK. I am going to stop. Machinery requires adjusting." She then hoisted "MG VI." If this was meant to be her number it was not in Wardle's copy of *Signal Letters of Ships Of All Countries*.

Alcantara's alarm gongs sounded Action Stations and all guns were trained on the stranger. The cautious Young in *Andes* had not closed the stranger, but had kept turning with her as she made several changes of course from a northerly direction round towards the south-east, with the range about eight miles.

Wardle could not see the smoke which he thought *Andes* had been chasing, and still did not think that the stranger was the enemy referred to by *Andes*. He signalled by searchlight to Young: "Am intercepting suspicious vessel. Is enemy still in sight?" The puzzled Young made no reply, but altered course to the southward and closed *Alcantara* and the stranger, then about four and a half miles distant.

When *Alcantara* was about two miles from the stranger Wardle altered course to port to hold off at this distance to signal her. Everyone could see quite plainly the Norwegian colours painted on her sides abreast her foremast and mainmast, and the two blue bands on her black funnel, but Lieutenant James Johnson RNR said, "She looks just like one of the new Hansa Line boats to me."

Alcantara signalled: "What is your name?"

"*Rena* of Tonsberg."

"Where are you from and where are you bound for?"

"From Rio de Janeiro to Trondheim."

These particulars, with her size and course, seemed to agree with *Lloyds' Confidential List of Ships*. Getting no reply from *Andes*, Wardle decided to put an armed guard aboard the stranger, who appeared quite normal, then go to help Young with the enemy as swiftly as possible, as meanwhile more smoke had been sighted to the south-sou'-east.

The "Return stores" was sounded, but the order given for guns' crews and control parties to remain at their stations. While Lieutenant-Commander Frank Main was getting his armed guard ready, Wardle reduced to 14 knots and kept clear of the stranger's stern, with one gun trained on her all the time.

Now Young in *Andes* signalled by searchlight:

"That is the suspicious vessel."

With a sinking heart, Tietze saw the enemy's boarding boat being hoisted out. They were lost. But they would not give up without a fight.

Across the water Jim Johnson got young Sub-Lieutenant Stanley and the crew into the boat, saw that a small amount of starboard helm was pre-set so as to give the boat an instant swing towards the other vessel's stern or port quarter the instant it hit the water, and waited for the armed guard to board.

In *Greif* Tietze shouted in a voice that resounded along the decks,

"Hoist the Naval Ensign! Man the guns and torpedo tubes!"

Wardle, watching the stranger, saw the ensign staff drop over her stern, and men clearing away a gun on her poop previously disguised by a dummy steering box. Flaps in her side covered by the painted Norwegian flags fell down.

"Fire salvoes!" Tietze shouted.

Wardle saw the gun flashes. Two shells screeched over the *Alcantara*.

"Salvoes!" Tietze ordered again.

Two shells hit the *Alcantara*. One damaged the boarding boat, setting it on fire and killing or wounding some of the crew. Johnson ordered them out of the boat and ran to his control station. The second shell burst in Wardle's cabin under the bridge, cutting the pipes for the telemotor steering gear and putting all the telephones on the bridge out of action, killing and wounding men there. Shells from a big 3.7-centimetre machine-gun under the enemy's bridge began hitting *Alcantara*'s bridge.

Wardle ordered "Full speed ahead. Hard-a-port. Open fire!"

"Controlled fire! Range 2,500 yards. Deflection 10 left!" Jim Johnson shouted down his telephone to quarters officers George Williamson and Wallace Kay.

Lieutenant John Howell-Price, the ship's Fire Officer, quickly assembled his fire parties. Seven men under Chief Stoker Good hurried off aft, seven more under Engineer Storekeeper Powell went for'ard. Howell-Price with eight men took the midships station, and there was a man at each of the fireproof doors on B, C and D Decks.

The ship would not answer her helm. Wardle sent Boy Seaman Eddy May aft to order the emergency steering gear connected up. While he made his way aft the ship was not under control. The helm automatically came amidships but the ship continued to turn to port, closing the enemy, who had also gone ahead and was turning to starboard, firing high-explosive shell, some falling short, others hitting the *Alcantara* near the waterline amidships, penetrating Number 1 stokehold bunker and the engine room, and below the waterline in the refrigerating room. The order for full speed reached the engine room but could not be carried out as steam began to fail immediately and continued to drop throughout the action. All Engineer Commander George Blay's telephone communications were out of action. He tried ringing the forebridge, the after control and both stokeholds, all without reply. But *Alcantara*'s three port 6-inch and the port 6-pounder had begun hitting the enemy almost at once. The first round hit the ammunition for the enemy's after gun and the explosion knocked the gun out. Another shell pierced the main steam pipe in the engine room and the Second Engineer narrowly escaped being scalded to death.

The *Andes* had also opened fire, with her starboard guns. Then Young saw that on this course he had the *Alcantara* directly in his line of fire on the other side of the enemy. He turned *Andes* on her starboard helm off the line and brought her port battery into action at a range of under four miles. He closed to three miles and held off to keep out of torpedo range. Then he saw *Alcantara* altering to port, and to clear the range again he did the same, and had to turn twice more to avoid firing on his ex-Royal Mail consort.

One of *Andes*' first rounds exploded in *Greif*'s lower bridge, which started to burn. Most of the officers there were disabled. Another shell exploded in the engine room about the same time, doing great damage and incapacitating everyone with gas fumes. Some of *Greif*'s guns engaged the *Andes*, most of the shots falling short but one round just missing the stern and one passing overhead.

Tietze transferred to the foc'sle to give the order,

"Torpedo ready for firing! Fire!"

Alcantara's Navigator, Lieutenant Harold Vivian, saw the splash of the torpedo as it was fired and shouted to the Captain. Wardle ordered "Hard-a-port!" but the steering gear was still out of action and she did not answer her helm. The torpedo just missed astern.

Frank Main got the after steering gear connected up and immediately put the helm hard-a-port to increase the range and bring the starboard battery into action.

In the *Greif* another torpedo left the tube. The *Alcantara* had just turned enough to allow the after starboard 6-inch to bear when the second torpedo hit her and exploded on the starboard side at the point where the bulkhead between the fore and after stokeholds joined the ship's side. Some stokers were scalded or wounded by splinters. Up on B Deck John Howell-Price felt the great shock and the deck buckle and surge under him. Wooden bulkheads blew adrift, blocking the port passages. There was a dense cloud of black smoke with a smell and taste like common black powder.

Both stokeholds started to flood fast and the young officers in charge had to order the men out before there was time to draw fires. Sub-Lieutenant Hazelton had to wade through three feet of water in Number 1 stokehold to get out. Reg Mackintosh coolly supervised the exodus from Number 2 in the eerie light from the emergency oil lamps. The engine room began to make water with increasing speed, and the emergency electric bilge pumps were overwhelmed.

Main eased the helm and gave the order to steady. The ship at once sheered to port with the erratic working of the propellers and began to list. In the engine room Blay shut the port main inlet valve. Shortly afterwards the ship took a slight list to starboard. Blay immediately closed the starboard main inlet valve and opened the starboard bilge injection valve. But this list was brief and the ship rolled back again.

All *Alcantara*'s port guns were firing, and about 10.32 the enemy was seen to be lowering boats. *Greif* was badly damaged. Her steering gear had been wrecked, only her forward gun remained workable, and all communication between fore and aft had been cut by a barrier of fire. Most of her guns' crews had been killed or wounded. Nebresky was dead, and a shell hit in her torpedo compartment had killed everyone there. But Tietze was determined. No Englishman was going to set foot on his ship. He ordered the explosive charges along her keel activated. This was done, and the ship began slowly to settle. Tietze sighted another ship on the horizon. Reinforcement for the British. It was time to leave her.

"Abandon ship!"

Undamaged boats and rafts were lowered, planks and empty shell boxes thrown overboard for swimmers to cling to. With three more cheers for the Kaiser, the last few officers and men jumped into the sea, sliding down ropes, Tietze last of all. Above the *Greif* and the cloud of smoke enveloping her the Imperial Naval Ensign still flew at the main. The empty ship drifted ahead, slowly turning to port, burning fiercely.

Wardle ordered "Cease firing", but the order did not reach the after gun, which continued firing until the increasing list prevented it. *Alcantara* began to turn to starboard, and the last guns to fire were Numbers 2 and 3 on that side.

The light breeze blew the smoke away from the enemy, and she fired one more round.

This was actually from a heated gun, but Wardle was not to know that and ordered "Open fire!" again, thinking that the exodus of men from the raider had been a panic party, Q-ship style. But *Alcantara* was listing badly now in any case and obviously sinking, and in a few minutes the orders came "Cease firing. Boat stations. Stop engines".

George Blay came up on the bridge. He found Norwegian Lieutenant Alva Hernandez in the charthouse and reported that the boilers would soon be out of action and that the water was gaining rapidly in the engine room. Hernandez told him that "Abandon ship" had been ordered.

John Howell-Price's fire party had been fighting fires on C Deck in the port cabin de luxe and the Social Hall on E Deck. Enemy shells were tearing through C and D Decks, opening six-inch holes in iron bulkheads but not exploding. He sent buckets to E deck and got hoses on C Deck, but the water pipes had been cut by shell fire. He closed the fireproof doors, isolating the fire to an area 120 feet by 30 feet, and had put out the E Deck fire when the ship took a lurch to port and the order "Abandon ship!" was passed. One of his coolest assistants, Chief Steward George Temple, stayed to help the wounded, and was not seen again.

In the engine room both telegraphs rang to "Stop". Steam was shut off on the starboard engine but the port engine stop valve could not be reached because of the height of the water and the angle of the foot plates. Water was pouring through the ship's side into the port forward side bunker.

From *Andes*, still well away to the east of the stricken ships, Young could see *Alcantara*'s heavy list to port and fires amidships and aft. Five minutes later he sighted the curling bow waves of Captain Alan Hotham's light cruiser *Comus* and the destroyer *Munster*, both brand-new ships capable of 30 knots, which had left Scapa Flow with the light cruisers *Calliope* and *Blanche* and destroyers *Magic* and *Noble* on the evening of 28 February to intercept the German auxiliary decoy ship reported as having left the Kattegat, possibly with a U-boat, about 7 a.m. that day. Shortly after reaching the Pentland Skerries the force had split up to hunt in pairs.

Young signalled them that the *Alcantara* was sinking. Then there was a hail of "Submarine Red 5–2!" from a lookout, followed by "Submarine right astern!" from After Control. Young held his course but on a second report of "Submarine astern!" with greatest reluctance turned away from the *Alcantara*.

At 10.55 a.m. the latter was clearly sinking. Aboard her every effort was being made to get those of her boats which were still sea-worthy turned out and the wounded put into them. With the ship listing sharply it was impossible for men to reach their correct boat stations, but officers did their best to get as many away as possible in the starboard boats, the falls of which were let go or simply cut with Pusser's dirks. Howell-Price had crawled out on to the starboard side from D Deck and up to the Boat Deck to try to help lower the boats. Many of the falls had been shot through, and parted, dropping boats at steep angles and throwing men into the water. Those that did reach the water on an even keel were dragged along awkwardly by the ship, which was still making three or four knots through the water and turning to starboard. Writer Bill Bond, who was suffering from a hernia, slid across the canting deck to the lee side to help a wounded man into the water, then jumped after him. John Howell-Price managed to let go the falls of two boats, which slid down the ship's side and took the water well, and were rapidly filled with men off the side. He followed them into the water. The ship was almost on her beam ends by then. She continued to list, and at a few minutes after eleven o'clock she rolled over and sank.

Andes turned back at once towards the spot, but *Comus* signalled that she had ordered *Munster* to steam on ahead and pick up survivors. The destroyer's three thin funnels belched more smoke as she went to her full 34 knots.

Some fifteen of *Alcantara*'s boats or Engleheart rafts and two rafts made on board floated clear of the ship. Swimmers immediately began making for them. Some port side boats, their falls cut or shot away, floated clear when the ship went down but they were badly damaged and most of them sank. Men helped each other to survive. Both John Howell-Price and young Horace Richardson, Boy 1st Class, jumped out of their boats and gave other men their places. Temporary Midshipman Hardress Waller D'Arcy Evans swam about helping men in difficulties to keep afloat, and Temporary Lieutenant-Commander Charles Williams supported a wounded man in the sea until one of the ships picked them up.

At 11.35 a.m. the enemy was still afloat and had not actually surrendered, so *Andes* and *Comus* attacked her with carefully controlled gunfire, manoeuvering so as to avoid hitting the German boats and swimming survivors. This was not always possible, and some men were hit. Tietze was killed by a shell splinter which took away half of his head.

The enemy did not return the fire. At 12.12 a.m. *Comus* ceased fire when the raider's main magazine blew up, with the ship in flames, listing heavily to port and settling by the stern. *Comus* closed *Munster*, put *Alcantara*'s surgeon John Berry aboard the destroyer, and Hotham sent her off to Scapa as there were no more *Alcantara* survivors, of whom *Munster* had two hundred aboard and *Comus* forty-one, to be picked up. Berry spent hours attending to the wounded in *Comus* and then in *Munster* before he changed his own clothes.

At 12.20 the *Andes* ceased firing, as the raider was on fire from stem to stern and sinking. At 1 p.m. the *Greif* listed further to port, her stern went down, and she disappeared in a cloud of steam and smoke. *Comus* made for her rafts and boats, spread out over a wide area. *Calliope* and *Magic*, patrolling to the south-west of *Comus* and *Munster*, had come up by now to head off the possibly altered course of the chase to the south-east, but seeing that *Comus*, *Andes* and *Munster* had the battle well in hand they returned to their patrol line, being joined there by *Blanche*.

Andes picked up three *Alcantara* survivors, then two German boats came alongside. While they were securing there a periscope was reported bearing Red 20, and the *Comus* was seen to open fire in another direction, signalling "Submarine in sight!" *Andes* went ahead at full speed, dragging one boat behind her, and stopped again at 1.25 when her "periscope" turned out to be the staff of a rammer blown overboard from one of the ships.

Comus steamed at full speed for her submarine, which was found to be an upturned boat awash, painted white, with small waves breaking over it. She ordered Young in *Andes* to pick up the last German survivors from the sea. Most of these were on a raft, which *Andes*' seaboat towed alongside. Getting wounded and exhausted men up the towering ship's side was a slow process. At 2.35 p.m. *Comus* signalled *Andes* to make one last search of the area, then set course for base. *Andes* steamed carefully through the wreckage. After rescuing one hundred and ten men and the German Assistant Navigator, the latter severely wounded, *Andes* made a thorough search and found one more man. At 3.37 p.m. she proceeded on patrol.

Lower deck prisoners were stripped and sent to the bathrooms to clean up, then were given dry clothes and confined in the starboard wing passage under guard. Officers messed in the wardroom or warrant officers' mess.

All the Germans rescued were surprised and pleased at their

treatment aboard *Andes, Comus* and *Munster*. One man said that he had held back from being rescued at first as he had been told that he would be shackled and beaten. After a diet of dry rye bread and sausage, white bread and butter was a revelation to them, though they missed their beer, and hospitality towards a beaten enemy did not go as far as the issue of tots.

Many of them spoke English, and *Alcantara*'s Lieutenant Hernandez had fluent German. They knew little about the course of the war and had been convinced by propaganda that Germany was winning until they read English newspapers on board the *Andes*. They were used to news which magnified a two-mile German advance at Verdun into ten, but they admitted that there were plenty of Army widows at home, where Allied prisoners of war were "eating up the food". Never mind – the Zeppelins would win the war.

Casualties in the *Alcantara* were two officers and sixty-seven men, most of them killed outright or dying of wounds aboard the rescue ships.

As for the *Greif/Guben/Rena/Auxiliary G*, "We came through the action with honour, and with pride will remember 29 February, 1916" ran the memorial document to those who died in the ship produced by prisoners of war at Handforth Camp on the occasion of the Commemorative Celebration on 1 March, 1917. "Near 100 German sailors died a heroic death for the Fatherland and, true to their oath to the flag, found a seaman's early grave in the waters of the North Sea."

5 "May I see your papers?"

Möwe had all the luck. When the brave but ill-starred *Greif* was going down to the guns of *Andes* and *Alcantara*, the Atlantic raider with a bag of 57,000 tons of Allied shipping recorded in her log was four hundred miles west of Rockall heading home, still in her coat of Swedish colours. She steered a wary course, and with all the extra ships across her path after the *Greif* panic, each one seeing a disguised raider in every innocent neutral vessel, she passed blithely a hundred miles south of Iceland, crossed both arms of the British Patrol Line A stretched out from the Faeroes, and dropped her hook in the Elbe on 6 March, 1916. The 10th Cruiser Squadron intercepted scores of ships every week, but not the lucky *Möwe*.

Nor were they catching those crafty Norwegians who were steaming at high speed without lights at night to beat the blockade. Trade was trade, after all. But the blockade *was* biting, and the storm-tossed AMCs were causing hardship in Germany. There had been poor harvests, and items like forage and fertilizer were badly needed to feed the livestock for milk, meat, wool and leather, and enrich the soil for wheat. Metals for weapons were always needed too, of course, and daring British submarines which had squeezed into the Baltic were cutting off the Swedish iron trade.

Admiralty Intelligence warned of minelayers, and rumours of more raiders gained the Northern Patrol more ships. On 31 May/1 June the Battle of Jutland was fought. The High Seas Fleet lost fewer ships than the British but was driven back demoralized to swing round the buoy in harbour. Jellicoe was able to detach fourteen cruisers and eighteen destroyers to watch the raiders' route west of St Kilda and beef up the patrol line between the Faeroes and Iceland.

And in September the Kaiser let his U-boats off the leash. They began to lurk in all the close approaches to the British Isles once more. The big supply sub *Bremen* left for New York to barter gold for foodstuffs. The AMC HMS *Mantua*, zigzagging west of Rockall on Patrol Line D, felt a bump and a grind below, which was the end of *Bremen*.

In mid-October Captain Booty's HMS *Otway* was patrolling north of St Kilda Island west of the Orkneys in rising seas when her barrel man sighted a ship flying Norwegian colours.

When challenged she claimed to be bound from Halifax, Nova Scotia, to Leith on the Firth of Forth. *Lloyd's Weekly Index* put her at Le Havre. Booty sent over a boarding party of two armed men under a young midshipman. They had difficulty getting aboard in the high seas and when they did they found themselves in the middle of an interesting situation. The ship was actually the fully laden British collier *Older* and she was in the hands of nine German sailors from the U-boat which had captured her in the Bay of Biscay who were taking her home to Germany for her valuable cargo and for conversion into a raider. Before they could be stopped the Germans set off explosive charges. Germans and British escaped in the boats but the *Older* did not sink and was taken round the Butt of Lewis into Stornoway.

Rumours of raiders haunted Scapa. The winter would favour them. The ice was creeping south but fog and foul weather would hide them. Grand Fleet cruisers and destroyers burned much fuel patrolling the Fair Isle gap and the other northern exits to the Atlantic. If a raider was reported heading for a run round Iceland, Operation ZZ would send these regular cruisers fanning out to the north and east, while the AMCs of 10CS would form a patrol line stretching north-east from the Faeroes, and send three ships up into the Denmark Strait between Iceland and Greenland, ice permitting. If a raider had already got through the Faeroes-Iceland gap when apprehended, auxiliary cruisers would activate Operation XX and form a line from the Butt of Lewis across to just south-east of Iceland, and send two ships round into the Denmark Strait. The Northern Patrol's last ditch was Operation YY, which aimed at throwing a line further to the west across the path of any raider that had got as far as the 59th parallel. The 2nd Cruiser Squadron stood by at Scapa under short notice for steam to back up the AMCs at any time.

On the chart this looked like a very tight net, but once again Dohna found the holes. In late November *Möwe* left Kiel, crept out of the Kattegat, up the Norwegian coast and probed the blockade well to the north of the Faeroes. Her alert W/T operator intercepted signals from one British cruiser to another ahead of *Möwe* – actually the AMC *Virginian* ordering the *Ebro* to a rendezvous with her. *Möwe* passed through the gap between the *Ebro* and the French-manned *Artois*, formerly the British HMS *Digby*, at dawn, and on 2 December, after a running battle in very rough weather captured and sank the Lamport & Holt liner *Voltaire*, steaming in ballast for New York. The Canadian *Mount Temple* was sunk next day with her cargo of 710 wretched horses.

On 7 December it was the turn of the Belgian steamer *Samland*. She got off an SOS before being sunk, and Admiral Tupper sent the light cruiser *Weymouth* and the AMCs *Almanzora*, *Arlanza*, *Orcoma* and the ex-Bibby liner *Gloucestershire* off in pursuit of the raider.

Other AMCs were hastily diverted to fill the gaps in the patrol lines, and before the *Otway* could take up the *Gloucestershire*'s station, another raider, Fregattenkapitän Karl Nerger's SMS *Wolf*, slipped through the hole, threaded the icebergs in the frozen Denmark Straits, and was off and running down the wide Atlantic, bound for a cruise in the Far East. With hidden guns and torpedo tubes and 465 mines, she was unique in that she also carried a seaplane, Friedrichshaven FF33-J No. 841, christened the *Wölfchen*, a small, two-seat, twin-float machine with a 150 h.p. engine, a top speed of 140 km/h (87 m.p.h.), and a range of 450 miles, flown by two intrepid airmen named Fabeck and Stein.

In the teeth of the pursuit the *Möwe* sank the small SS *King George* and *Cambrian Range* and the White Star cargo liner

Georgic. On 11 December Dohna captured the 4,652-ton steamer *Yarrowdale*, owned by MacKill of Glasgow and bound for Le Havre from New York, then the Norwegian *Hallebjorg*, which he sank, and on 12 December the valuable fully loaded collier *St Theodore*.

The *Möwe* was now grossly overcrowded with prisoners, so Dohna transferred all the men who agreed to parole from the *Mount Temple*, *King George*, *Voltaire*, *Cambrian Range*, *Hallebjorg* and the small British schooner *Duchess of Cornwall* to the *Yarrowdale* under Kapitänleutnant Bordewitz and his prize crew, and sent her back to Germany.

On 21 December, a fortnight after the *Möwe* had eluded the Northern Patrol, a third raider left Heligoland. Korvettenkapitän Graf Felix von Luckner was a sailor of fortune who had sailed round the world in many ships under many flags. Severely wounded at Jutland, he had been selected for command of a ship to go to the Pacific to destroy enemy ships there, mainly sailing vessels bringing food and raw materials to Europe from South Pacific and Australian ports. A secret raider's success depended so much on her camouflage. In August, 1915, the *U36* had brought the splendid three-masted clipper *Pass of Balmaha*, snatched from HMS *Virginian*'s armed guard, into Cuxhaven, and von Luckner saw her as the ideal vessel for his adventure. He used his convalescence to supervise her conversion. She was given auxiliary diesel engines, which were hidden in the hold, as were two 10cm guns and two torpedo tubes. The normal entrance to the holds was blocked by a deck cargo of timber, and access was only obtainable through secret doors. There were other devices which could be put into action if SMS *Seeadler* (*Sea Eagle*), as she was to be renamed, got into trouble with the blockade.

To avoid this she would borrow the name *Irma* from a genuine Norwegian vessel. To back up the disguise, von Luckner, who spoke some Norwegian himself, selected Norwegian-speaking Germans for his crew. Only Norwegian was spoken during training, and von Luckner grew a beard after the style of Norwegian captains, and studied their habits.

She sailed as the SV *Irma*, with a forged British Consular stamp on her papers, on 21 December. It was rough weather round the north of Scotland, but she sighted no other ship until Christmas

Day. At 9.30 in the cold and spray-lashed morning about 180 miles south of Iceland a big British armed merchant cruiser came over the horizon and signalled them to stop.

To add a little subtlety to his performance von Luckner ignored the signal like any blue-nosed Viking in a huff but stopped his secret engines and trimmed his sails to the light breeze prevailing, the while checking for blemishes in their presentation and getting his act together. It had better be good.

After ten minutes windjamming the AMC fired a blank, followed by a live round across their bows. Von Luckner took in sail and stopped.

The AMC circled them very close, all her guns manned and trained on the graceful clipper, lying to so innocently. Von Luckner had only his five more fluent Norwegian speakers on deck with him. The cruiser sheered off a little and stopped. A boat was lowered and came alongside. Von Luckner lowered a rope ladder, giving loud commands in his own rather shaky Norwegian, and two British officers and twelve armed ratings came on board.

"Are you the Captain?"

"Yes, Mr Officer. Happy Christmas."

"Happy Christmas. May I see your papers, please?"

They went below to the Captain's cabin. In the saloon lying on a divan was what appeared to be a woman with a scarf wrapped round her head. In fact "she" was a seventeen-year-old boy seaman whose clear complexion and effeminate appearance made him convincing in drag. Von Luckner hoped that he would divert the boarding officer from examining the saloon too closely.

"This is my wife," said von Luckner. "She has the toothache."

The officer looked sympathetic. "I hope you'll excuse me, madam, I'm only doing my duty. I have to look at the ship's papers. It won't take long." The false wife nodded. His boy's voice would have given him away, though there were Norwegian cushion covers in the cabins, photographs of the King and Queen of Norway on the walls, even one of the late King Edward VII of England, and the gramophone in the mess room was playing "It's a Long Way To Tipperary". The steward distracted the sailors of the British armed guard with glasses of whisky in his pantry.

The deck cargo of timber effffectively prevented a search of the hold, where engines, guns, a big wireless installation and extra accommodation for the large naval crew, not to mention most of the ship's company themselves, were hidden. But there was a secret much closer to discovery. As the British officer scrutinized the papers on the saloon table and von Luckner chewed tobacco and spat on the deck like a true Norwegian skipper, they were actually standing on the platform of a hydraulic lift which could, on the pressing of a button, be suddenly lowered by fourteen feet. Should the boarding officer not be satisfied with the fake *Irma*'s papers, the ship would be taken under armed guard to Kirkwall in the Orkneys, which would take some eight days. At a time when most of the armed guard were eating in the saloon von Luckner would press the button on the bridge that dropped the saloon floor. Twenty armed Germans hidden below in the hold would overpower the diners, the deck crew would grab rifles hidden in the hollow masts, and the ship would be theirs again.

The boarding officer straightened up. "Captain, your papers are all right. But you will have to wait until you get the signal to continue your voyage."

"Will I be safe from submarines?" asked von Luckner innocently. "Can you give me any advice?"

"I don't think you'll meet any as far north as we are."

The boarding party returned to the cruiser, which was actually HMS *Patia*. In about half an hour she signalled "Continue your voyage". The sea eagles breathed their relief steamily into the ice-cold air. As the AMC circled them once more they gave her three cheers and dipped the Norwegian flag. HMS *Patia* signalled "Happy voyage."

"Thank you very much," von Luckner replied. "That's just what we want."

Meanwhile, nearly three thousand miles further south down the long range of the Atlantic on 28 December *Möwe* surprised and sank the new 5,422-ton single-screw steamer *Dramatist* after looting her cargo.

The British Admiralty had assumed from such evidence as they had that a raider was steaming south on the rampage. From 1 January, 1917, the auxiliary cruisers HMS *Macedonia* and *Orama* and the small light cruiser HMS *Amethyst* began a search north of Ascension Island.

The Admiralty was right. *Möwe* was now in the search area. On

5 January she stopped the Japanese *Hudson Maru*, keeping the ship with her as a prisoner transport, and that evening in the moonlight captured the Royal Mail's *Radnorshire* with 7,000 tons of coffee and beans.

Some hundred miles to the north-west of them HMS *Macedonia* was heading for Pernambuco, and the *Orama* and *Amethyst* were steering for a rendezvous with their colliers *Minieh* and *Daleham* south-east of the port.

At ten past four on the afternoon of 9 January the *Minieh* was steering south-west for the rendezvous when she sighted a steamer heading towards her from the opposite direction. Through the glasses she looked like an ordinary tramp, and the standing orders were only to report anything suspicious, so the *Minieh*'s morse key was silent. But when the stranger came abreast of them she suddenly hoisted the "Stop" signal and ordered *Minieh* not to use her wireless. At the same time flaps dropped in her sides exposing a heavy gun for'ard and torpedo tube aft. *Minieh*'s operator tried to get a signal out but it was jammed, and the dynamo also broke down. She was boarded by Germans who took off everything they could carry, mainly tinned goods, whisky and tobacco, while the *Minieh*'s crew were taken aboard the raider, which one of the Germans said was named the *Vineta*, another of *Möwe*'s aliases.

Amethyst had actually sighted smoke twenty miles off, which had probably been the *Möwe*, but it vanished. *Macedonia*, *Amethyst* and *Orama* searched the last known position of the *Minieh*, then *Amethyst* hunted off the Abrolhos Rocks, and the two AMCs shaped course for Trinidade Island, to have a look there before steaming for the Plate.

The *Möwe* was now overcrowded again. Dohna put paroled men from seven prizes aboard the *Hudson Maru* and sent her off to Pernambuco, where she arrived on the evening of 15 January and landed 237 prisoners. As he left the *Möwe* Captain Williams of the *Minieh* noticed that the raider's telescopic funnel was a good eight feet higher than it had been when he had first come aboard.

Meanwhile Bordewitz had been conning the *Yarrowdale* cannily homewards through the long grass of the North Atlantic, wireless room keeping a sharp listening watch for all ships' transmissions, lookouts alert for smoke. Her holds were stuffed with goods as well as many of the four hundred crewmen and over a hundred officers from ships captured by the *Möwe*. These men were held down by eighteen armed German sailors. Meals were monotonous but sufficient – mostly macaroni and biscuits. The ship was worked by neutral seamen and stokers who drew wages in deutschmarks.

One of Bordewitz's worst nightmares was that they would be sunk without warning by one of the U-boats which were now infesting the British Isles. U-boats had sunk nearly two hundred ships in January, a score which seriously worried the Allies. But *Yarrowdale* had inherited some of *Möwe*'s luck. At the time when she was nervously threading the blockade south of Iceland a strike of boilermakers in Liverpool had reduced Admiral Tupper's 10th Cruiser Squadron, which had a nominal strength of twenty-three ships, to an effective six auxiliary cruisers. The *Yarrowdale* steamed on, her prisoners battened down. Underneath her boilers were two mines connected to the bridge. If apprehended, Bordewitz would have blown up the ship. But they sighted nothing until they reached the Norwegian coast, then kept to territorial waters, turned east through the Kattegat and into The Sound, to anchor on the night of 29/30 December in Swedish waters opposite the island of Hven, where they were met by a German patrol boat.

Here two young English sailors jumped overboard and swam to within thirty metres of the shore, but the patrol boat's searchlight picked them out and they were brought back to the *Yarrowdale* by a boat-load of marines.

The ship moved on south again and on 30 December anchored south of Drogden very close to a minefield. Here they were boarded by a petty officer from a Swedish torpedo boat. The Germans had changed from their uniforms into merchant seamen's gear, and Bordewitz had stuck a merchant skipper's cap rakishly on his head. Although the ship bore no name, carried no identifying colours, the Swede asked no questions and did not want to go below, where nearly six hundred prisoners of war were locked, kept silent by the guns of their guards.

Yarrowdale reached Swinemunde in the Baltic on the 31st. The Norwegian crew of the *Hallebjorg* had already been released. Allied prisoners were taken to Neustralitz Camp, where they were introduced to German blockade rations – cabbage soup, brown war bread made from corn, potatoes and a dash of wheat, coffee of crushed black beans and burnt barley. The Imperial German Navy was very pleased with the captured ship, and decided to turn her into another disguised raider.

So far *Möwe* had eluded all pursuit and met little opposition on her voyage home, having made seven more captures. On 10 March, about 2.30 in the afternoon, in heavy North Atlantic weather she sighted a large steamer heading west. She was Captain A. B. Smith's *Otaki* of the New Zealand Shipping Company, half-way to New York from London. She was in ballast but worth £301,000 of Lloyd's money.

Möwe came abreast of *Otaki*, which carried one 4.7-inch gun on the poop, then fell back astern again. About 4.30 she closed, but remained outside *Otaki*'s gun range, and signalled "Stop".

Dohna had picked the wrong man in Archie Bissett Smith. *Otaki* increased revs, Leading Seaman Worth got his 4.7's crew closed up smartly, apprentices Basil Kilner and William Martin doubled to their action stations on ammunition supply.

Through his binoculars Smith saw false bulwarks on the raider drop and torpedo tubes run out. He saw the big tinfish leave the tube, watched its bubbles as it streaked towards *Otaki*, swung her stern at the right moment, and the torpedo missed. The German fired another. Once again Smith combed its tracks and it sped away towards the Azores. Then it was his turn.

"Open fire!"

"Trainer on!" ... "Layer on!' Worth pressed the trigger.

Chief Officer Bob McNish, controlling the fire, saw the shell pitch in the sea, tossing up a fountain of foam. Out of range. "Up two hundred!"

Guns aboard the enemy opened up. Both ships were in lively motion in the heavy seas and the shells went over. But the raider was coming within range of Worth's sights. He opened fire again. Alf Worth was a good Whale Island man and he began to hit the enemy.

A shell tore through *Möwe*'s signal bridge. Leutnant Rhor was running along the upper deck past the funnel when he was flung full length to the deck. He scrambled up to see a thick cloud of smoke pouring from the ship's side. They had been *hit*, and by a merchantman's popgun!

This shell had smashed through the ship's side into the stokehold and set the coal in the bunkers on fire. The Chief Stoker and six of his men were badly burned. The flames spread fast, though water was pouring in through the jagged hole in the side.

Dohna shouted orders. Then he had another emergency to cope with. Locked up in the foc'sle were the English prisoners. As soon as they had heard the sounds of battle they had started to batter at the iron door to the well deck. Almost simultaneously with the bursting of *Otaki*'s shell in the stokehold the door burst open and the men rushed out on deck. Dohna saw them. Marines with hand grenades forced them back.

Worth scored hits with eight out of the nine rounds which he managed to get off before a shell from *Möwe* pitched near his gun and put it out of action, killing young Kilner and Martin as they were passing fresh shells up to the crew.

Another shell hit *Otaki*. With their gun knocked out, it was now surely only a matter of time. "Mr McNish," said Smith, "get the boats out. There's no point in staying until we sink."

Torn by *Möwe*'s shells, the brave *Otaki* hove to. Dohna saw her boats go down. "Cease firing." The first smudge of dusk was in the sky and he had a badly damaged ship, holed amidships and astern, steering gear erratic, the fire below getting out of hand and creeping closer to the magazine.

It was two hours before he could spare the time and attention to do something for his enemies, floating about in their damaged boats. Meanwhile *Otaki* had sunk, her Red Duster still flying. One man Dohna wanted very badly to confront was the English Captain. But Archie Smith had gone down with his ship.

The raider drew close to the lifeboats. Dohna shouted through his megaphone, "Do you want to risk coming aboard or would you prefer to stay in the boats?" The survivors looked at the enemy they had hurt so badly. She was listing to port and fires could be seen burning below decks. But they did not fancy the mid-Atlantic in open boats. McNish shouted, "We'll take our chances with you, Captain."

Then he wondered if there would be any reprisals for their action. The Germans were very touchy about merchant ships fighting back. But they could have simply been left to die of exposure in the boats. He need not have worried. They were treated fairly, and their wounded looked after, along with the ten injured Germans. Five men had been killed in the *Möwe*. In *Otaki* the two apprentices Kilner and Martin, Deck Boy Payne and Third Engineer Little had been killed, and Captain Smith and Chief Steward Willis had drowned. *Möwe*'s surgeon skilfully amputated Trimmer Glitz's mangled leg. *Möwe*'s engines were untouched, and with emergency steering gear rigged she limped from the scene of battle, though it took twenty-four hours to put out the fires and three days before she was in any sort of fighting trim again.

She still managed to capture Captain Spencer's armed steamer *Demeterton* on the day after the battle. The latter's 3-pounder gun was removed and she was blasted with explosive charges, but with all the American timber in her holds and on deck she refused to sink and was left derelict, a danger to navigation. After the *Otaki* battle *Möwe* had ceased using blanks, and on 16 March Dohna stopped Captain George Packe's two-year-old steamer *Governor* of the Charente Company with a lucky live shot which knocked her gun out of action, killed four men and wounded ten out of her complement of forty-six.

The *Governor* was *Möwe*'s last victim. Afterwards she stood round the north of Scotland, made Norwegian territorial waters unnoticed and arrived safely at Cuxhaven on 22 March. In this, her second, cruise she had captured twenty Allied ships.

As *Möwe* dropped her hook another disguised raider was leaving German waters. She was *Möwe*'s prize and prisoner transport *Yarrowdale*, now renamed SMS *Leopard* and armed with five concealed 15cm and four smaller guns, and two torpedo tubes.

Sailors are normally superstitious people, but she intended to pass herself off as the Norwegian *Rena*, the same alias which had brought the *Greif* no luck at all. Perhaps it was thought that the fortunate star of *Möwe* herself still shone on her protegée. If so, *Otaki* had dimmed its light. The real *Rena* had left Christiania on 2 January, reached the Tyne on the 16th and was now in Port Natal, South Africa.

On the morning of 16 March the armoured cruiser HMS *Achilles* and the armed boarding steamer *Dundee* were on a special search in company about midway in the wide gap between Iceland and Norway, steering north at 15 knots. The sea was moderate but visibility was blurred by snow and rain squalls. At 11.45 a steamer was sighted a few points forward of *Achilles*' starboard beam, steering west-nor'-west on a course which would take her round the north of Iceland into the Denmark Strait. Captain Leake in *Achilles* altered course to starboard to intercept and ordered Commander Selwyn Day in *Dundee* to conform.

At two o'clock the steamer, which had Norwegian colours at her masthead and painted on her side, was overhauled and directed to stop, which she did. Day was very suspicious of her as she closely resembled the picture of a German disguised raider in *The Daily Mail* of 3 March. She was directed to steer west-by-south and at 2.35 she was stopped again for *Dundee* to examine her.

With *Achilles* manoeuvering about three miles off, *Dundee* sent a boarding boat across to the steamer with Lieutenant Lawson, Able Seaman Alf Birchall and seamen Magnus Anderson, Henry Anderson, Henry James Anderson and Robert Anderson. *Dundee* was circling the steamer at a distance of about half a mile, and when she was at right-angles across her stern and the boat was alongside the steamer, Day, who was watching the suspicious ship closely through his binoculars, saw the sides of a deckhouse on her poop suddenly fall down and a gun emerge and open fire on *Dundee*.

But Day had his own gun manned and trained on the enemy.

"Fire!"

The panels in the raider's sides on which the Norwegian flag had been painted fell down and more guns, at least four on each side, Day estimated, opened up a brisk fire, mostly at *Dundee* but also at *Achilles*, which had also opened fire from 5,300 yards on the enemy's port bow with her six 9.2s and four 7.5s.

The raider put out a screen of light-coloured smoke, but Day could see that his shells were hitting her. In fact his first three rounds were all hits, disabling the enemy's port battery and creating a great jet of escaping steam.

As *Dundee* passed across the raider's stern the range closed to 800 yards and the enemy's starboard battery opened fire. But *Dundee* raked her and as the range opened again, her salvoes became wild. At 3.55 she fired a torpedo at *Achilles* which broke surface off the big cruiser's port quarter about the same moment that a lookout reported a submarine in the same direction. *Dundee* was still scoring hits and the raider was on fire for'ard, made worse when she was hit in the bow, on the gripe, by a torpedo from *Achilles*.

About four o'clock *Dundee* and *Achilles* checked their fire, the raider being well alight fore and aft, with occasional explosions erupting forward. Soon afterwards *Dundee* took station astern of the cruiser and Leake ordered her to steer west. At 4.23 Day reported a submarine between *Dundee* and the raider. Fire was opened again on the enemy and continued until at 4.33 she settled, listed to port and sank, a mass of flames and red-hot for'ard, leaving no visible survivors.

It was the end of the *Leopard/Yarrowdale/Rena*'s short-lived cruise. *Dundee*'s boarding party all died with the German crew. Selwyn Day had the sad task of informing Lawson's mother in Largs Bay, Adelaide, and the families of his boat's crew, most of them Scottish fishermen related to one another.

Allied merchantmen had to pay dearly for the escape of the *Wolf* and *Seeadler* from the cruisers of the British blockade. Tacking south across the sea lanes, Von Luckner's white-winged barque surprised thirteen ships with his engine and hidden guns in the North and South Atlantic, some of them steamers, and destroyed cargoes of coal, sugar, lumber, fish, maize and saltpetre, before rounding Cape Horn into the Pacific, where he destroyed three ships carrying loads of timber, copra and coal, then lost his beautiful ship on a reef off Mopelia Island in the Societies.

Karl Nerger's *Wolf* laid mines off Cape Agulhas, the southernmost point of Africa, in late January, then launched herself into the wide Indian Ocean. She sank the freighters *Jumna*, *Turritella*, and *Benlarig* and the barque *Dee*. Two small seaplane carriers HMS *Anne* and *Raven II* came from Port Said, and their handful of Short 184s searched for the raider in the Arabian Sea and over the Laccadive and Maldive Islands, off the Malabar Coast and Ceylon, but by then the *Wolf* was zigzagging her way across the South Pacific. Leutnants Fabeck and Stein made a daring early morning flight over Sydney Harbour in the *Wölfchen* and later saved the mother ship by reporting a warship nearby.

With the *Wölfchen* scouting for her, the *Wolf* took four more ships, laid mines in Cook Strait between the North and South Islands of New Zealand and sank an American barque and a Japanese liner in the South China Sea. Her guns sent the *Hatachi Maru* and her cargo of silk, copper and rubber to the bottom back in the Indian Ocean, and she sailed for home. Sinking two more ships on the way, she eluded the blockade and reached Kiel safely on 18 February, 1918, after a cruise of fifteen months, with scurvy and beriberi in her crew. The success of the *Wölfchen* led to the idea of a small aircraft which could be carried in U-boats, from which the 80 h.p. Hansa-Brandenburg W20 Kleinflugboot was developed.

6 Panic Party

At the beginning of 1917 U-boats were dotted round the Irish coast, especially in the approaches to the Irish Sea – the North Channel in the north and the St George's Channel in the south.

Captain Reg Norton's big ex-White Star HMS *Laurentic* left Lough Swilly, Donegal, at 5 p.m. on 25 January. Thinking it possible that there might be a U-boat somewhere near, sheltering from the south-easterly gale that was blowing, he had delayed departure. It was dusk now. He left harbour at 14 knots showing no lights and increased to 17½ knots as *Laurentic* passed Dunree Head, having got permission to drop the normal leaving harbour signal for fear of a submarine's listening watch, and went into zigzag, making good a course due north.

He had taken every precaution, but the U-boat lurking off the mouth of the Lough was a match for him, or luckier.

The ex-liner steamed on for about five minutes on her northerly course. Even in the dusk she loomed big as a haystack in the periscope's optic.

At exactly 5.55 p.m. there was a violent explosion on her port side abreast the funnel which threw Captain Norton off his feet, followed some twenty seconds later by another abreast the engine room to port, which blew all the lights out.

"Stop engines!" The telegraph clanged. The ship was listing to port.

"Full astern!" The alarm gongs rang. "Turn out the boats!"

Norton tried to call the engine room, the W/T office, but the telephones were silent. He said to Chief Yeoman of Signals Burke, "Fire a rocket." Jim Burke rushed to carry out the order. The flare whooshed up into the darkness and blossomed red high in the sky. Leaving the officer of the watch, Sub-Lieutenant de Blacquière, in charge on the bridge, Norton ran along the boat deck to the wireless room. There he found young Ordinary Telegraphist Bill Millam on watch. "Send out an SOS". Millam said, "Can't, sir. The batteries are all smashed."

Norton rushed back to the bridge. "Yeoman, call Fanad Point Signal Station on the lamp." He turned to de Blacquière. "Blackie, go down and see what's happening in the engine room." The Sub-Lieutenant rushed off. Burke steadied his Aldis in the crook of his arm and triggered the stuttering morse. There was no reply.

They were alone in the dark, and sinking. Norton saw that some of the port, lee side, boats had been swung out and lowered not fully manned. He grabbed his megaphone and shouted at them to remain alongside but they drifted off to leeward. Then he remembered something. He said to the Navigator, Lieutenant Walker, "There are those four chaps down in the cells. Go and let them out." Walker could not find the key to the cells, and had to get Shipwright Harrington to chop the men out with an axe.

The ship had now righted herself again, and the Executive Officer, Commander Rodgers, was able to get the starboard boats turned out. De Blacquière returned from the engine room. "It's full of water, sir. I couldn't see anyone." The eight officers and men who had been on duty there were all dead.

The ship was settling low in the water. Rodgers sent away the starboard boats with orders to steer for Fanad Head. The last remaining boat, No. 5, was lowered to abreast D Deck to wait for the Captain. Norton made a tour of the ship and found that the water had reached D deck from the engine room. There was no one left aboard so he went to his boat, now in the water and in danger of being swamped. He slid down a lifeline into it.

There were four hundred and seventy men in *Laurentic*'s crew, and she carried seventeen boats with a total capacity for eight hundred. Thirteen of these were large 63-man boats with airtight tanks; there were two 40-man boats, a steamboat and a gig. Each boat carried red flag, red lantern, sea anchor, axe, compass, a supply of beef, biscuit and fresh water.

All the boats got safely away except the steamboat, the gig and No. 11 lifeboat, though not all of them were full. They all pulled for Fanad Head. It was only a mile or so away but in the wind and heavy seas and darkness they could not weather it. With nothing but breakers to leeward they pulled back out, and were carried by wind and tide to the westward. In the Captain's boat they made a sea anchor with the mast and sail and rode to that. The boat was shipping water steadily. They managed to keep it in check until about midnight, then it began to gain rapidly on them. They burned a red flare, which luckily attracted the attention of the steam trawler *Imperial Queen*. *Skipper Royal* came up with them and picked up the men from theirs and the Bosun's boat. By 1 a.m. the *Imperial Queen* had rescued sixty-two men. She cruised to the westward until 6 a.m. but found no other boats, and returned to Derry, where they were told that eight other trawlers and small craft were out searching.

The sinking *Laurentic* was seen about four miles north of Fanad Point, about half a mile from where she had been abandoned, and finally went down about two miles from Fanad Head Lighthouse. Of the missing thirteen boats, numbers 3, 7, 8, 9, 14 and 16 were found with men alive in them. No. 6, which had been under the charge of Lieutenant Steele RNR, was picked up with twenty-seven men in it, all dead from exposure. No. 13 was found empty and waterlogged, and several other boats were drifting aimlessly, empty and awash. At 9.45 a.m. on the 26th the trawler *Lord Lester* picked up twenty-four men from No. 8 boat, seven others having died during the night. The last of the missing boats was discovered at 3 p.m. that afternoon with Engineer Sub-Lieutenant Evans and four men in it. In all, twelve officers and a hundred and fourteen men were saved. Three hundred and forty-four were lost. This was the price of the blockade.

In February 1917, U-boats sank 230 ships totalling 464,599 tons, a frightening score and an increase of fifty percent over the high January losses. Nearly 300 neutral ships were refusing to sail either to or from British ports for fear of U-boat ambush, and others were challenging the blockade.

Sir Maurice Hankey, Secretary of the Committee of Imperial Defence, was pushing for a system of "scientifically organized convoys", ships sailing in groups with all the means of anti-submarine defence, including warships with depth-charges and some of the new hydrophones for detecting U-boats' screws, even aircraft, concentrated round them, but the Admiralty thought that a convoy would be an open invitation to a massacre, and merchant skippers would not be capable of manoeuvering together or keeping station, especially at night. But the benefit of convoy began to assert itself. A clutch of colliers was escorted safely from Brest to Cornwall, and nine ships shepherded from Berwick across to Bergen without interference.

In March U-boat sinkings, for the first time in any month, exceeded half a million tons. This included two hospital ships, which inflamed American opinion, already outraged by the German Foreign Minister Zimmermann's infamous telegram urging Mexico to declare war on the USA and bring Japan in with her. On 2 April the American steamer *Aztec* was torpedoed and sunk off Cape Finisterre by a U-boat. On 6 April the United States declared war on Germany. On 8 April the notorious Kapitänleut-nant Werner in *U55* sank the British steamer *Torrington*, smashed her boats and left her crew to drown. On the following day Rear-Admiral Sims, President of the US Naval War College, met the British First Sea Lord, Admiral Jellicoe, in London, who prophe-sied a rise to a million tons sunk in April. On 12 April Werner murdered the crew of the steamer *Toro*.

A convoy of sixteen merchant ships escorted by three Special Service Vessels and three armed yachts sailed from Gibraltar on 10 May and was met a hundred miles from Ireland by six destroyers and a flying boat and brought in without loss.

Experimental convoys from the USA made safe passages. The ten ships of the first North Atlantic convoy left Hampton Roads, Virginia, on 24 May, and only one, a straggler, was sunk. Sixty ships in four convoys came over in June, with only one loss. Convoy gave the U-boats serious problems, though there were fifty boats deployed round the British Isles and still many Allied ships sailing independently.

By the end of June plans for a general Atlantic system had been worked out. Every eight days two convoys of from sixteen to twenty ships were to sail from Hampton Roads; one from New York; one from Sydney, Cape Breton Island, Canada; two from Gibraltar and one from Dakar, West Africa.

Each convoy would require an Ocean Escort to go with it all the way and a destroyer escort to meet it and take it through the submarine danger zone. Ocean Escort for a Hampton Roads (HH) convoy would be an American or British regular cruiser, the US Navy would look after New York convoys (HB mercantile or HX fast troop), and escorts for the Sydney (HC medium troop) convoys would be provided by seven armed merchant cruisers of the 10th Cruiser Squadron. HG convoys from Gibraltar would be the most difficult to organize as they both started and finished in a submarine danger zone. They would be arranged after the North American system had been set up, and sloops and smaller escort ships would mostly be used, both RN and USN. A full West African system would also have to wait, and fourteen cruisers and twenty-two destroyers would have to be found to cope with it.

Outward-bound convoys were not yet to be attempted. These were not so important, as outward trade could always be held up to avoid special danger from submarines, and it was advisable to establish an inward system on each route first. As soon as the Hampton Roads timetable was working with fair accuracy, outward-bound convoy would be commenced. Unless a raider was known to be in the Atlantic, it was not intended to escort an outward-bound convoy all the way across, but only with destroyers through the submarine danger zone, after which it would disperse.

The Americas system proceeded without any serious problems. Most merchant captains found station-keeping well within their competence and only stragglers seemed to be at risk from U-boats once the destroyers had taken over. Convoys for west-coast United Kingdom ports were brought in north of Ireland, those for the east coast by the southern route. HG1 left Gibraltar on 26 July for the UK, with HMS *Rule* looking after sixteen ships bringing Spanish iron ore, manganese and phosphate, and in mid-August HD1 from West Africa left Dakar, due to arrive at its destroyer rendezvous on 1 September.

Allied merchant ship losses in September were down to 315,907 tons, many of the victims small coasters sailing alone. Of sixty U-boats on station round the UK, eleven were sunk, but the U-boat arm was still a threat, uncontaminated by the mutinies which had broken out in some of the surface ships of the High Seas Fleet, and production was keeping ahead of losses.

The mutinies had been stirred up by deputies from the Reichstag who had begun a movement for peace, taking their cue from a hungry, war-weary public. Food and raw materials vital to the continuance of the German war effort were now being stopped on the quays by diplomatic methods and the need for the Northern Patrol had almost disappeared.

One of the last AMCs to sail for patrol with the 10th Cruiser Squadron was HMS *Champagne*. She had started the war as the *Oropesa* of the Pacific Steam Navigation Company, had been handed over to the French Navy and recommissioned in the RN on 23 July, 1917. She was an old ship, built in 1895, with a maximum speed of only 13 knots, and she was not in the best of condition. On docking the ship shortly after commissioning, Captain Percy Brown had seen plainly that the French had put her aground at some time. Part of the bilge keel was bent and there was a big dent in the bottom. The bilge keel had been repaired, and her holds were full of empty barrels for buoyancy, but none of her bulkheads had been shored up. To add to Brown's worries a U-boat had been reported about thirty miles off the mouth of the Mersey. A later report at 10.30 a.m. on 8 October suggested that the U-boat was moving out north-west towards the Isle of Man, but Brown had not been told this when he sailed from Liverpool Bar at 2.30 p.m. without an escort.

To avoid the U-boat he laid a course west to hug the coasts of Wales and Anglesey and detoured well towards the Irish coast before turning north-east to leave the Isle of Man to starboard. He tried to keep his W/T signals to a minimum but reported his position as ordered at 7 p.m. and 11.30 p.m. A U-boat might pick them up with her direction and distance-finding wireless, but there was a lot of traffic between Man and the Mersey. Why should *Champagne* be singled out? If the sub did pick them up she might decide to head for the twenty-four mile gap between Ireland and Man, but if she tried that from her last reported position she would have to fight a heavy sea dead to windward.

In fact the U-boat, already further to the north-east than Brown had been led to believe, did just that, lurked for a while under the lee of Spanish Head, southern Man, and was waiting for the *Champagne* when she came zigzagging through the Ireland-Man gap early in the morning in typical north-westerly weather, with blue skies but a squally near-gale blowing out of the nor'-nor'-west.

Four points to starboard of her normal course, turn eight points to make four points to port, another turn of eight points, then another of four points, and she was back on her normal course. She was on a port leg at 6.10 a.m. when AB Fred Murrin at the after starboard gun saw a periscope, shouted "Close up!" Then the first torpedo struck her in the engine room on the starboard side.

The shock smashed two of the masthead lookout's teeth. The engine room officer of the watch was blown to pieces, the engines stopped, the ship lost her way and swung off course, the wheel jammed.

First Lieutenant Hugh Bentley said, "Will you order Abandon Ship, sir?" Brown said, "No, not yet, she may float for some time, and we may bag the sub if she comes up." As he spoke there came a second explosion under the well deck to port. "Abandon ship!"

The ship remained on an even keel but began to settle rapidly. The main boats were lowered and got away, there was no time for the same davits to be turned in again to lower the collapsibles. Brown had asked for extra davits but they had not been provided. The Captain told PO Bill Ware to get spars and lever them over the side.

Other Captains in this situation had kept a gun's crew behind in hiding after abandoning ship, Q-ship style. Now Reserve Seamen Watkins, Ward, Cox and Ryan volunteered to stay with the two foremost port 6-inch guns. Ware saw the periscope and part of the conning tower of a submarine surface about three hundred yards away on the port beam. B Gun opened fire. The shell went over and the submarine dived. They all remained at the guns, and Cox was the only one saved.

Ware had got one port boat half over the side when another torpedo hit the port side with tremendous force, killing men and blowing others overboard. The ship broke in two, the mainmast fell and broke away, and she sank in no more than thirty seconds.

The port collapsible fell clear and some men scrambled into it, including Ware who said, "Out oars, and keep calm." A capsized boat bobbed up, men were killed by wreckage shooting to the surface. Cox and the Captain held on to a seaboat's empty biscuit tank. They were picked up by Lieutenant Bingham's boat an hour later, hoisted sail and ran before the wind in a very heavy sea to Port Erin, Isle of Man, where Brown telephoned the Coast Guard for help to rescue the others. Fifty-eight men were lost out of three hundred and five.

As the need for them diminished, the AMCs of the Northern Patrol were taken off blockade duties, and in November the 10th Cruiser Squadron was disbanded. The ships were used as Ocean Escorts to Atlantic convoys, especially on the runs from Cape Breton and Halifax, Nova Scotia, and from Dakar.

AMCs were looking after the convoys from West Africa. At 6 a.m. on 7 October HMS *Orama* left Dakar as Ocean Escort to HD7, a group of twenty ships, eleven for UK west coast ports, nine for the east coast. *Orama* had been recommissioned less than four weeks and her young crew, a third of whom were Hostilities Only ex-civilians, had not shaken down. Then at the last moment before sailing she took aboard from the pierhead 121 Merchant Navy men, seamen and firemen, from the *Caronia*.

For eleven days the convoy steamed through the empty Atlantic towards England. About 7 a.m. on 19 October in a position roughly two hundred miles from Ushant and about the same distance from the Scillies HD7 met its destroyer escort from Devonport. *Orama* had previously been zigzagging clear of the convoy, but now, in accordance with standing orders, she took station as the leader of the third column from the port flank. Captain Moorsom did not like doing this. It did not make sense to put a 19-knot ship at the head of a 7½-knot convoy, with no freedom to manoeuvre and forbidden to zigzag – though for a convoy to zigzag was not all that difficult, in his opinion. He would have preferred to have forged on ahead, as soon as the destroyers joined, to his home port, with a couple of destroyers as escort.

But he obeyed orders and eased into position ahead of the Commodore's *City of Chester*. Thirty miles ahead of the convoy steamed a Q-ship, trailing her coat. One destroyer pushed out to about five miles ahead, three more were spaced out, wing to wing, a mile ahead, with two on each flank and one more as tail-end Charlie half a mile astern. They steamed along in this tight box for two hours, until one destroyer was detached in response to an SOS from the American steamer *Luckenbach*, a straggler from another convoy under attack by a U-boat.

The submarine was Ernst Hashagen's *U62*. His 10cm (4.1-inch) cannon outranged the merchantman's gun, but she was giving him a hard running fight, pumping out distress signals all the time.

About 10.30 a.m. another destroyer was detached from the convoy to stand by the *City of Chester*, which had dropped out with machinery defects requiring an estimated thirty-two hours to repair. At 2 p.m. the *Luckenbach* was sighted approaching the convoy hull-down from west-nor'-west. She came up with them about 4 p.m. and took station astern of the fourth column.

Meanwhile Hashagen was in trouble. *Luckenbach*'s cries for help had brought the *Nicholson*, one of the US destroyers based at Queenstown, southern Ireland. Her second shell hit the *U62* in the bows. Hashagen dived and was kept under, but not damaged, by depth-charges. When he came up again and raised the asparagus for a cautious look round he found himself right in the path of a convoy of twenty merchantmen with nine destroyer escorts. Leading the third column was a big auxiliary cruiser. She was his target. He'd failed to get the straggler, the U-boat skipper's best bet these days. Now he had the more difficult and dangerous job of taking out a ship in convoy. If he had known that the *Clan Lindsay*, leading Column Number 2, had a cargo of torpedoes he might have switched targets. A hit on her and he could well have destroyed half the convoy.

And he had only one torpedo left. With such a big target he must get a hit in a vital spot or one might not be enough. He waited until the cruiser was almost broadside-on to them, and aimed for her engine room, blessing the fine, clear visibility.

In the *Orama* PO Jim Maple, Captain of the port forward 6-pounder, sang out "Torpedo on port side!" and flung his arm up to point. The quartermaster threw the helm hard over, but *Orama* normally took three minutes to respond and had a turning circle over two miles in diameter. There was no way Hashagen's last tinfish could miss.

At 5.55 p.m. it struck *Orama* on the port beam immediately

abaft the bulkhead separating Numbers 2 and 3 Holds. The engines stopped, the two for'ard 6-inch guns were jammed, and the ship listed heavily to port and settled deeply by the head, with the whole of the bridge and fore deck flooded by water thrown up by the explosion.

There was something of a panic. The drill of manning action stations automatically on submarine attack had not been made clear to the green hands. Greasers left the engine room, gun crewmen rushed for the boats, and the passengers milled about. There were insufficient boats for the ship's company alone, and only three rafts, which the passengers had brought with them.

The roar of steam escaping from the boiler room safety valves made giving orders difficult. Moorsom tried going slow astern to reduce the noise but the telegraphs were having no effect. He sent First Lieutenant Knowles and Navigating Officer Cooksey below to assess the damage, then, because of the list, ordered the starboard boats lowered to just clear of the water.

Knowles and Cooksey returned, faces black with the clouds of coal dust which the explosion had stirred up below, and reported Number 3 Hold full of water, with Number 2 filling, though Chief Engineer George Paxton was getting the pumps going on Number 2. Down below Paxton did get the pumps to work for a few reluctant strokes, then they choked on coal dust which had got in through a fracture in the pipes somewhere. The bulkheads, well shored up, were holding, but Knowles took another look below and saw that Number 2 Hold was filling rapidly. Some time previously the owners had had calculations made by their marine architects, who had come to the conclusion that Number 2 Hold's bulkheads should have been built right up to D Deck. They ended in fact just three feet short. The water in Number 2 Hold was now rising towards this gap above the for'ard bulkheads. If it poured over into Number 1 Hold, as it surely would, the ship would sink quickly by the head. Moorsom gave orders for the passengers and the sick to be put into the waiting boats, which were then lowered and tied up to the guest warp.

While all this was going on the USS *Conyngham* had closed the *Orama*. Then she saw a periscope, dropped astern and dropped depth-charges over the spot. The rest of the convoy was now well ahead of them.

HMS *Hecla*, the first British AMC. Converted from the SS *British Crown* and commissioned 7 March, 1878.

An AMC of the First World War, the ex P & O liner HMS *Macedonia*.

HMS *Changuinola*, an Elder & Fyffe banana boat, saw action in the First World War.

The AMC HMS *Carmania* lies in Valetta harbour, Malta, in 1915 after her duel with the German AMC *Cap Trafalgar*.

RMS *Lusitania* was listed as a British AMC and sunk off Ireland by U20 on 7 May, 1915.

Captain E. C. Kennedy, RN, lost with HMS *Rawalpindi* when she was attacked by the German battlecruisers *Scharnhorst* and *Gneisenau* on 23 November, 1939.

The German battlecruiser *Gneisenau*.

This painting by Norman Wilkinson depicts the action between the *Rawalpindi* and the *Scharnhorst* and *Gneisenau*.

Captain E. S. F. Fegan, VC, RN, of HMS *Jervis Bay*, sunk by the pocket battleship *Admiral Scheer*.

HMS *Jervis Bay*.

HMS *Alcantara* which did battle with the German commerce raider *Thor*.

The bridge of HMS *Alcantara* receives attention after the engagement with *Thor*.

Shrapnel damage in *Alcantara* inflicted by *Thor*.

A damaged Seafox aircraft and crew is hoisted aboard the *Alcantara*.

A victim of the *Thor*, the AMC HMS *Voltaire*.

One of the early AMC conversions in the Second World War, HMS *California*.

About 8 p.m. Number 2 Hold had filled and the water was lapping at the top of the bulkhead. Moorsom ordered the ship's company to abandon ship and make for the *Conyngham* and USS *Jacob Jones*, which were standing by. Then he signalled the *Conyngham* to come alongside, which she did in the most efficient and seamanlike manner and took off all the men who did not have lifeboat space. All 479 men in the *Orama* were safely rescued, or so Moorsom thought.

As the *Conyngham* drew clear, Max Cooksey thought he saw a light aboard the *Orama*. He and the Captain and PO Jim Finnis went back to the sinking ship in one of the destroyer's boats to find any man still aboard. They boarded the ghostly, dying vessel and searched her thoroughly, at some risk to themselves. Number 1 Hold was half full, and the old ship was labouring heavily, on the point of foundering. She was completely deserted. The light Cooksey had seen was a lantern left hanging on a stanchion. They left at 9.40 p.m. with the sea washing over the well deck.

At 9.55 the *Orama* sank. It was the sad end of a ship which had done much hard and useful seatime in northern and southern oceans. She had bombarded the *Dresden* in a Chilean harbour and hunted the *Möwe* off Pernambuco, and in times of peace had been a beautiful and popular ship. Amidst the lavish American comforts of the USS *Conyngham* Moorsom reflected. If only the hatch of Number 2 Hold on E Deck had been watertight... If the bulkhead between Numbers 1 and 2 Holds had been continued up to D Deck... Then the rescue tugs sent for from Queenstown might have been in time to save her... If only... If only... Somewhere away in an English grave the bones of dead Director of Naval Construction Barnaby turned.

In November there was a drop of some 50,000 tons in sinkings by U-boat, but in December the total rose again by 100,000 tons, partly due to a determined effort by the U-boat arm to single out American troop transports, the slaughter of Doughboys being thought by the German General Staff to be of far greater value than the winning of a major naval victory. UK-bound Atlantic convoys had just one armoured cruiser or AMC as Ocean Escort, which would be inadequate if the Germans started using battlecruisers. Battleships of the US Atlantic Fleet began escort duties, one or two per convoy.

Convoys from Sierra Leone (the HL series) were added to the HDs, and those from Halifax, Nova Scotia, to the HC and HX series from Sydney, Cape Breton, and all were covered by the overworked AMCs. The fast HX troop convoys from Halifax, so vital to the war in France, were increasingly covered by an auxiliary cruiser plus an armoured cruiser to allow for attacks by a German regular cruiser and a disguised raider together, which Intelligence thought might have been planned. The old *Teutonic* was paired with HMS *Leviathan*, then British with American, *Gloucestershire* with the USS *St Louis*, *Arlanza* with USS *Frederick*, *Otranto* with *Rochester*, *Edinburgh Castle* with two US cruisers, *Nebraska* and *Montana*, *Andes* with the *Rochester* and *Kansas*.

Outward-bound convoys from the Clyde (OB), the Mersey (OL, OLB, OLX, OE), Milford Haven (OM), Devonport (OD), Southend (OC), and Verdon (OV), were run. These were escorted by destroyers through the submarine danger zone and often had the additional protection of an AMC or armoured cruiser on her way across to pick up a homeward-bound convoy, before the ships were dispersed to sail independently.

Gradually convoy beat the U-boats. Escorts grew more skilled, their weapons more effective, while the nucleus of experienced submariners became spread out more and more thinly over the U-boat fleet. A largely green crew would find few soft targets, only the odd straggler, if they were lucky.

Acting-Captain Robert Newton had come out of retirement in 1914 and had commmanded a destroyer before being given the 16,000-ton *Calgarian*, sister ship of the *Alsatian*, both former Allan liners. Built in 1913, *Calgarian* was a 19-knot ship, and Newton chafed at having to hold down his speed for the convoy which he brought across from Halifax in February, 1918. As a small-ship man he envied the agile destroyers which joined them seventy miles west of Islay, though standing orders had now been changed, and he was free, unlike Moorsom with the *Orama*, to leave the convoy and head for Liverpool at full speed.

A U-boat had been reported working off Lough Swilly, but he saw nothing of her, and with Ratlin Island a few miles off his starboard bow he was feeling reasonably relaxed. There were plenty of friendly ships in sight, including two detroyers, several minesweeping sloops, half a dozen patrol trawlers and the ships of a big outward-bound convoy with surface escorts and two airships. But a U-boat, her asparagus just inches above the water, had picked out the bulky AMC from all the rest. The German commander was glad that the Britisher was making a rather tight zigzag, which made his attack that much easier. At 4.50 p.m. he put a torpedo into *Calgarian*'s fore stokehold.

The wheel jammed. Steam pipes were fractured. The stokehold flooded fast. Chief Engineer Cloud shut down the engines. The destroyer *Beagle*, which might have been better employed hunting the U-boat, and the trawler *Lord Lister* came up and tried to take *Calgarian* in tow, while Commander Harry Kendall got the AMC's emergency steering gear working, and Lieutenant Robinson's party shored up the for'ard bulkheads. The destroyer *Moresby* circled the ships, making a smokescreen. The ship had almost raised steam again when she was hit by a spread of torpedoes in the port side of both stokeholds and Number 3 Hold. Bulkheads gave way and *Calgarian* began to settle. The trawler *Thomas Collard*, which was towing alongside, was badly damaged and cast off. All *Calgarian*'s boats were lowered and manned, and everyone got away except those lost in the stokeholds. The AMC sank about an hour after the first hit.

Ocean Escorts for the eight-day HH convoys from Hampton Roads were usually US Navy or Royal Navy regular armoured cruisers, but *Virginian* brought home the nineteen ships of HH66 with cargoes of sugar, oil and nitrates. *Gloucestershire* looked after HH72, a wheat convoy, and *Victorian* the twenty-six ships of HH74.

In March, 1918, the HJ series, bringing South American meat, fruit and cereals from Rio de Janeiro, was started and escorted home exclusively by auxiliary cruisers. Ships like *Andes* and *Almanzora* found themselves back in the South Atlantic, though this time for war purposes. These convoys sailed without much trouble. HJ4 lost the SS *Valdivia* to a U-boat after the ships had been dispersed in UK waters, and apart from that about the only spot of bother was when the *British Transport*, which had sunk a U-boat in the Atlantic in 1917, was in collision early in the run of HJD15 and had to be sent back to Bahia Blanca by the Senior Naval Officer in HMS *Armadale Castle*.

The new series of HC, medium-fast, convoys from Halifax

which began in May, 1918, started badly. Ocean Escort for HC1 was HMS *Moldavia*, which was also carrying 614 tons of frozen meat and butter, eight tons of poplar lumber, twenty-five tons of stores for Chinese labourers working for the Allies – and a battalion of United States troops.

HC1 left Halifax on 11 May. On 21 May the destroyer escort joined it from Queenstown. At 2.35 p.m. on 23 May the AMC was zigzagging ahead of the mercantile contingent of five ships, all British liners, steaming in line abreast, with the destroyers disposed ahead and on the flanks, and was about to switch to the new leg of the pattern. Captain Smyth's afternoon doze in the chartroom was harshly interrupted by an explosion and the sound of breaking glass all round him.

He ran on to the bridge. "Hard-a-starboard!"

"Wheel's jammed, sir."

"What's the ship's head?"

"Compass unshipped, sir. Both of 'em."

"Mr Gray, make six blasts."

The mournful sounds boomed over the water. SO, Escort, in HMS *Grasshopper*, said, "Hello, *Moldavia*'s been tinfished."

In *Moldavia* Smyth was giving orders: "Mid, I want the signal '*Moldavia* torpedoed port side' sent at once. Number One, I want to know the state of the engines – and send the Chief Chippy to report on the for'ard bulkhead." He had had all bulkheads shored up with stout 14 by 12 pitch pine.

The ship had uprighted herself, then slowly listed to port. He sent an order to the Chief Engineer to use the trimming tanks to get her upright again, signalled the C-in-C for tugs, sent engineer Duncan to rig hand-steering gear, asked Navigator Unicume for a course to steer for Portsmouth. The ship was falling off to starboard but he must keep way on as the merchantmen were coming up behind him.

She was veering off to starboard. If she carried on she would hit either the destroyer *Scourge* or the liner *Persic* on the starboard wing. Smyth ordered the port engine reversed and switched on his "Not under control" lights.

He was feeling reasonably optimistic when young Midshipman Ken Burns, who had himself been torpedoed before, in the troop transport *Andoni*, returned.

"W/T's out of action, sir. Can't get a signal out."

"Not even a *short* one?"

"No, sir. Set's completely smashed, sir."

Behind him was a queue.

Engineer Commander Grant said, "The water's making in the stokehold, sir, and we shall lose steam very soon."

Chief Carpenter Chiswick said, "Number 3 and 4 Holds flooded, sir, water's up to the spar deck, and the bulkheads are going to go. The hit was right on Number 3 bulkhead. A lot of the Doughboys in Upper Number 3 copped it."

Number 4 bulkhead, only eighteen inches from a boiler, had no shoring. He was going to lose his ship.

"Signal *Scourge* to come alongside. Break out the towing hawsers." He would not give up yet. Lieutenant-Commander Law brought *Scourge* smartly alongside, and they got a tow going.

Smyth looked at the foc'sle. The guardrails were about three feet clear of the water. "Mr Simmons, pipe 'Abandon ship'." The First Lieutenant doubled away to supervise the lowering of the boats.

With most of the men clear in boats or on rafts, Smyth was on the bridge with Simmons, Grant, Unicume, Duncan and Chiswick. "Gentlemen, I see no useful purpose in staying aboard." They nodded their heads in agreement. "Mr Simmons, make one last search below, then cast off *Scourge*'s stern line." At 3.30 Smyth followed his officers aboard the destroyer. Twenty minutes later *Moldavia* slid her bows under, heeled to port, and disappeared.

The U-boats tried hard to get to grips with convoy. Michelsen, commander of the U-boat arm, noticed in reports of single attacks on convoys by veterans like Hersing and Hashagen that at the first sign of trouble several escorts left their stations screening the merchantmen to hunt down the U-boat, leaving gaps in the close defences which could have been penetrated if only the single attacker had been backed up in strength. Between 12 and 15 May 1918 nine U-boats were assembled west of the Scilly Isles to work in co-ordination against convoys, the first attempt at a "wolf-pack". But the teamwork was scrappy, and in the ensuing fortnight only three ships were sunk out of 293 which passed through the pack's area.

By the summer of 1918 the British armed merchant cruiser force had lost ten ships, a quarter of its total strength, nearly all of them to U-boat torpedoes, *Otranto* having been wrecked in a gale on Coul Point, Islay, with heavy loss of life among the United States servicemen she was carrying, and *Viknor* and *Clan McNaughton* being unaccounted for.

There was one to go. In the early evening of 22 July, 1918, HMS *Marmora* left Cardiff for Dakar, to take the transport *Boonah* out and escort homeward-bound convoy HD45 from Dakar as far as its junction with HJD17 in the Cape Verde Islands, hand over to HMS *Almanzora*, and drop down to Sierra Leone to escort a homeward-bound convoy from Freetown.

Leading Seaman Joseph Pinkney, Navigator's Yeoman, had watched their local escorts, the patrol boats *P66* and *P67*, come up and settle down on their flanks, then had gone down to his favourite kipping station in the storeroom right down for'ard, about twenty-four feet abaft the stem and some nine feet above the waterline. He had just dropped off to sleep when he was shocked awake by a tremendous explosion which threw him right off the bench just at the right moment to catch the full force of the grating which rose up from the deck and hit him, followed by the goods off the shelves. Dazed, he struggled to the door, but he could not open it. Then the whole ship shook with another explosion. He thought of opening a port and squeezing out. He tried the door again, put all his weight against it, forced it open, and saw that water was rising in the passageway outside. In fact from the noise of rushing water and the angle of the deck, the whole forepeak was filling up. *They were sinking.*

He reached for the ladder up to the well deck. It was gone, blown away. But the rope which he had slung there to help him up its steep rungs was still there. Panting, he dragged himself up on to the deck. He heard the water pouring into Number 1 Hold, where the for'ard guns' crews' shelter was. The explosion had blasted right up through the hold and blown the cover off. It was just like looking down a huge pit shaft. You could hear the water rushing in from down below.

The *Marmora* had been hit by a torpedo abreast Number 1 Port Gun and about five seconds later by another between the funnels. She settled quickly by the head. Captain Walter Woodward tried the engine room telephone but it had been wrecked. When the Chief came up he reported that both stokeholds were full of water and both engines stopped. By then the forward well deck was awash, and the ship was going fast. At 4.15 Woodward abandoned ship, and the *Marmora* sank half an hour later. All the ship's company were rescued, though Leading Fireman Bert Coleman was complaining in the boat that it was only seven months since he had been torpedoed in the *Champagne*. Both patrol boats dropped depth-charges, and *P66* fired on a periscope.

At the Armistice on 11 November there were thirty-nine armed merchant cruisers still in service, with HMS *Naldera* nearing completion. Many of them were scrapped in the years immediately following the war.

7 Emergency Equipment

After what a politician had called the "war to end all wars", British soldiers, sailors and airmen returned to what another politician called "a land fit for heroes". There was a honeymoon, when they felt simply lucky to be alive. Then the heroes tried to get jobs, in a market suddenly depressed by the abrupt loss of war production. Of course, it was all right for some. Fortunes had been made building guns, planes and ships. Now new ones were made scrapping them.

In ports all round Britain the Hostilities Only auxiliary cruisers rang down "Finished with engines". Older ones, like the pioneer *Teutonic* and the *Victorian* and *Virginian* twins, worn out by five years of punishing seatime, went to the breaker's yard, others swung round the hook, some were returned to trade.

As a result of the Washington Naval Conference of 1921 nearly two million tons of ships were axed from the world's navies, including British battleships, cruisers and destroyers – though the British motion to abolish submarines altogether was defeated.

The Admiralty reckoned that the Royal Navy would find itself seventy-five cruisers short in any future war – just supposing the optimists were wrong and history repeated itself after all. As a makeshift, they were once again allocated funds to subsidise shipping companies for the reserving of their ships to a total number of fifty as potential armed merchant cruisers.

Throughout the threadbare years of the Depression ships were stiffened, on the stocks or between voyages, to take the weight, and the operating stresses, of 6-inch and 4-inch guns, pedestals and mountings. In some ships the steel packing rings, on which gun pedestals would be mounted, were actually fitted to the deck and covered with teak planking, and rich cruise passengers trod them without knowing that they were sailing in an auxiliary warship. Others were stored. Transverse web plating from the "gun deck" to the deck below was fitted, with longitudinal brackets under the gun centre, and 6-inch portable pillars to shore up the decks were provided. Gun decks were allocated forty pounds of double plating, some of this portable and carried in the hold. In new ships, bulkheads near gun positions were constructed of heavy scantling.

The Admiralty had discovered in the Great War that the Blue Riband type passenger liner was impractical as an AMC, on account of size and high fuel consumption – with precious oil fuel having to be imported in a future war through a revival of blockade by U-boats, which the Germans began to build again, in defiance of an international ban.

The basic Admiralty specification was for a twin-screw ship which could be fitted with at least four 6-inch guns per broadside at a height above the waterline of not less than fourteen feet, could raise a minimum top speed of 15 knots, steam for at least 4,500 miles at 14 knots, with 6,000 miles desirable, and contain sufficient accommodation for conversion to take the naval crew's quarters. There was also a requirement, as in new regular cruisers, for the operation of one or more aircraft. Ships selected were usually passenger or cargo/passenger liners of 8,000 – 20,000 tons. Guns and mountings for them were stored in United Kingdom dockyards and in Empire ports at Gibraltar, Malta, Bombay, Calcutta, Colombo, Sydney, Simonstown in South Africa, and Esquimault in British Columbia, Canada. Many of the guns were old, some of them from Great War auxiliary cruisers.

The pale sun of Munich shone for a time, then faded. By the summer of 1939 the shadow of a possible conflict with Nazi

Germany was darkening again. In wartime Britain's great volume of sea-borne trade would become vital for survival. There were some 3,000 deepsea and 1,000 coastal vessels registered under the Red Ensign, with about 2,500 at sea at any given time.

To protect them the Royal Navy of the day was inadequate. Of its fifteen battleships and battle cruisers afloat, none was modern, and among its fifty-six cruisers, twenty-three dated from the Great War – though it was lack of numbers that counted most, in destroyers as well. There were also four large and three smaller aircraft carriers.

The German Navy was too small to face the RN in a fleet action, but it was new and well equipped for commerce raiding. There were the two fast battlecruisers *Scharnhorst* and *Gneisenau*, the three "pocket battleships" *Deutschland*, *Graf Spee* and *Admiral Scheer*, cruiser size but with 11-inch guns, one 8-inch heavy cruiser afloat and two more building, all these vessels able to cruise well out into the Atlantic and increase their range still further with the use of supply ships. There were five light cruisers armed with 5.9s. Under construction were two big 15-inch-gun battleships. Germany had also rearmed with the U-boat, and Kommodore Karl Dönitz had asked for three hundred.

To support Britain's battle fleets, man the blockade and hunt ocean commerce raiders, a force of fifty-six regular cruisers was far too small. Convoy, which had beaten the U-boat before, would be introduced from the start, but it would be very important to get the auxiliary cruisers into service quickly. To achieve this, some unstiffened ships would have to be used. Some twenty ships would be at UK ports, fifteen at Empire arming ports, inside ten days, available for conversion.

To speed up the entry of the AMCs into service, the first batch would be fitted with Emergency Equipment only. This included some very old 6-inch guns and mountings, only a light type of director, temporary wooden magazines and shell rooms, with no separate HA magazines. The stripping of a liner's expensive woodwork to reduce fire risk would be restricted to the removal of portable items such as furniture and easily removable bulkheads. The crew would use the original accommodation, which would be no hardship, and there would be no time to convert to naval "broadside" messes with stowable tables and hammocks. Bridges were to be protected with sandbags and plating, steering gear and machinery with steel plates.

It was intended to fit twenty ships in UK ports with the Emergency Equipment and another six abroad, to be hurried to sea, it was hoped, in as little as two and a half to three weeks. The ultimate aim was to fit all AMCs with Complete Equipment, including full director systems, watertight steel magazines and shell rooms, the open messdeck and hammock system of HM ships, paravanes (four per ship), with more complete stripping of the woodwork. It was planned to make use of thirteen sets of 6-inch guns, taken from C and D class cruisers, to be rearmed as anti-aircraft ships.

It was hoped that some ships would be at the right place at the right time for them to be taken in hand before war was declared, though the British Government tried to be careful not to contravene the Naval Limitation Treaties, covering the acquisition of new war vessels in peacetime by non-belligerents, which laid down that four months must elapse between the notice of acquisition of a completed ship "of the main categories" and its *actual* acquisition, and that no ship was to be taken up unless included in a previous declaration of acquisition.

These requirements could be side-stepped if armed merchant cruisers were treated as auxiliary vessels "not specifically built as fighting ships". Ships were required to be commissioned as vessels of war as soon as conversion work was started and prior to making any preparations for arming them, i.e. preparations to wage war must not be made "in merchant ships". This was a prohibition designed to prevent the secret arming of merchant ships before hostilities.

8 "Where is your steamer?"

And so it was that on 24 August, 1939, the Management of Shaw Savill & Albion Company at 88 Leadenhall Street in the City of London took a telephone call from the Admiralty.

"Where is your steamer *Jervis Bay*?"

"She's in London, preparing for a voyage to Australia."

"Has she begun to load?"

"No, not yet."

"Good. She is not to do so. We are requisitioning her for service as an armed merchant cruiser."

Further along the street at Number 122 the Pacific & Oriental Steam Navigation Company received the blunt telegram:

"Your vessel *Rawalpindi* is hereby requisitioned for Government service."

On the other side of the world, nearing New Zealand, Shaw Savill's *Arawa* was told by radio,

"Discharge your cargo without delay and proceed to Sydney for conversion to an AMC."

Similar messages went out to eighteen different shipping companies. On 25 August the Canadian Pacific Company's luxury liner *Montcalm* was taken over as an AMC in Liverpool, where she had just returned from a summer cruise round the Mediterranean.

On the 26th the Royal Mail Line's *Asturias* steamed up Southampton Water, also fresh from a Mediterranean luxury cruise. In a few hours she had disembarked passengers and their luggage, and was outward-bound again, this time for Belfast and a change of role. Her sister ship *Alcantara*, which had replaced the previous ship of the same name sunk by the *Greif* in 1916, was on her way to Southampton for conversion. The Scottish Anchor Line's 16,792-ton *California* docked in Glasgow and was taken over. *Caledonia*, 17,046 tons, came in next day and was immediately requisitioned. The smaller *Cilicia*, 11,137 tons, the Line's newest ship, launched in 1937, berthed and three days later was flying the White Ensign. The big 22,575-ton *Queen of Bermuda*, normally on the Bermuda luxury service, was chartered as an AMC on 29 August at New York, and left two days later for Belfast.

September 3 found the 15,000-ton *Dunnottar Castle* loading in London for South Africa. She was emptied, turned round quickly and sent to Harland & Wolff's yard in Belfast for conversion. Her stranded passengers packed the Union Castle Head Office in Fenchurch Street, demanding alternative arrangements for their passage. The veteran liner *Gloucestershire Castle* was brought out of reserve to take them.

Dunnottar Castle's sister ship *Dunvegan Castle* was in South African waters and reached East London on 3 September, bound for England via East Coast ports and Suez, with a full complement of passengers. Everyone on board listened to Mr Chamberlain's broadcast announcement of the commencement of war with Germany, and the ship prepared to sail for Durban that afternoon.

The pilot was on the bridge, the tugs were in position, and the last gangway was about to be lowered to the quay when someone noticed the small telegraph boy wandering round the boat deck asking for the Captain. The cablegram in his hand was an order to return immediately to Britain for conversion to an armed merchant cruiser. Passengers and their baggage were put ashore at once, and the ship sailed that night for Table Bay. At Cape Town the cargo for the East Coast was discharged and replaced in the holds by goods for Britain.

Lying at the adjoining South Arm Jetty was the Union Castle's new *Pretoria Castle*, also under requisition as an AMC. Both ships were hurriedly painted battleship grey and sailed via Freetown for Britain.

The 16,644-ton *Rajputana* of the P & O was in Yokohama, Japan, when war was declared, and had just completed loading for home. She received orders to unload and proceed to the Canadian port of Esquimault for conversion to an AMC. She had no charts to cover the voyage across the Pacific, but from the Japanese Chart Depot drew photostatted copies of Admiralty charts with Japanese names superimposed. Using these, *Rajputana* sailed, and for several days steamed through thick fog, picking her way through the dense Japanese and American steamer traffic. When she finally arrived in British Columbia, her 6-inch guns and mountings, director and searchlights, were waiting on the quayside under tarpaulins.

In different ports the conversion work was proceeding fast. In Belfast the big 22,048-ton *Asturias* was stripped of many of her rich appointments. Workmen removed all the fine mahogany and walnut furniture from saloons, lounges and smokerooms, the golden wickerwork chairs and richly carved cedarwood tables from the Winter Garden on the Boat Deck, still bright with the sunny colours of Moorish Spain, the small table and tiny chairs and the cuckoo clock from the First Class Children's Playroom. The Grinling Gibbons carvings remained to grace the First Class Smokeroom, which became the naval wardroom, the marble Adam fireplace still distinguished the First Class Reading Room, converted into the ante-room to the wardroom, the lovely panelling in peacock green and gilt continued to lend elegance to the First Class Lounge, which was to be used for Divisions in bad weather, Captain's Defaulters, and recreational purposes. *Asturias'* huge forward funnel was sliced off by oxy-acetylene torches, lifted in one piece by a giant crane and lowered on to the dockside. Eight old 6-inch guns, some of smaller calibre, searchlights and a fire control system were fitted.

In the meantime, *Asturias'* sister ship, RMS *Alcantara*, named after her fighting predecessor, had arrived at Southampton. She was stripped down there, valuable carpets being removed, cleaned and stored for replacement when the ship returned to peacetime service. To relieve the pressure on British shipyards she was hurriedly commissioned and sent in convoy to Malta for conversion to an AMC. Her only armament for the trip was one 4-inch fitted aft, and she carried over seven hundred officer and rating passengers for HM ships in the Mediterranean.

The *Queen of Bermuda* joined *Asturias* at Belfast on 8 September. As much care as possible was taken to preserve her beautiful fittings when they were stripped out of her, but much irreparable damage was done. She was fitted with seven 6-inch guns, all old and lacking the elevation and range of modern turret mountings. For anti-aircraft defence she was given two 3-inch guns of First World War vintage between her second and third funnels. Executive officers were allotted passenger cabins on the Sun and B Decks, engineer officers on B Deck, and many ratings slung their hammocks in the Dance Hall.

The 17,046-ton *Caledonia* was also converting at Belfast. She was renamed *Scotstoun* to avoid confusion with the old C class light cruiser HMS *Caledon*. The 10,515-ton Bibby motor liner *Shropshire* was also given a new name. She was in the Mersey loading for Colombo and Rangoon when she was taken over. Her cargo was off-loaded back on to the quay, and she was shifted to Cammell Laird's yard in Birkenhead for conversion. The Royal Navy already had a county class heavy cruiser of the same name. Lieutenant-Commander Harold Peate RNR, who was a Shropshire man, suggested Salop, the county's familiar name. My Lords made it *Salopian*, which seemed slightly less open to vulgarization, but her ship's company were soon calling her "Sloppy Anne". In the same dock was Cunard White Star's 14,013-ton *Ascania* undergoing Emergency treatment.

Carnarvon Castle, another 20,000-tonner, arrived in Table Bay from England in the second week of September with passengers for coast ports, and got no further. She too was requisitioned, passengers disembarked, cargo was off-loaded, and furniture removed from her public rooms for storage in a pre-coaling shed on the old East Pier in Cape Town docks. At 6 p.m. on 8 September the Union Flag was hauled down from the ship's main yard, and the White Ensign run up aft. She then went round to Simonstown for conversion.

The main armament of all the auxiliary cruisers consisted initially of from six to eight 6-inch guns, which the First World War had proved to be the minimum effective calibre for an AMC. Some of them had actually been fired then, and many of them were ancient and worn, some cast before the Boer War. At some stage two 3-inch or 12-pounder high angle guns, usually dating from the First World War, were fitted to most AMCs. The only anti-aircraft armament fitted at first to *Asturias* comprised two First World War Lewis machine-guns which jammed when they were tested. Eventually every ship had two 9-foot rangefinders, one for the main armament, one for the AA. Two depth-charge chutes and eight depth-charges were allocated to each AMC.

Ships' companies consisted mainly of Merchant Navy men who had signed T124 articles, which brought them under Royal Navy authority but preserved most of the MN conditions of service. T124 men continued to receive danger money for time spent at sea, the normal procedure for the MN in wartime. Many Merchant Navy petty officers and ratings were given temporary naval rank according to their work. Senior carpenters, bosuns and stewards became warrant officers, senior quartermasters being rated chief petty officers. An elderly engine rating in the *Queen of Bermuda* was given the rank of blacksmith RN.

Certificated Merchant Navy officers serving on in AMCs were usually given commissions in the Royal Naval Reserve, some uncertificated engineers being commissioned in the Royal Naval Volunteer Reserve. Bert Poolman, who had served as an engineer with the Bibby Line until beached by the Depression, volunteered for service at the age of fifty. This was above the normal age for acceptance, but he was allowed in on a Gentleman's Agreement. As he held a Second Class Engineer's Certificate he was given the rank of Sub-Lieutenant (E) RNR. As an ex-Bibby man it was entirely appropriate that he should find himself standing a watch aboard the ex-Bibby *Salopian*, formerly *Shropshire*. The first thing he noticed was that she had lost two of her distinctive four masts, a unique feature of the Line in peacetime. There was a sprinkling of RN ratings, mostly gunners, and an AMC was always commanded by an RN captain, normally a retired officer recalled for war service. Many men remained in the ship in which they had served before the war.

Emptied of cargo and passengers, the converted merchantmen were ballasted with pig-iron or stone for stability. Extra buoyancy was given by the stowage of thousands of empty, sealed oil drums of from fifteen to fifty gallons' capacity in holds and 'tween decks, although half the AMCs had to make do with wooden barrels and timber at the beginning owing to a shortage of drums. Coal-burner HMS *Antenor* from the China Mutual Steamship Company had 2,600 tons of rock, 35,000 cubic feet of wood and 22,000 steel drums in her; ex-Bibby liner HMS *Cheshire* carried bamboo bundles as well as oil drums.

Range always improved with the stowage of a proper buoyant cargo. HMS *Bulolo* of Burns Philp, at 6,500 tons the smallest of the Second World War AMCs, with seventy-five percent buoyant cargo and proper ballast had an endurance of 8,600 miles at fifteen knots using her main oil supply, with another 5,270 miles in hand in her reserve. HMS *Jervis Bay* was one of those ships which Admiralty shipwrights had originally declared too "stiff", that is too quick and sharp in her motion at sea, to make a steady gun platform, but additional buoyant cargo reduced the stiffness to acceptable proportions. In the *Queen of Bermuda* practically the whole of E Deck was filled with empty barrels.

The conversion work went forward with urgent speed, often in the teeth of great difficulties. The 18,724-ton triple-screw Cunard White Star *Laurentic*, whose predecessor of the same name had been torpedoed off the Donegal coast in January, 1917, had been laid up since June, 1937, first in Southampton, then for two years in Falmouth, rusting at her moorings. Her Load Line and Passenger Certificates had expired, and in her run-down condition some six to eight weeks would be needed to get her through the surveys necessary for re-certification. Permission was given by the Board of Trade to tow her coastwise with a crew of "runners", though she could not proceed under her own power. She was brought up to Devonport Dockyard, and completed on October 16.

Some ships underwent major surgery. *Rawalpindi* became a one-funnel ship when her afterstack was cut down to a stump, *Rajputana* lost her second funnel, *Carnarvon Castle* had her original foremast and most of her peacetime lifeboats removed. When the *Cheshire* was about to berth in Calcutta, where she was converted at the Garden Reach workshop of Mackinnon Mackenzie, the Berthing Master called out to Second Officer Williamson through a megaphone, "We are going to make a nice mess of your beautiful ship". They were some of the truest words ever spoken. *Cheshire* was left with only her original foremast, two stump derricks being fitted aft, and all four Bibby liners chosen for conversion lost at least two of their four masts.

In all the ships the trim lines of the decks were broken by the angular lumps of guns. White upperworks and the holiday colours of funnels, pink of Bibby, yellow of P & O, black, white and blue of Lamport & Holt, buff of Canadian Pacific with the red and white quarterings, all were defiled and extinguished by war's mud-grey drab.

While the P & O's *Ranpura* and *Carthage* were fitting out in Calcutta the monsoons broke. The drenching rain made the ships, each of which had been given over to a battalion of some eight hundred artisans, even less comfortable for their crews. There was no accommodation ashore, and no room in the crowded hospitals for the European crew members who went sick. The ships' doctors were seriously overworked.

The progress of 20,914-ton *Maloja*'s conversion at Bombay suffered from faulty or conflicting official instructions. Orders came for the immediate fitting of eight 6-inch guns, which would have ruined the ship's stability without the heavy hydraulic crane being first removed from the upper deck and the ship ballasted. Ballasting instructions from London, however, if carried out, would have had the ship down to thirteen feet of freeboard at the stem and aground in the harbour. There was a disagreement between two senior naval officers ashore over the sighting of a 4-inch anti-aircraft gun. One wanted it mounted aft, one amidships, and it was shifted at least three times. Eventually the ship's original deck and engine room officers were directing most of the work.

P & O ships in peacetime carried a large number of Asians in their crews. *Maloja*'s Goanese were willing to remain in the new ship's company, but were not allowed to do so. All the Asians in her engine room and deck departments stayed with her until she reached Britain and was about to join the re-established Northern Patrol for service in the freezing seas off Iceland.

While the *Chitral* was undergoing conversion at Glasgow before she too joined the Northern Patrol, the order came for the Punjabis among her engine-room staff to leave the ship. The Chief Engineer did his best to keep them, but the authorities did not think they could stand up to the chilling cold of the Denmark Strait. The lorry which took them away from the ship was piled so high with their gear that a railway arch caught the apex of the pyramid, and the Clydeside street was strewn forlornly with pots and pans, rice and curry powder.

In ports all round the world work was going on round the clock to rush to sea thirteen stiffened ships, *Asturias* and *Scotstoun* in Belfast, *Chitral* and *Transylvania* in the Clyde, *Montclare* at Barrow-in-Furness, *Aurania* on Tyneside, *Salopian* and *Ascania* on the Mersey, *Jervis Bay* and *Rawalpindi* in London, *Alaunia* at Gibraltar, *Carnarvon Castle* in Simonstown, *Letitia* at Esqui-mault. These were the new pioneers, the first of the shabbily armed, unarmoured stop-gaps that would once again have to help overworked regular cruisers counter the enemy's first moves at sea.

9 "Our big ships come tomorrow"

"Eventually we reached Scapa Flow and were surprised to find such a huge area of water with all kinds of warships dotted about all blinking away with signals and a great number of ships' boats all going the rounds."

Young Geoff Penny had joined a luxury liner as a purser's clerk and was now a paymaster sub-lieutenant RNR in an armed merchant cruiser. "We in *Asturias* were quite green in RN procedures." It was his job to make sure that the ship's company was properly clothed to face patrols up beyond the Arctic Circle. *Asturias*' store, which had been one of the First Class passenger suites on C Deck, sold thick vests and longjohns, shirts and shoes, sheets and hussifs, and he managed to borrow heavy fur coats, seaboot stockings, leather seaboots and oilskins from the naval stores in Kirkwall.

The first AMCs began to steam into Scapa from 29 September onwards, but none was sufficiently worked up to go on patrol.

The old C and D class light cruisers of the 7th and 12th Cruiser Squadrons formed the Northern Patrol. These small ships of under 5,000 tons had spent many of the falsely peaceful years showing the flag round the world, steaming lazily through tropic seas or displaying white hulls and funnels of daffodil yellow, draped in snowy awnings, in southern ports.

Now they were confined to the cold north, drab grey battered watchdogs, straining at their rivets, flogging their old engines through heavy seas, freezing fog, sleet and snowstorms, in the short hours of blurred daylight. Hatches, ventilators, deck plating and timber joints leaked. Boats, topmasts, bridge screens, booms, guardrails, were smashed. It was dangerous to use the upper deck, even with lifelines rigged aft along the waist. Below decks men subsisted on cold food, and slept with oilskins over their hammocks, but bedding and clothes were permanently sodden. Shaving invited mutilation. A flotsam of broken messtraps and personal gear washed about the decks as the ship plunged and rolled. Tables, benches and lockers broke adrift. Everywhere it was "one hand for the ship and one for yourself".

The cruisers *Caledon, Calypso, Cardiff, Colombo, Calcutta Delhi, Diomede, Dragon* and *Dunedin* formed a wide-meshed net between John O'Groats and Reykjavik, with an average of two ships in the Scotland—Faeroes gap, three between the Faeroes and Iceland at any one time.

The biggest hole in the net was the Denmark Strait, where the old cruisers could not patrol because of their low fuel endurance. Homeward-bound German merchantmen and neutrals were getting through there, and at any time a raider might slip out into the Atlantic. C-in-C, Home Fleet, helped by detaching a modern regular cruiser when he could, but even the *Sheffield* could only spend two days there. HMS *Belfast* bagged the German Hamburg-Sud-Amerika Line's cargo passenger liner *Cap Norte*, disguised as a Swede, on 9 October.

Savage seas made it barely possible to man the guns, especially in *Caledon* and *Calypso*, whose 6-inch were all at main deck level. When heavy weather made it impossible to board a suspect ship the cruiser had to leave station to take her to Kirkwall, where Vice-Admiral, Northern Patrol, Max Horton, a famous submariner in World War 1, had his HQ. Bad visibility made sightings difficult. The AMCs were trapped in Scapa, unable to work up or to take on stores. Ships which only a few weeks before had sweated in the tropics seemed to shrink and shiver. "A very eerie, cold and stormy time," wrote *Salopian* boarding officer Bill Jeffery, "chaotic, uncertain, anxious and bewildering". Vast areas of the ship were just open spaces where scores of passenger cabins had been torn out. The officers ate in the ship's old main saloon next to piles of the old furniture.

Just after one o'clock in the dark hours of the middle watch on 14 October men in the AMC *Chitral* were awakened by the deep explosions of torpedoes. Soon all the sleeping ships were awake, up-anchoring and shifting about The Flow. At her anchorage the 29,150-ton battleship *Royal Oak* had capsized, with a loss of 830 men. A daring U-boat* had got into The Flow through Kirk Sound, on the day before a blockship was to be sunk there, and put four torpedoes into the battleship. The submarine remained undetected, and no ship felt safe. All the big ships in the anchorage were ordered to sea out of harm's way. Extra precautions were taken to seal the entrances to The Flow.

There were no immediate repeats of the sinking, but four days later two squadrons of Junkers 88s flew over Scapa, to bomb the ships there. The main body of the Home Fleet was at sea, and the only British casualty was the old battleship *Iron Duke*, once Jellicoe's flagship at Jutland and now in use as a base ship and floating coastal defence battery, which suffered underwater damage and had to be towed into shallow water and beached.

But it was clear that Scapa Flow was no longer an impregnable base for the Home Fleet. In future the regular cruisers in the Northern Patrol were to use Sullom Voe in the Shetlands as their base, while the AMCs, with their greater range, would use the Clyde.

To fill the gaps in the blockade, particularly in the Denmark Strait, and get them clear of The Flow, the nine AMCs which had gathered there steamed out on 17 October, passing a patch of oil where the *Royal Oak* rested. *Asturias, Aurania, California, Chitral* and *Salopian* had not completed working up, but were sent on patrol. *Chitral* had had no gun drill at all, and practised on an iceberg, occasionally hitting the white floating mountain and knocking off big chunks. *Asturias* went on a convoy run to Halifax, Nova Scotia. The three ships which had completed working up, not without difficulties and hold-ups, *Rawalpindi*, *Scotstoun* and *Transylvania*, were sent up to the Denmark Strait

---

* U47, commanded by Oberleutnant-zur-See Gunther Prien, afterwards known in Germany as "The Bull of Scapa".

where swirling mists hid the sea, and the Arctic "day" spanned two and a half hours.

HMS *Rawalpindi*, the 16,697-ton, former P & O liner, already had the makings of a happy and efficient ship, and her oddly assorted ship's company had begun to shake down well. She carried thirty-nine officers and some two hundred and ten ratings. There were only three Royal Navy officers in the ship, including the Commanding Officer and the First Lieutenant, Lieutenant-Commander Molson. The other RN officer, Warrant Officer French, was the only one on the Active Service list.

Captain Edward Coverley Kennedy of the *Rawalpindi* came of a family which had had men in the Royal Navy for two hundred years. Captain Archibald Kennedy had commanded HMS *Flamborough* against the French in 1760; another had served with Nelson and had been commended by him in a letter which hung in a frame in Edward Kennedy's study at his home in Farnham Common. As executive officer of the battlecruiser *New Zealand* in World War 1, he had proved himself a brilliant officer. But in Newport, Monmouthshire, one morning in 1921 his battalion of Naval Reservists refused duty against striking Welsh miners, and Kennedy was court-martialled for not trying to force action on his men, almost all of them trade unionists and many of them miners themselves. When Geddes wielded his economy axe the following year Kennedy was one of the first to go.

He bore no resentment for his harsh treatment, and as soon as war was declared went straight up to the Admiralty and asked, at the age of sixty, for employment. Delighted and somewhat surprised at his reception, he rushed home and told his gardener, Harry Looker, "Harry, they've given me a ship. I never thought they'd give me such a big ship after being out of the Service so long. A big ship, Harry, so they must have confidence in me."

The big ship was the *Rawalpindi*. "I wondered from the start," he wrote to his wife Rose and son Ludovic, who was a midshipman in the RNVR, "if I had got too rusty. Some things certainly were a bit strange at first, but I feel now as if I was back in the last war and there had been no interlude at all. It has all come back and I find there is little I have forgotten. But I feel I must make good and I realise the responsibility of this command more than I ever did in my former command."

These were sentiments shared by many retired officers who had taken on a new fight to find themselves commanding a collection of Merchant Navy men and middle-aged Reservists in an armed liner. The feeling of *déjà vu* was also common, with names like *Alcantara, Laurentic, Voltaire* back in active service.

The self-confidence which Captain Kennedy quickly recovered spread equally fast to his ship's company. In another letter home he wrote, "Everything in the ship is slowly and surely shaping itself. It has been an interesting experiment trying to circulate the right spirit into such a mixed crowd... The mercantile firemen, who are usually very undisciplined, are coming quite into line and have expressed a wish to share the same recreation room as the seamen, to which the latter have agreed. They don't want to be different, a very good sign, and after my rounds this morning I was able to congratulate various people on the way they had cleaned up their departments. An excellent atmosphere is beginning to prevail."

Kennedy insisted on regular physical training for the ship's company in the form of a daily march round the decks, a routine he had introduced to the *New Zealand*. "I warned them we would do it and I myself led with Molson. Some of the mercantile men thought it a bit of a joke till I made them run the last lap of over 300 yards. They were all so pumped (except me) that they became quite subdued and appreciated that they were all the better for it."

There was trouble with the old guns fitted in the AMCs. Most of the 6-inch were on decrepit mountings. One mounting in the *Cheshire* was dated 1901, another 1902. *Rawalpindi*'s 6-inch were 1901 and 1909 models, *Alcantara* had one made in 1898, and her newest guns were her 3-inch HA, dating from 1914. One of *Canton*'s mountings and one of *Cilicia*'s went back to 1895, and the latter was the ship's newest. Many of these guns had bores worn by firing in the First World War.

These relics had been taken out of storage, where some of them had lain for decades without attention, and were not even overhauled when brought out for service. It was not surprising when defects developed, most of them caused by wear in pivots and mountings. Even when the Gunner's party and the ship's engineers managed to get the working parts in motion, it was impossible to keep the guns in proper order, as most of them, like *Rawalpindi*'s eight 6-inch, had previously been fitted behind the protection of casemates as the secondary armament of battleships and heavy cruisers, and had no shields. On the open decks of the AMCs the mechanism was exposed to the savage northern weather. The forward guns were the most badly affected. Water got betwen the upper and lower bushes of the centre pivots of the mountings, which seized up along with other moving parts of the mechanism. Some of the guns could only be trained with the help of two or three members of the gun's crew shoving on the barrel.

Deck strength, space and stability for accuracy of fire dictated the postitioning of the guns, which often had a poor field of fire. *Rawalpindi*'s two forward guns were on the well deck, their arc of fire obstructed by the foc'sle. All her four after-guns were on the main deck, two each side, their elevation restricted by the deck above, which stretched aft right to the stern, and there was an arc round the stern which could not be covered at all. In *Jervis Bay*, less decked and with clearer and less obstructive upperworks, two of her 6-inch, all of which had shields, were mounted on the foc'sle, two were on the open after well deck and one up on the deckhouse right aft with an unrestricted field of fire astern.

Gunnery control systems were also primitive. In the *Salopian* there was a small rangefinder clamped on the rail, by means of which it was supposed to be possible to work out the deflection, and one very old destroyer director which always got out of step as soon as the first 6-inch shell was fired.

The gun control platform was linked to the guns by inter-connected telephones to port and starboard which gave endless trouble. Eventually they fell back on the old battleship type of range and deflection clocks. One of these was fitted on the control platform. This one could be seen by the foc'sle head and poop guns' crews, who repeated the information on other boards which could be seen from the waist guns. This arrangement worked after a fashion in daylight, but was not much use at night. Much later a system of voicepipes was installed as well, but Harry Peate, *Salopian*'s Mate of the Upper Deck, said, "I don't think we shall ever be classed as a first-rate gunnery establishment." *Alaunia*'s working up in October was delayed by gun defects. *Asturias, Aurania* and *Rawalpindi* all had some unserviceable guns and untrained guns' crews.

Retired officers recalled to the Service and Reserve telegraphists and bunting tossers did not understand modern Fleet communications. Two AMCs missed a signal, crossed cruiser patrol lines at night, and were nearly fired on. *Asturias* was off the Faeroes at night on her way to a patrol area off the Denmark Strait when she was challenged by a regular cruiser. A confused signalman made the wrong reply. A starshell burst in the sky and lit up the big grey-painted former Royal Mail liner. Just in time she flashed the right code. She had just reached the Denmark Strait when a radio signal ordered her west into the Atlantic to look for a German raider, thought to be the pocket battleship *Deutschland*.

On 19 October *Rawalpindi* intercepted a strange ship south of Iceland. The AMC's best 6-inch, made in 1909, fired a round across the stranger's bows. The ship stopped and her crew scuttled her. Her Master identified her as the German *Gonzenheim*. In thanks for his kind and courteous treatment on board *Rawalpindi* he gave Kennedy his binoculars, which he passed on to Boarding Officer Anderson.

The *Biscaya* was in the Denmark Strait running for Germany. Suddenly a grey ship loomed out of the mist and a signal lamp flashed. It was HMS *Scotstoun*.

She signalled "What ship?"

Biscaya's Chief Engineer rushed to the bridge. "Permission to scuttle, sir?"

"No. If we do that she'll fire on us." Lieutenant-Commander Clark's prize crew took *Biscaya* to Leith, with the German engineers sullenly working the engines at gun point.

On 20 October HMS *Transylvania*, ex-Anchor Line, stopped the German tanker *Bianca* in the Strait, put a prize crew under RNR Lieutenant-Commander MacLean on board.

As *Bianca* headed for Leith MacLean thought the prisoners seemed strangely cheerful. The German Captain approached him. "Commander. I think it would be best for yourself and your men if you allow me and my officers to escape in one of the boats." He would not give a reason for this suggestion, and MacLean refused anyway. As the voyage south wore on the Germans' good spirits deteriorated. When the *Bianca* reached Scotland the German Chief Engineer confided that they had sent a signal on being stopped by the *Transylvania* and had been expecting a rescue by a U-boat north of the Shetlands.

On 21 October in this heavy weather *Scotstoun* intercepted a merchantman giving her name as the *Virginia*. Closer scrutiny exposed her as the German *Poseidon*. For twenty-nine hours *Scotstoun* escorted her, unable to get a boarding party across in the rough seas. Then, in the lee of Iceland, the German crew abandoned ship. A prize crew, which the ship could not really spare, having sent one away in the *Biscaya*, under Lieutenant Armstrong was put aboard her. The Germans refused to return and work their ship, and Armstrong anchored *Poseidon* while his men raised steam.

Scotstoun lost *Poseidon* in a thick snowstorm, but early on 25 October *Transylvania* intercepted the prize, found her unable to steam, and took her in tow. Next day a southerly gale sprang up, and the tow parted at *Poseidon*'s end of the cable. It was so rough at dawn that *Transylvania* slipped the towing wire and took off the prize crew, though they were only eleven miles from Iceland. No sooner were the men safely on board than the wind increased again, and *Poseidon* had to be sunk by gunfire.

Patrolling a roughly SW-NE line between the south coast of Iceland and the northern Faeroes, *Salopian* stopped a Scandinavian ship, but the weather was so bad that it was impossible to board her. The AMC escorted her into the calmer waters of the Faeroes, where she was handed over to an armed trawler for boarding and examination.

On patrol south of Iceland, *Delhi* sighted a steamer, fired a round to stop her, and sent over a boarding party. The ship was a German merchantman, H. Vogemann Knohr & Burchard's *Rheingold*. Her crew had their lifebelts on and were in a very nervous state. The boarding party investigated below and found the ship set up for scuttling. Most of the condenser door bolts had been removed and the door shored up but fitted with lanyards for quick removal. The German Captain had given the order not to scuttle, however, because, "In six or nine months, when Germany has won the war, I will get my ship back."

Armed trawlers were plugging the gaps Orkneys – Fair Isle, Fair Isle – Shetlands, Shetlands – Faeroes, and were kept busy by neutral Scandinavian ships trying to sneak home.

Neutrals hated going into Kirkwall. Their charts did not show dangerous tidal streams and currents, there were no shore lights now and no qualified pilots to guide them in. Two ships grounded on Sanday and became total losses.

At Kirkwall itself there were queues of ships and long delays. The Master of the Swedish MV *Uruguay*, held up in port for three weeks said, "It's a dash through the Denmark Strait for me after this." His company, Rederaktieb Nordstjernan of Stockholm, made this official for their faster ships. Time was money. Another resentful skipper wanted to know, "How was it that a submarine got into Scapa Flow and sank the *Royal Oak*? Is Kirkwall any better protected than Scapa?"

There was by this time a serious threat to British shipping at sea in the North Atlantic. On 21 October a ship brought into Kirkwall the crew of the Norwegian *Lorentz W. Hansen*, which had been sunk by the *Deutschland*. Shortly after this the American SS *City of Flint*, captured by the *Deutschland* on 22 October, was taken over by the Norwegians when her German prize crew were trying to sail her through Norwegian territorial waters to Germany.

Deutschland, with her sister ship *Graf Spee*, had left Germany in August before the beginning of war, the latter for the South Atlantic. They both remained inactive throughout September to give Hitler a chance to patch up a peace with the Allies after the conquest of Poland, but at the end of the month there had been no reply to his overtures and both ships were given the all-clear to begin attacks. *Deutschland* intercepted three ships in the western North Atlantic, sinking the British SS *Stonegate* and the *Lorentz W. Hansen* in the first fortnight of October.

HMS *Dunedin* had worked out the best boarding drill:

"Bridge – R/T office. Strange merchantman in sight.'

That was the first step. Germans stopped by British cruisers had been known to tip off U-boats, and next the cruiser closed to flag-wagging range, signalled,

"Do not use your radio."

"What ship? Where from? Where bound?" was flashed or flagged slowly.

When a name was given, the cruiser's W/T operator looked up that ship's call sign. If he heard her transmitting he jammed it at once.

On the bridge they checked the name and the ship's position with Lloyd's *Shipping Index*, Talbot Booth's *Merchant Ships*, *Lloyd's Register*. Then...

Boarding for a cargo or identity check needed caution. There might be a U-boat paired with the stranger. If so the submarine captain would be expecting the cruiser to stop herself and the merchantman and send a boat across. A sitting duck for a torpedo.

But *Dunedin* would steam ahead of the merchantman, and only then lower a boat. This made it harder for a submarine, easier for the boat to reach the target, especially in a rough sea. Only when the boat, with boarding officer and armed guard, was close aboard was "Heave to!" signalled to the quarry.

The boarding officer was probably young and overworked. He was on Max Horton's staff, not in the ship's company, but kept watch on the bridge, commanded several guns in action, and was a divisional officer as well. He needed rare commonsense, tact and judgement to deal with awkward and unco-operative masters and crews.

HMS *Scotstoun* was on patrol between Iceland and the Faeroes on 7 November. The four forward 6-inch guns, entirely unprotected by any gunshields, became unworkable sculptures of frozen spray. At Action Stations, held regularly at daybreak and dusk, they were manned, but whether they could be fought was doubtful.

The former Anchor liner spent the 8th running before a wind blowing at 30 mph from nor'-east-by-north, raising a sea too steep for boarding. At night a gale howled out of the north-east, cutting her speed to 8 knots. The daylight brought snow flurries and ice, with visibility down to about four miles. During the forenoon the ship passed an iceberg three miles to the southward. She was dodging pack ice and growlers on the return patrol at 7.40 next morning when there was a grinding shudder.

Inspection revealed leakage in the fore peak and Number 1 Hold at the rate of about two tons an hour. *Scotstoun* manned the pumps and continued the patrol, still maintaining radio silence.

A gale hit *Laurentic* on 15 November and damaged the big liner. Several of her vintage 6-inch guns jammed at their mountings and could not be trained. Three boats were holed, furniture smashed. In the C and D cruisers boats were swept away or shattered, Carley floats lost overboard, depth-charge fittings and shell racks washed away. In one ship the tail of a paravane was snapped off like a carrot. Electrical defects multiplied. Water got between decks, and the lack of drying facilities made life miserable.

A very severe gale blew up while there were forty-one neutral ships in Kirkwall, and there was nearly a disaster when several of them began to drag their anchors. Two trawlers did drag ashore but were later refloated. The necessity for a trot where trawlers and other small craft could lie in comparative security became more apparent after every gale.

Behind the wall of hostile weather lurked the other enemy. On 12 November the Norwegian ship *Tvrifjord* was brought into Kirkwall by an armed guard. Her Master reported to the Contraband Control Base Boarding Officer that on 4 November they had been stopped by the *Deutschland* seven hundred miles west of Ireland. He had not reported this before as he did not want to be overheard by the Germans. He said that if the name of a neutral ship was mentioned in an Admiralty message, neither officers nor crew would dare sail in her again for fear of reprisals.

At 3.30 p.m. on 17 November the limping *Scotstoun* had finally left her patrol area for the Clyde when she sighted a vessel hull down about fifteen miles away and altered course towards her. The strange ship turned away and increased speed.

By 4.45, in the dusk, *Scotstoun* had closed to flashing distance and ordered her quarry to stop. There was no reply, and at 5.10 the AMC fired a shot across the stranger's bows at a range of 10,000 yards. The vessel hove to. *Scotstoun* came up with her at 5.25 and she claimed to be the Swedish *Isa Trellborg*, bound from Murmansk to Boston.

Captain Hardy was suspicious. She had the correct colours on her black funnel, a white band with a blue circle, and the appropriate deck cargo of timber. But if she was genuine she was not where Lloyd's said she should be. It was getting dark, there was a heavy swell running, and both ships were rolling and pitching heavily. Hardy signalled the suspect *Isa*,

"Keep your lights burning. Prepare to be boarded at daybreak."

At 9.45 in the morning Hardy stopped both ships to board but the weather was too rough. At half-past three in the afternoon he managed to get a boarding party across, who flashed back,

"She is the *Eilbek* of Hamburg."

The German Master was willing to work his ship into port and had sufficient bunkers for three days, though he had been reduced to burning his cargo of pulp wood. Hardy put young RNR Sub-

Lieutenant Ramsthorne aboard her, with one RNVR sub-lieutenant, one midshipman, one engineer officer, one petty officer, one leading hand, eight seamen and one signalman to take the prize into Glasgow.

On 20 November the *Chitral* sighted and chased a steamer off the coast of Iceland. On her side were painted the name *Ada* of Bergen and Norwegian colours, an obviously amateurish job done at sea. The clumsy disguise hid the 4,100-ton German SS *Bertha Fisser*, bound for Hamburg from Pernambuco. She was slow to heave to. Her wireless operator tried to get off an SOS but this was jammed by *Chitral*'s operator. Her crew tried to escape on her landward side away from the *Chitral*, but a shot across the bows stopped them. By the time the boarding party got on board, her engine room and stokehold were half full of water, the condenser cover and inlet valve having been fractured. Forty of her crew surrendered, but the ship herself sank with painful slowness, as if reluctant to go. Before darkness fell the AMC fired seven rounds of 6-inch into her, and the blast from the guns shattered glass in the village of Hoefn on the Icelandic coast and even windows in farmhouses as far as six miles inland. The *Bertha Fisser* burst into flames but still would not go down. Morning found her aground on the rocks, broken in two, just to the eastward of Horne Fjord.

Chitral's Chief engineer interrogated the German Captain and First Officer, with the two prisoners standing stiffly to attention. He instantly disliked the arrogance of the latter, and deliberately kept him standing in a position where the melting snow on the edge of the Sun Deck dripped down the German's stiff neck.

"This ship – no good," said the German. "Our big ships come tomorrow. They take us away."

10 "We'll fight them both"

In bad weather on the night of 21 November the AMC *Transylvania* intercepted a merchantman which signalled that she was the Swedish *Gunor*. Next morning the weather was still bad. The ship was heard using her W/T. *Transylvania* jammed this and ordered her to stop signalling. The freighter then scuttled herself. The sea was still so high that although the crew were picked up from their lifeboats, the AMC's boarding boat could not be hoisted and had to be cut adrift. The sunken vessel was the German SS *Tenerife*.

At 6 p.m. on the 22nd the *Laurentic*, which had only joined the Northern Patrol at the beginning of November, left her patrol line, which was immediately to the south of the Faroes and north of *Rawalpindi*'s patrol line, to proceed to Liverpool for refuelling. At quarter to eight she closed the Swedish steamer *Lulea* bound from Narvik to New York, and an hour later she had just checked the credentials of the trawler *Milmir* when the keen eyes of the AMC's Gunner, Mr O'Brien, sighted a strange ship in the darkness.

Laurentic challenged the ship but got no reply, and the stranger began transmitting on W/T. *Laurentic* fired starshell over her. The bright pyrotechnics revealed her as a freighter. *Laurentic* signalled "Cease transmitting", and her operator jammed the other ship's signals.

With the stranger preserving a sullen silence, the AMC signalled in succession.

"Stop." No response.

"Proceed course south." There was no change.

"If you sink your ship I will not be able to pick up your boats."

Two warning rounds of 6-inch were then fired.

The last signal was either not received or the bluff was being called. The freighter's crew abandoned ship in a large lifeboat. The ship was rolling heavily beam-on to a very heavy swell, and *Laurentic*'s boats' crews were too inexperienced to be sent away. *Laurentic* remained near the other vessel all night in the hope that she could be boarded in the morning if still afloat, and towed in if it was not possible to steam her.

Daylight revealed a ship with black hull and white upperworks, black funnels with two widely separated white bands, a yellow foremast and a black and yellow mainmast. She called herself the *Flora* of Amsterdam, and Dutch colours had been freshly painted on her sides. The sea had moderated, *Laurentic* made a good lee, and the men were taken aboard from the boat. Their ship was the German *Antiochia*, Hamburg-Amerika Line. Her Master, Captain Joseph Winand, told *Laurentic*'s officers that his ship would sink, as the condenser inlet had been removed.

Laurentic had been warned by radio of U-boats off Iceland, and kept on the move. At half-past four in the snow blizzard that was now blowing hard *Antiochia* was still afloat. The AMC put several rounds of 6-inch into her, then left the scene but steamed in the area all night. In the morning the stubborn *Antiochia* was still floating.

Waterlogged and on fire, she was a danger to navigation. *Laurentic* gave her two more salvoes, and she sank shortly afterwards. At 7.50 *Laurentic* shaped course for Liverpool. On passage Surgeon Commander Elder, who spoke fluent German, and Commander Hartley talked to the German officers and crew, and discovered that the *Antiochia* had left Hamburg on 8 August bound for the West Indies with cement, fertilizers and general cargo. On the declaration of war she was ordered by radio to go to the Azores. She made Ponta Delgada and stayed there for two months. On receipt of further radio instructions she left on 12 November for Hamburg, with her original cargo still on board. She was on the eleventh day of her passage when she met the *Laurentic*, having made poor time, Winand said, because of the marine growth on her bottom accumulated during her long stay in port.

The old C and D cruisers were in need of refit, but newly commissioned AMCs were joining the Northern Patrol to replace them. On 19 November the *Montclare* arrived in the Clyde. HMS *Worcestershire* commissioned on the 22nd, *Andania* and *Forfar* would be joining in a matter of days. *Asturias* left Halifax, Nova Scotia, in mid-November to return to the Northern Patrol as part of the escort for a large convoy to Greenock. Half-way across the steep Atlantic stream they ran into a gale "with waves as big as office blocks", Geoff Penny said in a letter home. The convoy had to be scattered, *Asturias* was hove-to for two days and strained her expansion plates.

When she eventually arrived at Greenock she was sent up-river to a Glasgow dock for repairs, and *Rawalpindi* went on patrol in her place. The *Asturians* were to bless that gale.

Under Captain Kennedy, *Rawalpindi*'s ship's company felt a responsibility to maintain high standards. Guns' crews were exercised as often as the northern winter weather allowed. In her first ten days of active service at sea she stopped an average of one merchantman a day.

Entertainment was organized on board to help keep morale high. When she left the Clyde on 16 November and headed north for her third patrol, a concert party went into rehearsal. The first performance was a great success. Captain Kennedy himself did his party piece. His version of

> Here a sheer hulk lies poor Tom Bowling,
> The darling of our crew

received loud applause. It was decided to give a second performance on the following evening, 23 November.

In the forenoon of the 23rd a Swedish ship was sighted. *Rawalpindi*'s Boarding Officer, Lieutenant Anderson, was ordered to take her into port under armed guard. Anderson was appearing in the concert party, so he spun a coin with Lieutenant Pickersgill, the Second Boarding Officer. Anderson lost and left the ship to take over the neutral vessel, taking his German binoculars from the *Gonzenheim* with him. *Rawalpindi* continued her patrol.

At 3.30 p.m., about the time of sunset in that area, *Rawalpindi* was about mid-way between the Faeroes and Iceland, when she sighted a ship. The silhouette quickly established her as a large warship.

Captain Kennedy looked at her through his binoculars. She looked like a German battlecruiser.

He ordered Action Stations, a change of course, and an enemy sighing report to be made immediately. The alarm bells rang as *Rawalpindi* headed for a fog bank to port. Smoke floats were lit and thrown into the water, but they failed to burn. Kennedy thought that an iceberg about four miles away to starboard looked like better cover and ordered another alteration of course in that direction.

The enemy warship altered course to head off the British AMC, and closed her rapidly. A signal lamp flashed on her bridge.

"Heave to!" It was *Rawalpindi*'s turn to be on the receiving end of the signal which she herself had made to enemy ships many times already.

Rawalpindi ignored the order. After a few minutes there was a flash from one of the German's forward guns, and a warning shell hit the sea two hundred yards ahead of the AMC's bows, sending up a geyser of white water.

There was some doubt about the identity of the German ship. Some thought her to be, not a battlecruiser, but a pocket battle-ship, probably the *Deutschland*, thought to be still at large. Which-ever she was, she was closing rapidly.

Kennedy examined her through his binoculars agan. "It's the *Deutschland* all right." He ordered an amended signal to be sent out to C-in-C, Home Fleet.

The German flashed "Heave to!" for the second time.

At that moment a lookout in *Rawalpindi* reported another warship about four points on the starboard bow. Believing their original pursuer to be the *Deutschland*, which previous victims had described as operating on her own, Kennedy thought this second ship to be another Northern Patrol cruiser, and ordered a change of course towards her.

The Engineer Commander arrived on the bridge to report relief firemen closed up. The Chief Yeoman of Signals called out: "I think the second ship's a battlecruiser, sir!"

Kennedy said, "We'll fight them both, they'll sink us, and that'll be that." He held out his hand to the Engineer Commander. "Goodbye."

As he spoke the second enemy warship was altering course to get on *Rawalpindi*'s bow again. The AMC, with her frail, unarmoured liner's hull, was about to do battle with the *Scharnhorst* and *Gneisenau*, the most modern and most powerful warships on active service with the German Navy. Here *déjà vu* did not apply. No auxiliary cruiser in the First World War had had to face a regular warship, let alone two capital ships. Once again Victorian bones could be imagined turning in the grave, in this case those of the two Navy captains, the colonel of Marines and the assistant master shipwright who had thought that auxiliary cruisers "would not make efficient substitutes for regular men of war". Here was the case in point illustrated in the extreme. Eight ancient 6-inch guns faced eighteen new 11-inch rifles in the hands of well-trained gunners.

Scharnhorst, the leading pursuer, flashed "Abandon your ship!" The AMC took no notice.

The signal was repeated, and again ignored.

Captain Hoffmann, who had been watching from the battlecruiser's foretop, ordered, "Try her once more." The signal went out for the third time. "Abandon your ship!" There was no answer. She was going to put up a fight. "So be it," said Hoffmann. "Open fire."

It was 3.45, only fifteen minutes since the *Rawalpindi* had first sighted *Scharnhorst*. The range was four miles.

Rawalpindi opened fire with a salvo aimed at the *Gneisenau* from her four starboard 6-inch guns and hit the battlecruiser, Admiral Marschall's flagship, amidships. With her port battery she fired at *Scharnhorst*.

Then *Scharnhorst*'s first salvo struck *Rawalpindi* on the Boat Deck just below the bridge, killing nearly everyone on the bridge and destroying the wireless room, making it impossible for her to send any further reports.

Gneisenau opened up a cross-fire, and soon her shells hit *Rawalpindi*'s main control position, killing everyone there and knocking S3 Gun out of action.

Kennedy, who had survived the hits on the Boat Deck, sent Chief Petty Officer Humphries round the seven surviving guns to tell the officers in charge to continue firing independently as long as possible.

A shell exploded in the engine room, destroying the dynamos and the electric power supply to the shell hoists from the magazines. Kennedy ordered Humphries to put all the spare hands on to carrying the heavy 6-inch shells up from the magazines and humping them to the guns.

C-in-C, Home Fleet, in the Clyde received *Rawalpindi*'s first signal reporting contact with an enemy battlecruiser at 3.51 p.m. He immediately signalled HMS *Newcastle*, which was twenty-five miles away from *Rawalpindi* on the next patrol line, and *Delhi*, which was also nearby to the south-west chasing a merchantman, to close her. *Calypso* and *Ceres* too were not far away to the south. All AMCs on patrol, including three in the Denmark Strait, were recalled. Heavy cruisers *Norfolk* and *Suffolk* were ordered down from the Denmark Strait to the scene of action.

Rawalpindi was now badly on fire, though all guns except S3 and P1 were firing. One badly wounded loader was crawling his way to the gun with a shell in his arms. In his shocked brain he remembered lugging a 6-inch shell up and down Laundry Hill at HMS *Ganges* for farting in gunnery class during his initial training. Another 6-inch gun jammed after scoring three hits on the enemy. The gun captain shouted, "Come on, lads, give me a hand to free it!" but they were all dead.

In the after magazine down in the bowels of the ship the lights went out. When the hands there were told that the ship was on fire they flooded the magazine to stop it going up and made for the upper deck. Up there they found cordite sticks and 6-inch shells rolling about the deck in the path of the flames, picked them up and threw them overboard.

Kennedy took two ratings aft with him to try to get a smoke-screen laid.

Chiefie Humphries was trying to get some of the wounded men into the boats when one of the men who had gone aft with Kennedy appeared through the smoke and flames, "The Captain's been killed, Chief."

Petty Officer Shipwright Pyndar Wyniatt had his axe ready to cut free anything that would float. Fires were burning everywhere, the water supply was cut off, the steering gear was useless. Commander Molson ordered him to get the convention valves closed, which might keep the ship afloat a little longer. One lifeboat was being prepared for lowering, with some thirty to forty men in it, but it broke away from the falls and hit the sea upside-down, throwing the men, most of them wounded, into the water to struggle helplessly.

A shell hit the carpenter's shop, about twenty feet away from Wyniatt, and blew him and his mate into the scuppers. Wyniatt picked himself up, bent down to help the other man, and found that the latter had one leg broken in two places. He lifted him up and carried him to the Boat Deck.

At that moment, about four o'clock, *Rawalpindi* was hit in the forward magazine by a shell from the *Scharnhorst*. There was a devastating explosion, which broke the ship's back. One gun went on firing.

Wyniatt found it very unhealthy on the Boat Deck, with a rain of shrapnel coming down and the ship's ammunition blowing up in the racks. *Rawalpindi*'s last gun was now out of action. Wyniatt and the bosun tried to get the cutters launched but there was no steam to power their hoisting derrick. Wyniatt hacked away with his axe at anything floatable. He cut free the three tons of timber lashed down on the poop and tipped sand bins overboard. Then he and the ship's baker made one of the port lifeboats ready for launching. The starboard lifeboats were wreathed in smoke. Wyniatt went to chop through their falls so that they would still float. There was fire and smoke everywhere. He tripped over a body. The smoke became unbearable and he turned back.

Half the port boats were also burning, but one was launched with twenty-one men in it. Wyniatt protested that none of the men should be in that particular boat, but the lieutenant in charge there said, "That's all right. Get in any lifeboat down – take this one if you like." Wyniatt dropped his axe, stepped into the boat and clung on to one of the falls.

The boat had just begun to descend when the after fall broke. Wyniatt was left hanging from a fall, with the boat below him. Men on the ship shouted to him to "Hang on!" The boat went down a few feet more, then a wave tore it free and it dropped behind the ship. Turning his head Wyniatt found himself looking through the porthole into his own cabin, which was glowing white-hot from fire. He let go the fall and dropped into the trough of a wave.

He narrowly missed *Rawalpindi*'s screws. Looking up towards the surface he saw the shape of a lifeboat. He swam upwards, caught hold of the keel amidships, searched for the bilge rail and found a hand hold on the gunwhale, shouting "Save me!" over and over again. He was hauled aboard the boat, where he found a broken oar and paddled hard to get warm after his immersion in the ice-cold water.

A group of men and one officer, Second Boarding Officer Pickersgill, who had almost gone to the Swedish ship instead of Anderson, had gathered on the poop, the only place on the sinking after part of the ship not swept by fire. Some of them were wounded and in great pain, but no one complained. The men here shared out cigarettes and waited calmly for the end.

Then they saw a waterlogged lifeboat drifting down the ship's side. Most of the men could not face jumping thirty feet into the rough sea, but eleven of them went over, and one climbed up into the boat. As the blazing wreck of what was left of the *Rawalpindi* drifted away from them into the gathering darkness, a chief petty officer and a rating could be seen trying to get one of the forward guns into action.

The huge grey bulk of the *Scharnhorst* approached the lifeboats. She swung round and nearly swamped Wyniatt's boat. They could see the eagle and the swastika on her stern. Then Captain Hoffmann reduced speed and stopped. With a struggle the survivors managed to bring their boat alongside the battlecruiser's port side, and the Germans lowered rope ladders. Wyniatt's hands were almost useless, but he climbed up somehow. As he was being carried below by two German sailors he looked across the darkening water and there in the dusk saw the after part of the *Rawalpindi* sink, with the White Ensign still flying. The fore part had already gone.

Another boat was being manoeuvered alongside the *Scharnhorst* when a signal lamp in *Gneisenau*, which was also picking up British survivors, began to flash.

"Break off rescue operations at once. Follow me."

Captain Hoffmann looked questioningly at his Commander, who had just reached the bridge to report on the progress of the rescue operations. The masthead voicepipe buzzer whirred. The lookout's voice sang out,

"Shadow dead astern!"

Hoffmann rushed to the wing of the bridge and looked anxiously down. Survivors were still scrambling out of *Rawalpindi's* boat.

"Let go the painter!" Hoffmann shouted, then turned.

"All engines full speed ahead!"

Scharnhorst made off east with gathering speed, following Admiral Marschall in *Gneisenau*.

HMS *Newcastle* had picked up *Rawalpindi's* enemy sighting reports and altered course eastwards at full speed. Two hours later, in company with *Delhi*, she had sighted gunflashes and a searchlight on the horizon, then at 6.15 p.m. a darkened ship six and a half miles away. Two minutes after this she saw a second ship signalling to the first.

The range was closing too rapidly for *Newcastle*. It was not the job of a 6-inch cruiser to fight two heavily armed capital ships, and the old *Delhi* would not be much help. Her role was to shadow and report them to Admiral Forbes, who had sent three destroyers from Scapa to assist the cruisers. HMS *Sheffield* was on her way from Loch Ewe to the enemy's last known position, and Forbes himself was heading north via the Minches and the Pentland Firth with the 16-inch battleships *Nelson* and *Rodney*, the heavy cruiser *Devonshire* and seven destroyers towards a position mid-way between the Faroes and the Norwegian coast.

The three 6-inch *Southampton*, *Edinburgh* and *Aurora* were on passage from Rosyth to search in the Fair Isle Channel area. *Caledon*, *Colombo* and *Cardiff* were hurrying south from patrol lines between the Shetlands and the Faeroes to join *Diomede* and *Dunedin* off North Rona and cover the western approaches to the Fair Isle Channel, heavy cruisers *Norfolk* and *Suffolk* were heading for Bill Bailey's Bank south-west of the Faeroes. A convoy which had just been leaving the Firth of Forth for Norway had been turned back and its escort of three destroyers sent to the Shetlands to join the cruiser *Glasgow* and her two destroyers diverted from a search for the German liner *Bremen*, and search to the north. Four destroyers which had left Belfast escorting two dummy battleships were detached and ordered to join Forbes' main force. One destroyer guarded the Pentland Firth between Scotland and the Orkneys in the unlikely event that the German force would attempt to break back to Germany that way. The battleship *Warspite* had been detached from a Halifax convoy and was on her way to the Denmark Strait. The battlecruiser *Repulse* and the aircraft carrier *Furious* were steaming east from Halifax, the big battlecruiser *Hood* and the French battlecruiser *Dunkerque* were heading towards a covering position in the North Atlantic.

Newcastle tried to hang on to the German raiders until the big ships of the Home Fleet could reach them. Admiral Marschall made no attempt to engage the British cruisers, which he could have disposed of without too much trouble. *Rawalpindi* had delayed him two and a half hours. He knew that he must have been reported and that the Home Fleet would be out looking for him.

The bad weather was kind to him. With darkness deepening, a curtain of rain came down between the British cruisers and their quarries and they lost sight of them. They carried no radar at that stage of the war, and when they emerged from the squall, *Scharnhorst* and *Gneisenau* were nowhere to be seen. *Newcastle* and *Delhi* searched to the north-west and north-east until dawn, but they never regained contact.

Steaming east until midnight on the 23rd, Marschall then altered course to the north-east, and waited on the 66th parallel until he felt it safe to strike south for the North Sea, hoping the bad weather would last and hide his movements, and relying on patrolling Luftwaffe flying boats to give him warning of the enemy.

There was an anxious period on the evening of 25 November when the visibility cleared too much for safety. He retraced his steps and waited. Next morning the weather obliged, visibility thickened, and *Scharnhorst* and *Gneisenau* sped south, looking for a Norwegian landfall, with double lookouts watching for British cruisers, now concentrated on a line from the Shetlands to Norway, and for hostile aircraft.

Off Stadlandet they sighted the *Glasgow*, but she did not see them. The Home Fleet had no aircraft carrier immediately available to make a close search, and aircraft of RAF Coastal Command from Scotland failed to make contact. The hostile weather which made *Scharnhorst*'s bridge untenable also blinded all pursuit. A gale on 26 November savaged the C and D cruisers at sea and they all suffered damage. One had a motor boat on the shelter deck torn away, another had a funnel badly dented by a heavy sea. In all of them the upper deck was almost continuously awash.

Marschall was met by destroyers off Jutland, and on the 27th the two battlecruisers were at anchor in the Jade River. Two days after this Admiral Forbes was still waiting for a sighting report from his cruisers and reconnaissance aircraft. When none was forthcoming he took his ships, minus *Rodney*, which returned to the Clyde with a rudder defect, on a sweep to the north, returned south empty-handed on 30 November and was entering Loch Ewe on 4 December to refuel his destroyers when his flagship *Nelson* hit a magnetic mine and had to be sent to Portsmouth for repairs.

The *Deutschland* had long vanished from the scene, having slipped back home through the Denmark Strait on 8 November aided by the dim light of the short northern day and the German weather, and had reached Kiel by the 15th. She had intercepted nothing since the *City of Flint* on 22 October, in contrast to the* *Graf Spee*, which had sunk five ships in the Atlantic and was now worrying Whitehall by cruising in the Indian Ocean.* Shortly after *Deutschland* had returned to Germany she was renamed *Lutzow* by personal order of Hitler, who was worried about the effect on German morale if a ship bearing the sacred name of The Father-land should be sunk.

The *Chitral* and the trawlers from the Faeroes patrol cruised round in the area of the *Rawalpindi* battle on the evening of 23 November and throughout the night, looking for survivors.

At 10.30 the following morning it was snowing a blizzard when the AMC sighted a boat with a white shirt flying at an improvised mast, and ten wet, cold and exhausted and wounded men in it. Other lifeboats were sighted, damaged or capsized and empty of life. At mid-day an upturned boat was sighted with a man draped

---

* *Graf Spee* cruised for ten days south of Madagascar, sank one ship, and returned to the Cape-Sierra Leone route, then switched to the waters off The Plate to attack the thick concentration of British ships there. She met the cruisers *Exeter, Ajax* and *Achilles*, and subsequently scuttled herself off Monti-video on orders from Hitler.

over the keel. *Chitral* sounded her siren, but there was no response. She lowered a boat in the rough seas and swirling snow, and sounded another blast on her steam whistle. This time the man on the boat raised his forearm feebly in recognition. It was Harry Fleming, a steward from Bethnal Green. He had hung on at first by gripping the jagged edges of a shell hole in the bottom of the boat, then only his cork lifebelt, which had caught on the keel, prevented him from joining four men who had been washed away during the night or blown off by the blizzard that followed in the morning. When he was lifted into the rescue whaler his body was frozen into the curved shape of the boat's hull. That made eleven men picked up by *Chitral*, and twenty-seven by *Scharnhorst* and *Gneisenau*. Two hundred and thirty-eight *Rawalpindi* sailors had been lost.

11 On Their Own

Admiral Marschall had disrupted British sea traffic and frustrated the Home Fleet. Certainly *Rawalpindi* had forced him to abandon his sortie without any further success, but the Admiralty was now very sensitive about the use of armed merchant cruisers. However, there were no replacements to be had and the vulnerable vessels were sent back to the Northern Patrol lines. Five of them left the Clyde on 30 November for patrol south of Iceland in the area where *Rawalpindi* had been cut down.

The former Bibby liner *Worcestershire*, commissioned on 20 November, went on her first patrol. She had been in the eastern Mediterranean bound for London via Marseilles when war was declared. From Marseilles she was routed independently to Gibraltar, and sailed on alone to Liverpool. There were several U-boat warnings, but she arrived safely. After the discharge of cargo she went to the Clyde where she was berthed at John Brown's yard in Dalmuir for her conversion.

Her boarding whalers were handled by tough and experienced Newfoundland fishermen of the Canadian Naval Reserve, but even they found the job hard and dangerous in foul weather. Twice it was impossible to board. The two neutrals were ordered to

Kirkwall, and actually arrived there. At this time a written under-taking by the master of a neutral merchantman to put into the Con-traband Control Base was sometimes accepted, if the ship was a known Scandinavian "regular". If this agreement was broken, the ship was put on the Northern Patrol's "Black List".

On 3 December the AMCs on patrol were temporarily ordered to steer south when an aircraft reported a possible enemy warship. It was a false alarm. On the 13th the submarine HMS *Salmon* reported sighting enemy heavy warships in the North Sea. Home Fleet cruisers were disposed to meet another breakout into the Atlantic. C and D cruisers at sea were concentrated west of the Faeroes, except *Colombo*, which remained in the North Minch. But they were chasing ghost ships again.

In spite of the upheaval caused by the *Rawalpindi* battle and the bad weather, contraband control was doggedly maintained. In the period 24 November – 21 December 125 ships were sighted, of which forty-seven were sent into Kirkwall, and seventy-six went there voluntarily.

On 20 December Max Horton handed over command of the Northern Patrol to Vice-Admiral Raikes.

Only *Colombo* and *Ceres* of the C and Ds were available for patrol, and the original Emergency-Equipped AMCs were also becoming due for refit, including important modifications to armament and re-equipping with Semi-Complete or Complete gear.

At least the weather was improving. Christmas Day brought ex-ceptionally fine, mild conditions. On deck at Divisions in the *Asturias*, back on patrol in the Denmark Strait up amongst the ice, they sang "From Greenland's Icy Mountains" with the latter actually in sight. The good weather lasted for some days. There were a few passing showers of fine snow or rain, and a rather heavy swell, but visibility was good, and there was a record run of sight-ings.

U-boats, too, found the fine weather to their liking. Just before noon on 28 December a British fishing trawler was torpedoed and sunk in the North Rona area. Armed trawlers searched but sighted nothing. Later on in the same day the battleship *Barham* was hit by a torpedo.

Montclare spent the first eight days of 1940 up in the Denmark

Strait and reported, "The weather has been the best on any patrol so far... There was no day when we could not have boarded." Elsewhere in the Northern Patrol area, however, conditions began to deteriorate in the second week. Gales were reported on several patrol lines, and on 10 January the *Scotstoun* had to heave to, with the ship rolling forty degrees. On 6 January the *Laurentic* grounded south-west of Islay, not fifty miles from where her namesake had foundered twenty-three years before almost to the day, and on the 10th the *Canton* ran on to the west coast of Lewis. Both AMCs got off without assistance, but returned to port badly damaged.

They could not be spared. On 12 January *Ceres* left for Belfast, on the 14th *Colombo* headed for Devonport, both to refit, but by the 18th *Delhi* and *Diomede* had rejoined. They and *Dunedin* were now the only C and D cruisers left with the Northern Patrol, and they would be the last.

From the first week in January drafts of Newfoundland ratings of the Canadian Naval Reserve became available to all the AMCs of the Northern Patrol. It was taken for granted that all these men were fishermen, ideal for boarding crews, but it was found when they reached the ships that only some of them were seamen by profession. The remainder had been mineworkers, farm labourers and other types of landsmen.

By the end of January one regular cruiser and one AMC were maintaining patrols in the Denmark Strait, nine or ten AMCs patrolled south of Iceland, and two cruisers south of the Faeroes, as well as the usual patrols off the Faeroes and Orkneys.

Gaps were left in this net when a cruiser had to leave her patrol line to escort an untrustworthy neutral to a rendezvous point where an armed trawler could take over and see the ship into Kirkwall. This happened whenever the cruiser could not spare an armed guard or found boarding impossible.

Before the end of January the last of the D class cruisers left the Northern Patrol. The AMCs were now on their own, taking the full weight of the Patrol, and urgent modifications were in hand. *Chitral* and *Montclare* were fitted with Complete Equipment. *Worcestershire* and *Scotstoun* had gun defects corrected. Old gun mountings in some of these ships were modified by spring rollers and improved lubrication as temporary measures. *Chitral* had her

6-inch replaced by later models. *Laurentic* and *Montclare* were given the much newer 5.5-inch. In *Chitral* and *Montclare* the two 3-inch HA guns were replaced by three 4-inch, and better fire control gear was fitted.

All this work took time, and six AMCs were in dock for repairs. But new ships commissioned. The Anchor Line's *Cilicia* joined the Patrol on Boxing Day, 1939. HMS *Derbyshire*, another Bibby liner, commissioned at Christmas, left Portsmouth for Greenock, and was soon patrolling the Denmark Strait.

The ex-Donaldson Atlantic Line's 13,475-ton *Letitia* joined the Patrol on the 29th. HMS *Carinthia*, 20,277 tons, late of Cunard, joined on the 18th and left the Clyde for her maiden patrol on the 21st. The China Mutual Steamship Company's coal-burner *Patroclus* joined on the 22nd and, after being delayed in the Clyde by fog, sailed for patrol on the 24th.

In spite of these additions, there was a drop in the number of ships on patrol. Armed trawlers replaced C and D cruisers on four patrol lines and were badly missed further south. Two AMCs patrolled the Denmark Strait, ten more south of Iceland, one south of the Faeroes.

There were signs of fresh enemy action. On 3 February German aircraft attacked anti-submarine trawlers in Shapinsay Sound, off the eastern entrance to Kirkwall, while there was a neutral freighter with an armed guard on board nearby.

U-boats featured in signals to and from the Northern Patrol. On 4 February the Admiralty warned Admiral Raikes that they expected U-boats to try to come to the assistance of German merchantmen trying to break home through the patrols. The ships *Arucas* and *Rostock* were thought to be on their way, escorted by U-boats. On 7 February a U-boat was sighted near Sule Skerry. The following day a Fleetwood trawler reported a U-boat escorting a large merchant ship on an easterly course. Cruisers were ordered to intercept, and destroyers to co-operate with them.

Circassia sighted a merchantman but there was no sign of a U-boat and the ship turned out to be the Norwegian *Solferino*.

U-boats were reported between Shetland and Bill Bailey's Bank, to the west. The trawler *Northern Isles* reported one on 10 February. On the 11th a motor ship was torpedoed sixty miles north-east of the Shetlands. Five new patrols were mounted, including one off the east coast of Iceland, one from Siglunes Light on the north coast of Iceland northward for a distance of sixty miles, to catch German merchantmen which might have passed through patrols NP41 and NP42 in the hours of darkness. On 13 February the Norwegian tanker *Albert L. Ellsworth* was torpedoed between Bill Bailey's Bank and the Faeroes. Her crew abandoned ship but returned on board later and found her navigable.

Nine destroyers and the 10th Anti-Submarine Striking Force now reinforced the Northern Patrol to carry out Operation WR, the interception of the homeward-bound German merchantmen.

Weather for the search was very bad, with freezing cold, easterly or north-westerly gales, and visibility down to less than half a cable in snow showers. Conditions in the Denmark Strait were even more severe. For over three days it blew a blizzard and a full north-easterly gale.

At 1.30 a.m. in the dark hours of the graveyard watch on 2 March about forty miles north-east of the Butt of Lewis a U-boat opened fire on the Norwegian motor vessel *Belpamela* of the Belships Company which was being brought to Kirkwall under an armed guard from the *Scotstoun*. *Belpamela*'s crew abandoned ship immediately. The boat in which the armed guard intended to get away was lowered prematurely and lost, but the *Scotstoun* men managed to launch a raft and get clear. Meanwhile the U-boat left the *Belpamela* and went off to stop the *Lagaholm* of the Svenska Amerika Mexiko Line. The latter's crew were given half an hour to abandon ship. The U-boat then fired about thirty-five rounds at the *Lagaholm* and left her burning. British aircraft sighted the *Lagaholm* and *Belpamela* at 10.30, and attacked a U-boat to the westward.

Lagaholm sank during the day. The U-boat did not return to the *Belpamela*, and when daylight came some of her crew went back aboard her. At 3.15 in the afternoon they sighted the British armed guard and rescued them from their raft. One boatload from *Lagaholm* was also picked up. The men in a second boat shouted that they preferred to sail to the Orkneys, about eighty miles away. They arrived at North Ronaldsay at 3 p.m. the following day. *Belpamela* made Kirkwall safely, but her armed guard were suffering from the effects of exposure on the raft.

At 10 a.m. on 13 March the big, 20,914-ton ex-P & O liner

Maloja, making her first patrol as an AMC on NP51, was sixty-five miles south-east of Seidisfjord on the east coast of Iceland, when she sighted a big ship coming out of the snowstorm.

"What ship?"

"*Taki Maru* of Kobe."

Maloja was suspicious, but the sea was too high for boarding and the merchantman was ordered to steer west for the Faeroes trawler rendezvous.

At 3.40 p.m. *Maloja* ordered; "Heave to. I will send a boat."

Almost immediately men were seen falling in abreast the lifeboats, and the ship began to transmit wireless signals. *Maloja* fired a shot across her bows, but her men continued to man and lower the lifeboats. Before these had touched the water, there were explosions at each of the four hatches, smoke poured from the ventilators, and the ship appeared to be settling. *Maloja*'s boarding party were on their way across but the ship's gunwhale was already under water by the time they drew close, and they did not attempt to come alongside. Eighteen officers and fifty men were taken on board *Maloja* from the boats, and the sinking ship was named as the German *La Coruna*.

The Northern Patrol continued its hard grind, with eighty percent of eastbound traffic being intercepted. After a long patrol, "the sight of Ailsa Craig was wonderful," wrote young Geoffrey Penny from *Asturias*, "and it was shortly after that point that we considered ourselves home safely and the engineers would fill the swimming pool with warm water." The main recreation was taking one of the ship's boats up the Gare Loch for a walk over the heather finishing up at the pub at Rosneath.

Then as spring came their load was lightened. Britain made trade agreements with Denmark, Norway and Sweden, by which the Scandinavian countries would no longer carry contraband.

The last of these had hardly been signed when, on 7 April, there came reports of the movements of German heavy warships in the North Sea. *Scharnhorst* and *Gneisenau* were out again. The spectre of *Rawalpindi* arose, and all AMCs on patrol were ordered to steer west or south-west at their best speed. The two which had left the Denmark Strait were sent back to patrol south-west of Iceland, the others were ordered to the Clyde.

At noon on 8 April the Polish submarine *Orzel* intercepted and sank the German SS *Rio de Janeiro* off Kristiansand on the Norwegian side of the Skagerrak. Among the men rescued from the ship were German soldiers. Reports of the incident went to Oslo and to the Admiralty in London, but neither recognized the significance of it, and it was not repeated to Admiral Forbes until late that night.

The Admiralty and C-in-C Home Fleet were fully occupied with what looked like a threatened breakout by the two battlecruisers, and their ships were concentrated to block the northern exits from the North Sea into the Atlantic.

At 3.37 a.m. on 9 April Admiral Whitworth was cruising with the battlecruiser *Renown* and nine destroyers off the Lofoten Islands, when he sighted *Scharnhorst* and *Gneisenau*. At 4.05 in heavy seas, with snow squalls, *Renown* opened fire. At 4.17 a hit from her put *Gneisenau*'s main armament control system out of action.

Further south at that moment the pocket battleship *Lutzow* (formerly *Deutschland*), the 8-inch cruiser *Blücher*, the light cruiser *Emden*, three torpedo boats and a swarm of smaller vessels were approaching the narrows of Oslofjord, with 2,000 troops for the occupation of the Norwegian capital. Similar invasion squadrons were approaching Trondheim, Bergen, Kristiansand, Arendal and Narvik. To the south the German Army was entering Denmark unopposed.

The two German battlecruisers managed to shake off *Renown*, although the older British ship worked up to twenty-nine knots in pursuit and inflicted heavy damage on *Gneisenau*. The German Navy put the invasion troops ashore in Norway without serious loss. The Allies moved quickly to send an army to oppose them.

12 "How long can you float?"

The sea off north-western Ireland was tranquil in the early afternoon of 6 June, 1940, the weather fair. Former Cunard White Star liner HMS *Carinthia* was on course homeward from Spanish waters.

The war was going badly for the Allies. The Germans had taken Denmark, Holland, Norway, Belgium and France. The British Army had been rescued from Dunkirk, minus its equipment and at the cost of heavy losses in destroyers.

With all the ships of the Home Fleet engaged off Norway or Dunkirk, the AMCs and armed trawlers of the Northern Patrol had had to cope alone with the job of stopping all incoming Danish and Norwegian ships from falling into German hands.

When it looked as if Mussolini would join the conquering Hitler, five of the hard-pressed AMCs were detached and sent south to intercept Italian ships entering the Mediterranean.

Carinthia had been on this duty. Mussolini had held back, the Italian Patrol had been cancelled, and she was on her way back to the Clyde.

Lieutenant-Commander Jim Blake RNR was on the bridge. U-boats, which had sunk eleven British auxiliary cruisers in World

War 1, had so far left the AMCs alone, though Dönitz's meagre twenty-one operational boats had sunk a million tons of Allied merchant shipping. They were a growing threat, and the unescorted 20,000-ton ex-liner, a big target, was zigzagging.

Blake had just ordered the helm put hard over to port to turn her on to the next zigzag when the whole ship suddenly jerked, shuddered, and gave a heave to starboard, and there was a tremendous explosion aft.

In the engine room the noise deafened Lieutenant Arthur Husband, who had his ear to the bridge voicepipe. Bits of metal flew through the air. Something hit his left temple, stunning him. The port engine stopped. The lights went out. He felt water swirl round his ankles, grabbed the handrail of the ladder above him and climbed.

On the bridge Jim Blake gaped at the column of black smoke and debris thrown up to port from the after engine room.

"Action stations!" He pressed the alarm buzzer.

The ship was listing to port and shearing away to starboard against the helm.

"Stop port engine!"

"Port telegraph to STOP" repeated the quartermaster. "No reply, sir. Helm jammed hard-a-port."

"Stop starboard engine!"

In three minutes engine room and after holds were flooded, stokehold, magazines, shell rooms and messdecks were filling. All power gone, the ship settled aft, listing to port.

Captain Barrett, still sick from bad gastro-enteritis, struggled to the bridge. On her emergency batteries *Carinthia* signalled:

"Torpedoed by submarine!"

Jim Blake rushed to his action station in control of the after guns. He had just got there when a rating shouted,

"Sub bearing Green 170 crossing starboard to port!"

Blake saw the periscope.

"Open fire!"

Two guns opened up. Four shells fell close round the periscope, which disappeared.

Minutes later it rose on the port quarter about two miles off. Blake's guns opened fire again, and the U-boat vanished.

Twenty minutes later a torpedo missed the bows by five yards. A periscope appeared near the port beam. *Carinthia* opened a heavy fire and drove the German down again.

The ship was still afloat three hours later when a Coastal Command aircraft appeared and flashed: "How long can you float?"

"We hope to be towed into harbour as we are not making any more water," Barrett replied cheerfully.

In the small hours next morning three destroyers came up with them, and HMS *Gleaner* took up the tow. The water began to gain again. Barrett transferred most of his crew, and the tug *Marauder* took over the pull. Fog came down. The water was creeping forward and upward, and at ten clock that night *Carinthia* was abandoned. An hour and a half later she broke up and sank, thirty-five miles off Bloody Foreland, taking the bodies of four men with her.

Scotstoun, once the Anchor Line's *Caledonia*, left the Clyde for patrol at noon on 12 June. At 4.17 p.m. she was zigzagging north of the Scottish coast at 15 knots when a torpedo hit her aft on the port side.

A hatch cover blew off, smoke and spray shot upwards. The port shaft stopped and the ship began to circle slowly under port wheel and starboard engine.

Four more torpedoes were fired at the ship. Two missed but the other two hit her aft on the starboard side, and *Scotstoun* settled quickly by the stern. Most of the ship's company took to the boats. Fifteen men remained at the guns, but the ship was going down fast. The sea washed the gunners overboard, and she sank just after 7 p.m. in a calm sea and a long swell. Just after noon the destroyer *Highlander* came up and rescued all but six of her men.

Three days later, 15 June, *Andania* was torpedoed and opened fire at her attacker, putting her off her aim so that three more torpedoes missed, and the ship's engineers fought through the darkness of the graveyard watch to keep her afloat, but she sank at dawn. On 17 June *Canton* was narrowly missed by a torpedo when returning to the Clyde from the Italian Patrol.

On 22 June France surrendered to Germany and Hitler gained control over the whole great arc of coastline from the northern tip of Norway to the Spanish border. With U-boat bases and Luftwaffe airfields on the Atlantic coast of France, the Allies could expect a great increase in enemy submarine and air attack, as a prelude to invasion of Britain.

It was decided to expand the Allied blockade to cover the Atlantic coasts of France, Spain, Portugal and French North Africa. The Northern Patrol was to set up a new branch for this purpose to be called the Western Patrol.

Six AMCs and four of the new Armed Boarding Vessels were initially allocated to the Western Patrol. The ABVs were small converted merchant ships armed with one or two 4-inch guns. Other, larger ships, intermediate between ABVs and AMCs, called Ocean Boarding Vessels, were to be added when ready. These would be fast ships equipped with two 6-inch and lighter anti-aircraft guns.

The CO of the Northern Patrol, Vice-Admiral Raikes, transferred his headquarters from Kirkwall to the Clyde. All ships sent in by the Western Patrol were to be routed there, via the North Channel, or to Gibraltar.

On 7 July Fritz Lemp, who had sunk the liner *Athenia* on the first day of war, became the first U-boat commander to use the newly captured French Biscay port of Lorient when he brought his *U30* in off patrol. It was a welcome change to steer south, past Ushant, then east and up the winding Scorff Estuary, instead of the long haul up round the Irish coast and through the British patrols between the Scottish islands back to Wilhelmshaven. With the new berth so much nearer the happy hunting grounds of the Western Approaches to the British Isles it would mean much less time on passage, far longer on patrol. When *U30* berthed, U-boat Headquarters had already been set up in the former Préfecture, and the Hotel Beau Séjour taken over for officers' quarters. In the cellars were 100,000 bottles of good vintage champagne.

Already established at Mérignac airfield near Bordeaux was the Luftwaffe's Kampfgeschwader 40, with a Staffel of four-engined Focke-Wulf Fw 200 Condor long-range maritime aircraft. Developed from a commercial airliner, they could operate beyond the Azores to the meridian of 20° West and reach the coast of Iceland to assist the U-boats on patrol by reporting Allied ships, as well as using their own 250kg (551 lb) bombs on them.

Other salt-rimed U-boats began to come into the Breton ports, some of the few which had sunk more than a hundred Allied ships, over 500,000 tons' worth, that winter, commanded by young veterans like Otto Schuhart, who had sunk the aircraft carrier *Courageous* in the second week of the war, Gunther Prien, whose *U47* had got into Scapa Flow and sunk the *Royal Oak*, Vaddi Schultz, Knight's Cross, first man to sink 100,000 tons, handsome, swashbuckling Joachim Schepke in *U100*, with over 20,000 tons to his credit, and Otto Kretschmer, nicknamed "Otto the Silent", in his *U99*.

From Brittany these aces were back in action much sooner than they would have been from the Wilhelmshaven base, and fourteen U-boats were reported in the Western Approaches, others as far north as 35° north of the Shetlands and as far south as the Azores. The quiet, undemonstrative Kretschmer in *U99*, the boat with the two inverted golden horseshoes painted on the conning tower, returned with seven victory pennants flying from his periscope standard and a record total of 65,137 tons sunk in one patrol, to receive the Knight's Cross from Grossadmiral Raeder himself.

The ex-Anchor line *Transylvania* sailed from the Clyde for patrol at 12.30 p.m. on Friday, 9 August. Once clear of the mine-field, south-west of Ailsa Craig, she went to her full speed of 16½ knots and began to zigzag. She was still criss-crossing through the darkness at midnight and was expecting to meet AMCs *Circassia* and *Wolfe* in the middle watch. She altered course and a minute later was still swinging under starboard wheel, almost on the new leg. The port lookout was staring aft at that moment and saw a flash and a column of black smoke near P4 gun, which was followed by a reverberating double explosion.

The engines stopped. All the lights went out. After about five minutes reports came in that the engine room and the after end of the ship were flooded. C Deck was awash, the depth-charges and P4 gun, which was canted outboard as a result of the explosion, were under water. The ship had taken a list to port and was well down by the stern and lying broadside-on to the freshening westerly wind.

At 2 a.m. a distress signal was sent out. In another half-hour the water had reached B Deck, the list had increased, and the ship was slowly sinking. Captain Miles ordered the boats away. Six men were lost in a lowering accident and two overcrowded lifeboats capsized, trying to get alongside the rescue destroyer HMS *Achates*. *Transylvania* sank at 4.25 a.m.

The Royal Navy's Western Patrol of AMCs and Armed Boarding Vessels had been established at the expense of its parent Northern Patrol. Rear-Admiral Spooner, who had replaced Vice-Admiral Raikes, asked the Admiralty for a minimum of ten trawlers or corvettes to tide him over in the north, but was told there was none available. He asked Flag Officer-in-Charge, Iceland, if *he* had any trawlers to spare to patrol inshore waters, but got the same answer.

On 11 and 12 August, when the Battle of Britain was raging over the south of England, with the Luftwaffe trying to destroy the Royal Air Force and invasion barges massing in the German-occupied Channel ports, German aircraft made long-distance reconnaissance flights over Northern Patrol's area from the Faeroes to 16° West and to the southward – a possible prelude to a breakout through the weakened British patrols by surface ships. The heavy cruisers HMS *Norfolk* and HMAS *Australia* were sent to patrol north of the Faeroes. On the 13th there were reports that German troops were embarking in ships and fishing boats in Norwegian waters. Refits and boiler cleaning were suspended, and the battlecruiser *Renown*, on passage to Gibraltar, was diverted to patrol Icelandic waters for two days.

At 12.30 p.m. on 16 August ex-Bibby liner HMS *Cheshire* was 150 miles west of the Hebrides returning from patrol when she sighted a periscope bearing Red 45°, two hundred yards away. She altered course, increased to full speed, and steered an S along the estimated track of the U-boat, dropping two depth-charges each time she crossed it. After the explosion of the second charge the rangetaker sighted a periscope at five hundred yards, which then disappeared. The destroyers *Arrow* and *Achates* quickly arrived to hunt the submarine.

At 7.15 p.m., about 450 miles west of Finisterre, on the night of 18/19 August, *Circassia* tried unsuccessfully to ram a U-boat which surfaced so close to the ship that her guns would not bear. Three depth-charges were then dropped at fifty-yard intervals. Later a U-boat broke the surface, then disappeared stern-first. At 1.45 in the middle watch *Circassia* sighted a darkened ship. There was no response to her signals, and she fired a warning shot. This was also disregarded, and the suspicious vessel made a large alteration of course. *Circassia* opened fire and had delivered several broadsides before the stranger identified herself as the British *Rowallan Castle*.

On the night of 28 August HMS *Dunvegan Castle* was steaming west of the Irish coast. At ten minutes to eleven the Captain was in the charthouse discussing with the Navigator the course to steer after the ship had stopped zigzagging, when the ship shook to an explosion on the starboard side where a torpedo struck her just abreast the refrigerator and generating rooms, stopping the engines and dousing all lights. The emergency generator cut in with power for lights, steering and pumping the bilges, but the ship listed to starboard. A distress signal was sent and the crew went to action stations. A submarine was sighted on the port bow, but there was not enough power for the electrical gun circuits, and the gunlayers could not see the target through the telescopes. Two more torpedoes hit the AMC and she sank with the loss of thirty men.

Auxiliary cruisers were losing the battle against submarines. Did the uneasy ghost of Mr Barnaby murmur that he was "afraid it would not be wise to employ such ships as men of war" ...?

He would have been even more emphatic had he been able to foresee the maritime bomber. HMS *Cilicia* and HMS *Wolfe* left the Clyde on 10 September for the Western Patrol, but at 8.45 p.m. on the 11th an Admiralty signal ordered them to take over Ocean Escort for Convoy AP3, bound for Freetown, West Africa, from the regular cruiser *Sheffield*. At Freetown they were to top up with fuel and water and return to their patrol areas.

Wolfe, formerly the Canadian Pacific's *Montcalm*, was 250 miles west of the Donegal coast, western Ireland, at 2.20 p.m. on 12 September on passage to the rendezvous with the convoy when she was attacked by a KG40 Condor from Bordeaux-Mérignac.

The big four-motor bomber roared in from astern not much above masthead height and flew along the centre line of the ship. The first 500-pounder fell short and exploded in the ship's wake. The second hit the Boat Deck but failed to explode and bounced overboard. The third smashed through the fiddley casing, bounced back on to the Boat Deck and lay there, unexploded and lethal. The fourth bomb hit the sea ahead of the bows and went off with a geyser of foam.

Lieutenant Sydney Gorrell RNR was Fire and Repair Officer, Upper Deck. Checking along the decks for damage he found the big third bomb lying with quiet menace on the deck. He "legged it round the other side of the fiddley casing in case it went up," and looked round for help. The Navigator, Lieutenant Eric Rhead, joined him, looked at the bomb and said, "Why don't we roll the thing over the side?"

The *Wolfe* had bulwarks round the Boat Deck with doors which led to the lifeboats. Gorrell opened the door nearest to them; they got hold of a plank and pushed the bomb towards the scuppers, assisted now by the ship's young bugler, whose bugle still hung round his neck and got in their way. The bomb reached the edge of the deck at the open door, they gave a last heave and "took off for the scuppers on the other side of the deck in case hitting the water from fifty feet up set the thing off." But the bomb sank without exploding. At 10 a.m. on 13 September the two AMCs took over their escort duties. *Wolfe* reached Freetown on the 23rd, while *Cilicia* was off looking for stragglers and came in next day.

Both ships left again on the 26th, *Wolfe* to the Western Patrol, *Cilicia* to escort the old aircraft carrier *Argus* homewards as far as 50° North, thence to the Western Patrol. *Cilicia* was with *Argus* shortly after 4 p.m. on 2 October in the North-Western Approaches, when a torpedo track passed about fifty yards from her stern. She sighted a periscope and altered course to bring her port guns to bear, opening fire at a range of about 2,000 yards. The submarine, which looked like an Italian of the *Argonauta* class, one of those which had been sent to join the German flotilla at Lorient early in August, surfaced, then dived hurriedly. *Cilicia* fired thirteen rounds of 6-inch and straddled the target but observed no hits.

Enemy aircraft bombed Convoy WS3 on 8 October west of Ireland and disabled the transport *Oronsay*. *Salopian*, on passage to the Western Patrol, picked up her distress signals and altered course to close her. *Cheshire*, heading for the Clyde, was much nearer *Oronsay* and went to give assistance. *Oronsay* reached the Clyde safely on 9 October escorted by *Cheshire* and the cruiser *Cairo*.

Cheshire was on passage back to the Western Patrol at 7.30 p.m. on 14 October when a torpedo struck her on the starboard side abreast the centre of Number 2 Hold, tearing a rectangular hole thirty-six feet long and twenty feet wide. The destroyer *Skeena* and the corvette *Gladiolus* were sent to assist, and tugs ordered out from the Clyde. *Cheshire* crawled along at four or five knots until 7 a.m. on the 15th when she reported that she was stopped, with Numbers 1, 2 and 3 Holds full of water and her fore deck awash. *Skeena* took off all but a steaming party, and *Cheshire* was taken in tow by the tugs *Superman* and *Seaman*. By the early forenoon of the 16th *Cheshire*'s Boat Deck was almost awash. At 12.30 a.m. on the 17th she was beached five cables from Kilroot Point, Belfast Lough.

There was still a great shortage of ships for convoy escort, and armed merchant cruisers were increasingly used for this job, as in the First World War. *Letitia* provided Ocean Escort for two troop transports from the Clyde to Reykjavik, and brought them in safely on 24 October. On 1 November *Salopian* was on passage to Western Patrol when she was diverted to act as Ocean Escort to Convoy OG45.

The auxiliary cruisers were being hit hard by the determined U-boat campaign. Used like warships, they were suffering like merchantmen. Like so many of the latter, with their small, single guns, the AMCs fought back whenever they could.

On 3 November HMS *Laurentic* and *Patroclus* were returning home in company after Western Patrol duty. Captain Vivian was in *Laurentic*'s chartroom at 9.45 p.m. when she received a distress signal from the SS *Casanare*, which had been torpedoed about thirty miles away. Vivian remarked to Commander Richard Daintree that it would mean a big alteration to starboard. The gyro compass had been giving trouble, and the Navigating Officer, Lieutenant-Commander John Jones RNR, was sent for to check the ship's position.

Laurentic was a big ship, with a high hull and very tall funnels, and on a clear, dark night such as this was visible at a distance of up to eight miles. She was also a coal-burner, and it had never been possible to keep her smoke down to really safe proportions.

The ship was zigzagging at 15 knots, and the Navigator had just shown Captain Vivian their position on the chart when they were hit by a torpedo on the starboard side.

The tinfish had come from Kretschmer's *U99*, the sub with the golden horseshoes. Otto the Silent was now the top-scoring U-boat ace. Towards the end of September he, in company with Prien in *U47*, Heinrich Bleichrodt in *U48* and Joachim Schepke's *U100*, had used Kommodore Dönitz's new Pack Attack on poorly escorted Convoy HX72 and sunk eleven ships with 100,000 tons of supplies from the USA. In a pack attack in mid-October on the thirty-four ships of SC7, Kretschmer, whose motto was "One ship, one torpedo", sank seven of the twenty ships destroyed in a bloody action which became known as "The Night of the Long Knives".

On the bridge of *Laurentic* Captain Vivian pressed the buttons of the alarm gongs, sending the ship to action stations and the two guns' crews who were on watch to man one forward 5.5-inch gun and one 4-inch to fire starshell.

He went out on to the bridge from the chartroom. The Engineer Commander reported that the ship had been hit in the engine room, and Vivian sent the Chief Yeoman of Signals to the wireless room to get a signal off to the Admiralty. The Chief returned on the double and reported that there was no power. Vivian told the engine room to start the emergency dynamo. The ship was listing to starboard and pumping was impossible, though the sea was calm, with a moderate swell.

The Captain gave the order to turn out all boats, and for everyone except the two guns' crews already closed up to go to their Abandon Ship stations. He told the Commander that the boats should keep together in the water and steer to the east. Then he went to the Boat Deck and repeated his instructions. He returned to the bridge, saw the *Patroclus* coming up on the port quarter, and fired a series of red Verey lights, the signal for a ship torpedoed, to warn her of the presence of a U-boat.

Lieutenant Jones, Midshipman Nicholson, the Chief Yeoman and Leading Seaman Roberts were also on the bridge, and as the scarlet fireworks blossomed in the night sky they sighted a submarine on the starboard bow. The Captain shouted from the bridge to the forward guns to open fire, but someone had apparently given the order for the men there to fall out. He sent young Nicholson to get the 4-inch into action, and he and Roberts went aft. Nicholson got the 4-inch crews together, and Roberts took over as gunlayer on the starboard gun. They fired one round, and

Nicholson shouted to the after 4-inch to open fire but its training had jammed. Nicholson shouted to the starboard gun's crew, "Take over firing starshell!" just as the second torpedo struck.

Captain Vivian ran to the wireless office, made sure that the Confidential Books were in the safes and certain to sink, then rushed down to the starboard forward gun, but there was no one with him.

Roberts' starboard 4-inch was now firing starshell to illuminate the U-boat. On the after 4-inch the shock of the second explosion had freed the jammed training, and they also began firing starshell. Nicholson switched the starboard 4-inch back to firing high explosive at the conning tower of the U-boat. It was enough for Otto the Silent, who took *U99* down out of harm's way.

Captain Vivian went to the Boat Deck. Number 7 boat had not yet got clear, Number 3 was leaking, and Number 1 cutter, the boat for the bridge party and guns' crews, had been smashed by the second explosion, but Jim Wilford, the Damage Control Officer, was releasing rafts. Vivian went back to the bridge, ordered the Chief Yeoman to jettison the signal books, and helped Engineer Donaldson and two seamen to release the Carley float under the bridge. Then he, Donaldson and John Jones went below to make one last check on the state of the ship. The engine room was flooded and the ship was obviously sinking.

On A Deck Vivian found some men and ordered them up into Number 3 boat. They held back when they saw that the boat was leaking, but Wilford got some buckets and oars into it and Vivian ordered them to get in, with Wilford in command. Vivian and Jones went round making sure everyone had got away, collected a few more stragglers, then climbed down into the Carley which Nicholson was holding ready. They paddled off round the bows behind Number 3 boat.

When they got round to the port side they saw a light on board. They closed, and Vivian shouted,

"How many men are there?"

"Three."

"There's a raft secured near the after funnel on the port side. Go and get into it."

"We know about the raft, sir, but we'd rather stay with the ship."

"Get into the raft! That's an order."

Jones was just repeating the order when there was a third explosion. The ship sank quickly by the stern, to join her namesake in World War 1, and these men were lost.

Patroclus had come up with the stricken *Laurentic*. She circled the position for some time until Captain Wynter judged it dark enough for them to close safely, and pick up survivors. As she came up, *Patroclus* dropped two depth-charges to scare away any U-boat nearby.

At periscope depth *U99* shuddered as the shock wave bounced off her outer hull, but Kretschmer and his hard-case crew were not to be put off by a couple of ash cans. Otto the Silent had watched the second big auxiliary cruiser approach and had waited patiently, reading her captain's mind, for her to give him the best shot from the best angle.

The *Patroclus* men saw the boats in the water and hailed the nearest one, *Laurentic*'s Number 6. This boat was just coming alongside the ship at her for'ard well deck when a torpedo struck the *Patroclus* right underneath the boat, blowing the latter to pieces. Few men were saved from the boat, and some *Patroclus* men were killed instantaneously by the explosion. Some were blown overboard, and the well deck turned into a shambles. Lieutenant Piddock had both legs broken. Lieutenant Atkinson dived overboard to rescue some of the men swimming about, before climbing on board one of the ship's cutters which had been lowered, to take charge of it.

Patroclus' ship's company went to their Mine and Torpedo stations, falling in abreast of their respective boats with lifebelts and warm clothing on.

Every patrol Commander Ralph Martin had given them lectures on the course of the war, and he had always got an ovation at the end. Now he picked up a megaphone.

"All right. Now, there's no need to abandon ship yet, but I want you to stay where you are by your boats until further orders."

There were loud cheers and handclaps and someone shouted,

"That's right, you tell us, sir!"

They were still applauding when another torpedo hit *Patroclus* in Number 4 Hold.

The Captain said, "Abandon ship. Flood the magazines."

Martin said to Lieutenant-Commander Hoggan, "Get the boats away."

He turned to Vivian. "Well, goodbye for now, sir." Martin never saw him again.

Then he went down to the Boat Deck. He saw Sub-Lieutenant Howarth, the Signals Officer. "CBs all ditched?"

Howarth was busy lowering the starboard cutter. "Yes, sir." Martin went to the wireless room and stuck his head round the door. "Make a signal to C-in-C Western Approaches, 'Hit by second torpedo.'"

"Been done, sir."

The ship had a big list on her, and launching boats in the dark was tricky. But they went down smoothly, all but Numbers 1 and 5 lifeboats, which had been damaged by the second explosion and some of the men in them killed. Martin grabbed his megaphone. "Lie off to port and keep well clear. And wait for orders!" There was a faint cheer. "You tell us, sir!" He noticed men already swimming about.

On the bridge Vivian saw that the boats and rafts were clear. "Both engines slow ahead."

The telegraph had barely clanged when the ship was hit by two more torpedoes simultaneously, one in the cross bunker and one in Number 6 Hold, the latter blowing Number S3 gun overboard.

"Stop engines! Finish with engines. All hands into the water."

Martin was on the Boat Deck with Hoggan, Lieutenant Murchie, Lieutenant Kirkpatrick, Sub-Lieutenant Davie, Senior Wireless Op Johnson, Chief PO Creasey, PO Kemp, PO Naylor and two or three ratings.

"How long do you reckon she'll last?" Hoggan asked.

"Better ask him," Martin said, and pointed out over the water.

Out of the sea rose the conning tower of a U-boat, white water running out of her scuppers and off her forward casing as she surfaced. Men tumbled up out of her hatches and manned her gun, which swung round on them. There was a bright flash, a muffled bang, and a shell whistled over them.

There was a rush to the nearest gun, the starboard 3-inch AA. Creasey, a Whale Island man, naturally took over gunlayer, AB Ellis trainer, Martin made himself loader, Hoggan ammunition supply.

They fired four rounds at the U-boat, which hit the sitting duck

Patroclus twice, starting a small fire in the after well deck over the magazine, before diving again.

"I reckon we hit him with the fourth round," Creasey said.

"Yeah, dead on target," said Ellis. "He didn't like it."

Then they waited on events. "Well, she's taking her time to go," Martin said, "Yeah," Ellis said, "she's a stubborn old cow, sir."

Kretschmer thought so too, and about 4 a.m. the helpless ship shook to the impact of a sixth torpedo, underneath the bridge. The whole bridge collapsed.

"The silly bugger has put four tinfish in the same place," said Martin, and they all laughed.

This hit broke the back of the ship forward of the bridge, but five minutes later came another hit amidships in the engine room. So much for "One ship, one torpedo".

The ship began to list steeply, and they realized the end had come at last.

"Come on," said Martin, "over the side." They had already swung in lifelines and made them fast. Now they unlashed them and slid down them into the water. Martin shouted "Push away from the ship!" Don't get caught by the suction!"

"We swam away," he reported later "and when we were about twenty yards off we could feel all kinds of disturbance going on in our rear, and could feel the suction and the ripples of the ship going down and a terrific noise as all the girders twisted and bent, and the drums rolled about and crunched together. I turned and looked over my shoulder. She was halfway down. She rolled over on her starboard side and slid into the water, and when I looked at her practically only the bows were sticking up.

"I swam away and when about 150 yards off I got everybody I could round me in a cluster. We supported ourselves on the wreckage and held on to each other as far as we could. The ship's bows were still in sight and they did not seem to go down for a long time. I don't think they disappeared for two hours. We did not try and swim much as there was no point in it, we just stayed together, moving our legs up and down, and paddled. At one moment we started a song, but came to the conclusion that we'd better preserve our energy, but we wisecracked the whole time and joked each other and jollied about." In his party were Murchie, Kirkpatrick, Davie, Creasey, Kemp, Ellis and AB Rondean.

The AMC HMS *Asturias* intercepts a neutral coaster on Northern Patrol during the Second World War.

nterception. A boat crew from HMS *Asturias* pulls alongside the Vichy-French vessel *Mendoza* in Northern waters.

A gun crew closes up aboard HMS *Asturias*. Note that the old gun has no protective shield.

MV *Shropshire* before the Second World War. She was quickly converted into the AMC HM *Salopian*.

After conversion. The AMC HMS *Salopian*.

Iced up. HMS *Salopian's* bridge in the Denmark Straits.

The view from the bridge. HMS *Salopian* in Northern waters.

Torpedoed. Men from HMS *Salopian* abandon ship in an orderly manner.

Two life boats pull away from the sinking *Salopian*.

The remains of *Salopian's* starboard seaboat hang from davits after it has been smashed by a column of water thrown up by the first explosion. The Captain and Commander can be seen leaning over the rails before entering the boat secured alongside.

The end of HMS *Salopian*.

The author's father, Sub-Lieutenant (E) B. Poolman, RNR, who served aboard HMS *Salopian*.

Friedrickshaven FF33-J No. 841 Seaplane, with crew, aboard raider *Wolf*, 1916.

The German raider *Atlantis* in one of her disguises.

The eyes of the German submarine fleet, the Focke Wulf Condor 200C-I

The AMC HMS *Queen of Bermuda*, veteran of the Second World War. Note the Seafox
aircraft aft.

HMS *Pretoria Castle* after conversion from AMC to aircraft carrier.

The best-equipped AMC of the war, HMS *Corfu*. This picture was taken after her last refit. A Kingfisher aircraft sits on her catapult.

"The time we got into the water was about 4.30, and I estimate we had to wait until 8.30 for daylight, with no chance of being picked up in the dark.

"From time to time I could hear Hoggan's voice in the darkness, yelling out, 'Boat ahoy' and we kept yelling 'Boat ahoy' back."

"After we had been in the water an hour and a half I produced my brandy flask out of my Gieves waistcoat, and we all had a tot. That revived us a lot.

"About seven o'clock we each had some whisky from a bottle which Murchie had brought. About 7.30 Murchie died, quite peacably. There wasn't anything I could do. His voice had been getting weaker and weaker, and I realized he was dying from exposure, but he went out quite peacably.

"PO Kemp was also getting very weak at this time. It was a pity because starshells were being fired all round us, and we knew destroyers were on the scene looking for us and would find us as soon as daylight came.

"Daylight started to break about 8 o'clock. At 8.30 HMS *Achates* stopped close to us and we made our way alongside. They got them all on board with the exception of PO Kemp who had, I think, by this time gone, and myself. I unfortunately was the last man to come up out of the water. The Sub-Lieutenant of the *Achates* had come down to give me a hand, and I was about halfway up the side when I think HMS *Achates* got a 'ping' and went ahead with both engines, I think she went full ahead because I dropped back into the water, and I remember being hit on the head by what seemed to me to be every bit of wreckage in the sea. I bobbed up astern and remember somebody firing a depth-charge.

"After what seemed half an hour afterwards, another destroyer came alongside and I yelled to them and they saw me. They lowered a whaler and hauled me into it. I told them there was another officer further on and we picked up Lieutenant-Commander Hoggan."

13 "QQQQ!"

While the AMCs of the Northern and Western Patrols were supporting the blockade, others were logging plenty of seatime and taking similar risks as substitutes for regular warships on convoy escort or patrol in other theatres of war.

Ascania, Alaunia, Ausonia and *Laconia,* all Cunarders, joined the Halifax, Nova Scotia, Escort Force for duty in the North Atlantic.

Antenor and *Voltaire* went to the Mediterranean, *Carthage, Cathay* and *Ranchi* to the East Indies, *Arawa, Kanimbla* and *Moreton Bay* to the China Station. The Royal Australian Navy's *Manoora* and *Westralia,* and the New Zealand Division's *Hector* worked in the Pacific. Another New Zealand ship, the *Monowai,* and three Royal Canadian Navy AMCs, *Prince David, Prince Henry* and *Prince Robert,* were late conversions and went into service in the spring of 1940.

It was intended to base a number of AMCs on Freetown, Sierra Leone, West Africa, for patrol work and the escorting of convoys to and from the United Kingdom, to augment C-in-C, South Atlantic's meagre force of regular warships. In the beginning he had only the modern 6-inch light cruiser *Neptune* based at

Freetown, two old D class cruisers, the 4th Destroyer Division (four, later seven, H class ships), the two sloops *Milford* and *Bridgewater*, the two big Fleet submarines *Severn* and *Clyde*, and a few armed trawlers. One cruiser was based at Montevideo as the flagship of the South American Division of his Command.

The first Freetown – UK convoy, SL1, sailed at 4 p.m. on 14 September, 1939. Its eight ships, crawling along at 8 knots, were escorted by the cruiser *Dauntless* as far as a rendezvous 150 miles south-west of the Canary Islands, where the cruiser *Capetown* took over as Ocean Escort to the north of Madeira, enabling *Dauntless* to return to Freetown, refuel, and escort SL3.

It was thought that the AMCs, with their high endurance, would be able to take one convoy to the UK and bring another one out without topping up, but when the first AMC, HMS *Montclare*, came out on 30 October, 1939, it was found that she could not carry enough fresh water to last a round trip, so after she had taken SL7 home she was sent back to the North Atlantic.

On 4 November, 1939, HMS *Cilicia* arrived at Freetown and four days later sailed as the sole Ocean Escort for the twenty-eight ships of SL8. There was a great shortage of fresh water at Freetown, and it was arranged that AMC escorts should call at Dakar on the outward trip to top up there.

HMS *Salopian* joined the Freetown Escort Force on 13 November from the Northern Patrol. When she arrived at Plymouth to fuel and store for West Africa there were no white tropical uniforms to be had, but bolts of white duck material and sewing machines were available, and some of the RN pensioners in the ship who had been lower deck tailors in their active service days volunteered to make the uniforms provided they were excused all other duties. They worked night and day, and by the time the ship reached Freetown had managed to make a suit of tropical rig for every man, though most people had to sew on their own buttons.

Most of the middle-aged and elderly pensioners and Reserve men in the ship had been pleased to discover that they could cope with their duties as well as the better practised younger men. Engineer Sub-Lieutenant Bert Poolman found at the age of fifty that, like Captain Kennedy of the *Rawalpindi*, it had "all come back", and keeping a watch again down among the pounding engines now seemed normal. He had been a Territorial Army gunner in France in the First World War, then had been one of those with civilian engineering experience detached to work on new submarine trials back in Blighty. That should have been a rest cure after France, but in reality he found it more dangerous and nerve-racking when the new boat was reluctant to surface or her diving planes stuck. After the war he had joined the Merchant Navy. He was one of those beached by the Depression, spent two years on the dole, endured the humiliation of the Means Test, then got a job as Chief Engineer with a firm of pork butchers and pie makers in Bath, his home town. He would have spent his second World War there, but volunteered for service on the first day of hostilities. He preferred the tropics to the Denmark Strait, where *Salopian*, covered in frozen snow and spray, had resembled an ornate iceberg or a sailor's wedding cake. His blood was still warm from the trips he had made to Ceylon for tea or Rangoon for rice with the pre-war Bibby Line. He struck up a friendship with *Salopian*'s Captain, Sir John Alleyne, Bart, himself a volunteer from retirement.

On 16 November *Salopian* took over the eleven ships of SL9. The destroyer *Havoc* sailed in company as far as the latitude of the Canaries, then left to go to Gibraltar for repairs. *Carnarvon Castle* arrived on 17 November and joined Convoy SLF10 on the 25th, HMS *Dunnottar Castle* steamed in on the 29th and took out the nine ships of SLF11 on 3 December, and six more AMCs followed at frequent intervals, *Pretoria Castle* on 29 December, *Esperance Bay* on 1 January, 1940, *Cheshire* on 3 January, *Jervis Bay* on the 16th, *Bulolo* two days later, and *Dunvegan Castle* on 19th January.

On 14 January, the day after she had arrived at Freetown, HMS *Alcantara* was sent out again for urgent patrol off the South American coast. She was routed across to a position off the Brazilian coast north of Pernambuco, then down the coast to rendezvous with the Rear-Admiral, South American Division, Sir Henry Harwood, whose three cruisers had fought the raider *Graf Spee* on 13 December and forced her to scuttle herself in the River Plate.

The regular convoys continued, usually with an AMC as sole escort, with one or two destroyers sailing in company, when available, as far as the Canaries, then breaking off for Gibraltar to refuel. Occasionally there would be a submarine as well.

On 4 February the AMC *Comorin* intercepted the Portuguese merchantmen *Nyasa* and removed ten Germans, including two women. On the 5th the five ships of SLF19 sailed, with the AMC *Mooltan* as escort. On 11 February former Furness Withy HMS *Queen of Bermuda* arrived at Freetown after working up on completion of conversion. She sailed again next day, steaming out of harbour at 15 knots for a rendezvous with Harwood, now in the 8-inch cruiser *Hawkins* patrolling off the Brazilian coast in the Rio–Santos area. Harwood had to cover the Rio–River Plate stretch with his one regular cruiser plus *Alcantara* and *Queen of Bermuda*, the latter on her first war patrol, switching them about as one or the other went into Rio or Montevideo for fuel or provisions, where they were allowed twenty-four hours before another patrol of five or six weeks. *Dunnottar Castle* took over the Rio patrol from 8 to 15 March while *Alcantara* went for a boiler clean.

In mid-May the Admiralty had become suspicious that another German raider, perhaps more than one, was operating in the South Atlantic when mines were discovered off Cape Agulhas, the southernmost point of Africa.

In fact there were three raiders. With a numerically inferior force, and caught unprepared by the Allies' declaration of war, especially in the strength of the U-boat fleet, the German Navy had felt an even greater need than the Kaiserliche Marine of 1914 for a force of disguised armed merchant cruisers to prey on commerce and tie down already understrength Allied escorts and hunting groups. Though the Army and the Luftwaffe had priority in material for the conquest of Europe by Blitzkrieg, the Naval Operations Staff acted quickly, and on 5 September took over three merchantmen, the Hamburg–Amerika Line's *Neumark* and *Kurmark*, and the Hansa Line's *Goldenfels* for conversion into AMCs.

The decks were stiffened to carry the 5-ton weights of six 15cm (5.9-inch) guns, which were sited inside folding deckhouses or behind false bulwarks, as in the First World War, but mostly below the weather decks behind moveable panels. The old First World War type of hinged flap had been clumsy, far from weatherproof, and too easy for a keen eye to spot. This time a more sophisticated sort of flap was evolved, which was moved by the touch of a lever like an "up-and-over" garage door. From two to six 50cm (21-

inch) torpedo tubes were also fitted, and up to forty 20, 37, and 40-millimetre quick-firing cannon, as well as a load of mines. Hundreds of gallons of paint, and materials for false structures to alter their appearance were stowed away in their holds as well as dummy ventilators and king posts. Advising on the whole project was Karl Nerger, Captain of the famous raider *Wolf* in the First World War. His ship had been the first disguised raider to carry an aircraft, the little Friedrichshaven FF33J *Wolfchen*. The new raiders were to have one or two Heinkel or Arado seaplanes apiece.

The conversion work, on low priority, took time. Originally meant to be in action that winter, the first ships were not ready until March, 1940. Schiff 16, *Atlantis*, ex-*Goldenfels*, and Schiff 36, *Orion*, ex-*Kurmark*, sailed at the end of the month.

On 2 May the *Atlantis* passed the British liner *City of Exeter*, whose Captain reported something suspicious about the apparently Japanese *Kasii Maru*, even with Fregattenkapitän Bernhard Rogge's smallest, darkest and most inscrutable crewmen on deck and the pilot of his seaplane pushing a baby carriage along, accompanied by a young seaman disguised as his wife. Perhaps the upperworks looked too brilliantly white for a ship on the other side of the world from her home port. Anyway, there was something not quite right.

Rogge did not interfere with the big ship, as he did not have room for all those passengers and crew, but next day he surprised and sank the British SS *Scientist*, after a running fight in which the raider out-gunned the stubborn freighter, with her single gun, and a lucky 5.9 shell hit the latter's radio room just as she was starting to signal "QQQQ..", the signal for an attack by enemy merchant raider.

On the night of 10 May, a few hours after German troops had moved into Holland, Belgium and Luxembourg, the *Atlantis* laid her mines inside the 120-fathom line twenty-five miles off Cape Agulhas Light, then turned east into the Indian Ocean, where Rogge found that shipping had been alerted to his presence in the southern hemisphere. By that time Korvettenkapitän Kurt Weyher's *Orion* was approaching Cape Horn, after a secretive passage down the Atlantic, on her way into the Pacific to lay mines off New Zealand ports, and a third raider, *Widder*, ex-*Neumark*, commanded by Korvettenkapitän Helmut von Ruckteschell, a ruthless First World War U-boat captain, was feeling her way into the North Atlantic past the ships of the Northern Patrol.

On 15 July Harwood's flagship *Hawkins* entered Montevideo for a twenty-four hour stay. Next day she sailed to patrol the Plate area.

There had been more indications of enemy raiders in the North Atlantic. Unidentified vessels had been reported off the coast of Ireland. The British tanker *British Petrol* and the Norwegian freighter *Krossfonn* had gone missing. On 17 July the Admiralty received a report that D/F bearings had placed a German ship to the westward of the Cape Verde Islands on the 15th. It looked as if a raider was moving south.

Back with the South American Division was Captain Jack Ingham's *Alcantara*, the 22,209-ton former Royal Mail luxury liner, at this time patrolling the Rio–Santos area. Admiral Harwood came up from the Plate with *Hawkins* to take over this patrol and sent *Alcantara* north to the Pernambuco watch. If they found nothing hostile, he intended to move both ships down to the Plate in the assumption that the raider was heading that way and that they had missed her.

On 18 July Harwood received a report, gleaned from survivors landed in the West Indies, that two British merchantmen had been sunk by a raider in that area, the 6,433-ton SS *Davisian* on 10 July 450 miles north-east of Barbados, and the MV *King John* of 5,228 tons on the 13th further to the westward.

This was the work of the *Widder*, slow and poorly engined, which had suffered the indignity of being chased three times by submarines (British) on her way out of the North Sea, but had reached the Trinidad–Azores sea lane thanks to two refuellings by supply ships in mid-Atlantic. Von Ruckteschell shelled the *British Petrol* into submission without warning, captured the *Krossfonn*, then used his rough tactics on the Charente Company's *Davisian* from Liverpool, which had showed some signs of resistance, and *King John*, which had ignored his command not to use her radio.

British Intelligence reported that the small German tanker *Rekum* had sailed from Tenerife on 17 July, almost certainly to meet and top up a raider. They presumed, rightly, that the raider was the one which had been doing all the recent damage. *Widder* was a very thirsty ship.

From the 19th to the 21st *Hawkins* patrolled off Rio. On the 22nd Harwood estimated that if his raider had come south from the position given by the D/F bearings on the 15th she would be south of the latitude of Pernambuco.

At 4.30 p.m. on the 22nd he signalled *Alcantara*, which had reached her Pernambuco patrol area on the 20th, ordering Ingham south to examine Trinidade Island, haven of raiders, where *Carmania* had found the *Cap Trafalgar* in 1914. If the anchorage was empty this time, *Alcantara* was to patrol an area south-west of the island, keeping a distance of 250 miles from the South American coast.

On 23 July the *Hawkins* received a report that a U-boat had sunk a Norwegian tanker near the Cape Verdes on the 18th. It seemed likely that this was the ship pinpointed to the west of the Islands by D/F bearings on the 15th. But reports from the West Indies, and the routes of three ships which had been reported overdue at Freetown indicated that there was a raider in West Indian waters, and another in the South Atlantic. *Hawkins* continued to watch the sea lanes between Rio and the Plate throughout the 26th and 27th.

Alcantara inspected Trinidade Island during the forenoon of the 26th in the welcome coolness of a fresh trade wind, found nothing hostile, and proceeded according to instructions on patrol K33 south-west of the Island across the likely track of any raider making by the shortest route for the Plate.

At noon on the 27th Ingham's lookouts had a clear view all round to the far horizon. The sea was calm, with only light breezes. *Alcantara* steered a south-westerly course during the night and reversed course at dawn.

At 10 a.m. she was cruising along at 11½ knots. The weather was still fine and clear. The crow's nest voicepipe whirred on the bridge.

"Two masts bearing due east, fine on the starboard bow!"

The hull was not visible, but the stranger was estimated to be steering about nor'-nor'-west, away from them. *Alcantara* at once altered course to intercept. Cruising station guns' crews were closed up.

Fregattenkapitän Otto Kahler had been watching the other ship from a discreet distance since nine o'clock, uncertain of her identity. Liner or auxiliary cruiser? One was fair game, the other was poison. In his secret operational orders was the warning "Engagements with enemy warships, even auxiliary cruisers, must be avoided."

His own ship looked, he hoped, like an innocent banana boat. She was in fact a fourth disguised raider, the fast 3,862-ton Schiff 10, the *Thor*, ex-fruit carrier *Santa Cruz* of the Oldenburg-Portugiesische Line, at this time masquerading as the *Vir* of Split, Yugoslavia. She had left Germany on 6 June, and prisoners from five ships, Lamport & Holt's *Delambre*, the Belgian *Bruges*, the *Gracefield* from Newcastle, the British *Wendover* and the freighter *Tela*, were locked below, and a prize, the Rotterdam-Lloyd freighter *Kertosono*, was on her way home to Germany. In the hold was the *Thor*'s rather unreliable Arado 196 seaplane, ready for action if needed.

Forty-six year old Kahler was the son of a Merchant Navy captain and had served in U-boats in the First World War. In peacetime he had commanded the sail training barque *Gorch Fock*, and was a fine seaman and navigator.

Stocky and square-faced, the inevitable cigar stuck between his teeth, he watched the big grey ship coming up. What was she? The single funnel baffled him.

About 1 p.m. *Thor*'s radioman intercepted a coded message coming from the other ship. She was reporting him, calling in help. *Thor* jammed the signal.

Just under an hour later Kahler saw that the liner was gaining on him. He increased speed.

Alcantara was making 15 knots. The range opened.

"Full speed!" ordered Ingham.

The range began to close. *Thor* went to her full 18 knots.

But *Alcantara* was touching 20 knots now, and still increasing.

Kahler knew he would have to make a fight of it. To regain the initiative, about 2 p.m., when the range was about 17,350 yards, *Thor* altered course to starboard. The flaps in her sides slid up and over to expose her 5.9s, and signalman Hans Baasch hoisted the battle ensign at the main.

Alcantara's signal lamp was blinking "What ship?" when *Thor* opened fire, first with two guns, one forward and one aft, then with the first four-gun salvo.

Before these shells reached *Alcantara* she fired two return salvoes at extreme range. The first fell short and to the right, the second could not be observed because of the murderous hail of metal splinters flying round *Alcantara*'s control position from the German shells.

Thor's guns had been obsolete in the First World War, but they outranged *Alcantara*'s, one of which dated back to the Boer War, by a good 2,000 yards. Both ships made up for the inaccuracy caused by wear and tear with rapid, sharp drill.

One shell fell about a hundred yards over *Alcantara* on her port quarter. A second burst over the quarter deck, killing the trainer of P4 6-inch gun, severing the range, deflection, fire gong and cease-fire gong leads at the gun, short-circuiting the entire system at all the guns, and bringing down the W/T aerials. *Alcantara* switched to auxiliary W/T, to keep in touch with Harwood. "Enemy approximately 8,000 tons," Ingham signalled. "Speed 19 knots. Armament four 5.9-inch guns." Another shell burst in the air just abaft what had been the Tennis Deck, damaging the deck, smashing the skylights, boat hoists, fans and ventilators and cutting the searchlight feeds.

Two shells from the German's third salvo hit *Alcantara*'s thin, unarmoured starboard side aft, tearing two holes nearly four feet square, gutting the stokers' messdeck, severing pipes, leads, fire control circuits, ventilators, starting fires. Another burst on the ship's side about four feet above the waterline and caused damage on the orlop deck.

Immediately after *Alcantara*'s second salvo her Transmitting Station reported that the range and deflection instruments were not working. Sight-setters then worked to orders from the control position on the bridge, passed through telepads over the ears, ignoring the now useless mechanical receivers.

The German's cordite smoke was now blowing directly down the range. This made *Alcantara*'s fall of shot more difficult for gunners to see, but *Thor* had a director high above the smoke, and Gunnery Officer Werner Koppen-Boehnke kept up a rapid and regular rate of fire, straddling the British AMC consistently.

Just after 2 p.m. a hit on *Alcantara*'s waterline abreast the fore end of the engine room on the starboard side tore a triangular-shaped hole two feet wide at the top and four feet deep, and the sea poured in at high pressure, short-circuiting three out of four condenser water extractor pumps and seriously reducing the speed of the engines.

Petty Officer Pollard, who was right aft disposing of the depth-charges, saw shells falling in *Alcantara*'s wake, rarely more than a hundred yards astern. Enemy near-misses falling short burst on impact with the sea, throwing up geysers of white water heavily speckled with black which drenched the guns' crews. Shrapnel and anti-personnel shells with time-and-percussion fuses were bursting in a continuous fusillade of sharp explosions overhead or on impact, sending jagged metal shards whistling through the air close to the unprotected heads of men on deck, including the men at the guns, which had no shields.

One shell hit the old Promenade Deck just to starboard of the funnel, damaging the deck, bulkheads and alleyways and the wardroom, slicing electrical leads and engine room voicepipes, starting a fire which was energetically doused by the Midship Fire Party. Its companion tore a four-foot hole in the funnel, inner funnel and the waste steam pipes inside. Seven boats and three life rafts were holed, the starboard cutter wrecked.

All the loud racket of the shell bursts, coupled with the ship's own guns firing, made it difficult for sight-setters to hear orders from the Transmitting Station over their headphones, and the fall of shot soon indicated that the sights at the different guns had got out of step with one another, preventing salvo firing. The order "Check" went round. Firing was stopped while range and corrected deflection were passed to the guns, then re-opened. This had to be done repeatedly.

In spite of these interruptions, *Alcantara* straddled the enemy with several salvoes, and at 2.13 p.m. a bright flash was seen, quite distinct from that of a gun firing, abreast the German's foremast. Her foremost starboard gun ceased firing, her salvoes became ragged, and her rate of fire decreased.

Two 6-inch shells had hit the *Thor*. The first had not exploded but had ripped away electrical cables, pipes and the forward ammunition hoist. The second smashed the starboard motor boat and its jagged splinters killed men at the torpedo tubes below.

By 2.20 *Alcantara*'s speed had dropped to 15 knots as a result of the hole in the engine room. At 2.30 the raider altered course away from the AMC and opened fire with two stern guns. *Alcantara* continued firing, but the range, which had closed to 9,800 yards, was opening again. Her reduction in speed caused the deflection at the guns to be thrown out, which was particularly noticeable when the German turned stern-on. Not all the sight-setters heard the spotting correction, and one gun continued to fire wide of the target.

At 2.35 *Alcantara* turned to starboard, opening fire with her port battery. Splashes were observed very close for line, and at least one hit was seen on the raider's stern, leaving black smoke pouring from her starboard quarter.

Thor replied with three of her port guns, and dropped three smoke floats which gave off dense white smoke. She continued to fire her stern guns until the smoke had almost completely hidden her.

One German shell, the last to hit the ship, blew away part of the starboard side of *Alcantara*'s bridge, seriously wounding the rate officer and the time-of-flight operator, and slightly wounding the control officer and the rangefinder trainer, all of whom were knocked down and dazed, the rangefinder being damaged. The order "Quarters firing!" was given. The Gunnery Officer was cut on the chin and the blood filled his telephone mouthpiece. The engine room voicepipe was destroyed.

By this time *Alcantara*'s speed had dropped to 10 knots, and the raider, steaming at something between 12 and 15 knots, drew swiftly away until only her topmasts were visible. *Alcantara* continued to fire a few rounds at extreme elevation, but the target soon became obscured. The Gunnery Officer tried to re-establish contact with the guns and take over control again, but some of the sight-setters had taken off their telepads to hear local spotting corrections.

Guns then asked Captain Ingham's permission to go forward and take control of the forward guns. By the time he reached the fo'c'sle firing had ceased, then he heard a shouted order from the bridge.

"Close up the port battery, she's coming out of the smoke-screen!"

Thor burst out of the smoke. *Alcantara*, slowing down all the time, fired several rounds at extreme elevation. The crow's nest lookout reported a hit on the raider's stern. The raider replied with three-gun salvoes, all rather ragged. Firing ceased as smoke obscured the range, then *Thor* fired a few rounds which fell short.

The *Alcantara* was now practically stopped. The raider turned as though to close her, then made a thirty-degree turn and steamed off at about 15 knots, with a distinct list to port. Kahler had been tempted to go in and try to finish off the badly hit enemy AMC, but there was still plenty of fight left in her. He dared not risk taking any more punishment himself, and there were probably more British cruisers just over the horizon. *Thor* fled south and east.

Alcantara was in no condition to give chase. As soon as it became clear that the enemy had no intention of re-opening the action, temporary repairs were begun. Wooden patches were fitted over the two holes aft abreast the stokers' messdeck and secured from outboard by bolts and strongbacks. Oil was transferred from starboard to port tanks to list the ship and reduce the part of the hole in her engine room which was below the waterline. Pieces of plate were slipped between frames, and bales of cotton waste wedged in. This helped, but water still poured in. The Repair Party then built a wooden caisson round the damaged area and filled the space with hammocks. A bottom line was passed from for'ard and a collision mat fixed over it. The Electrical Party patched up the fire control circuits and fixed temporary electric leads all over the ship. The engineers worked on the condenser pumps, three of which were working when the ship reached Rio de Janeiro on 1 August.

There she was allowed by international law to make only such repairs as were necessary to make her seaworthy again. Half-inch plate was welded over the holes in the hull, and a cement box fitted inside the bad gash in the engine room in lieu of permanent repairs. The British Red Cross were allowed on board with medical supplies and fruit.

Alcantara went to Freetown for further repairs to her electrical leads and fire control circuits, and had a boiler clean before returning to Britain for proper repairs and the fitting of better guns, with shields and a longer range. Her sister ship *Asturias* came out from Britain and took over the patrol of the Rio–Santos stretch. *Canton* and *Carnarvon Castle* patrolled between Freetown and The Cape, another AMC covered the Freetown–Pernambuco route.

These dispositions were the best that could be made in the circumstances, with a general shortage of ships of all categories. And there were other raiders out. Schiff 33, the *Pinguin*, ex-*Kandelfels*, sister ship of the *Atlantis*, had left Germany on 15 June and had begun what was to be a very successful rampage by sinking the Liverpool freighter *Domingo de Larrinaga* on the other side of the Atlantic from *Thor*'s battle. Schiff 45, the *Komet*, ex-*Ems*, was at that time at anchor off Novaya Zemlya in the Barents Sea, waiting for Russian permission to try the icy North-Eastern passage round the north coast of Russia into the Pacific, where she was to join the *Orion*.

In August five ships, including two precious tankers, were lost between Bermuda and the Canary Islands, victims of the impatient von Ruckteschell in the limping *Widder*.

On 28 September the Admiralty received evidence from enemy radio transmissions that the German heavy cruiser *Admiral Hipper* had put to sea. Admiral Forbes took heavy units of the Home Fleet out to look for her.

On 28 October Convoy HX84 left Halifax, Nova Scotia, for Britain. It comprised thirty-eight ships, carrying valuable cargoes of benzine, gasoline, kerosene, lubricating oil, fuel oil, crude oil, lumber, wool, steel, pitprops, scrap iron, maize, newsprint, and trucks, but the shortage of warships was so acute that only one Ocean Escort could be provided, the armed merchant cruiser HMS *Jervis Bay*.

The convoy was organized in nine columns, with the Commodore, Rear-Admiral H. B. Maltby RN, leading the fifth column in the *Cornish City*, and *Jervis Bay*, commanded by Captain Edward Fegen RN, in the centre between the fourth and fifth columns.

The *Jervis Bay* was a 14,164-ton cargo/passenger liner built in 1922 which had carried British engineering products to Australasia and brought wool and refrigerated meat and fruit back for the Aberdeen Commonwealth Line, controlled by the Shaw Savill & Albion Line. She had become temporarily newsworthy in 1928 for a "mutiny" by eight stowaways discovered trying to return free to England, who had started a fire on board. She was a good seaboat, trim and steady, handsome with her buff and black funnel, white upperworks and dark green hull.

Now she was a grey auxiliary. She had been for a time on the sweaty West African run but was now back in the Halifax Escort

Force. Her ship's company were the usual AMC mixture of RN regulars, Reservists recalled, Merchant Navy men on T124 articles or with temporary RNR commissions, and ex-civilian Hostilities Only ratings or RNVR officers. There was torpedoman PO Charles Castle, a Kentish man, who had last served in the gunboat *Moth* in the Canton River; the ship's former Chief Officer George Roe, now a lieutenant-commander RNR and Navigating Officer; thirty-year-old Chief Quartermaster Walter Wallis, peacetime RNR, a married man from Hull; the two radio officers, big Hugh Williamson, a Scot from Portsoy on the Banffshire coast, and his friend and former colleague in the *Mooltan*, Dick Shackleton; senior watchkeeping engineer John Robertson, twenty-seven, from Ilford, Essex, a former Shaw Savill man who had gone ashore after his marriage and returned to the line in 1939; Commander John Blackburn RN, back from retirement at the age of fifty, who had served in submarines in World War 1 and won a DSC for his part in the sinking of a U-boat.

Dominating them all was the tall, rugged, aloof figure of Captain Edward Fogarty Fegen RN. An Irishman, son of Vice-Admiral F. Fogarty Fegen of Ballinlonty, County Tipperary, he was a bachelor, and the complete professional naval officer, a born leader who had commanded training ships, strict but unpretentious, inspiring instant confidence. When he joined the *Jervis Bay* on 1 April, 1940, he said to the waiting Blackburn, whom he already knew, "I wonder whose April Fool's Day this is – yours or mine?" Blackburn was put on his mettle. "I sweated out my soul to turn her into an efficient fighting unit," he said later.

The convoy proceeded without incident for some days, and was steaming at 9 knots through a smooth sea in good visibility when *Jervis Bay* sighted a warship almost due north about fifteen miles away, steering towards them. The *Empire Penguin*, leading the fourth column, also called attention to the stranger.

Dennis Moore, Portsmouth pensioner, *Jervis Bay*'s Chief Yeoman of Signals, challenged her by Aldis lamp. Her only reply was to alter course to present her port side to the convoy.

PO Charles Castle was standing outside the Transmitting Station. He said to another PO standing next to him,

"She's one of ours. A battler. *Ramillies* class."

The other man had a look. "You're right. R class battlewagon."

165

The guns' crew ran to their action stations.

At S2 Gun, starboard on the well deck between foc'sle and bridge, AB Fred Billings said, "What's the panic, then?"

The PO Gunner's Mate said, "It's only the *Ramillies* over there. False alarm."

Fred felt slightly relieved. When he'd been fired on by the Turks in the Dardanelles in 1915 he had had the sturdy armour and the 12-inch guns of the old *Agamemnon* around him.

On the bridge Captain Fegen said, "Make the challenge again – on the 10-inch this time."

Moore worked the shutter of the bigger lamp. As he was passing the signal he said, "She looks like one of the *Ramillies* class, sir."

Fegen said, "There's nothing like that reported in the area. No reply?"

"No, sir."

"Make it on the thirty-six. She can't ignore that."

The big searchlight flashed out.

Fred Billings looked through his gunlayer's telescope. "Single funnel, cowl on the fore end... Looks like the *Resolution*."

On P1 Gun AB Alf Handley had the same thought. "It's the old *Resolution*. Come to give us a hand."

At the same gun Sam Patience, son of a Scottish fisherman, who had been relieved at the wheel by the Chief QM Walter Wallis, had served in the *Resolution*. He said,

"It's not the *Reso*. It's another class."

Still peering through the telescope he saw three flashes bloom for'ard on the strange warship, another three aft.

Commander Blackburn had his binoculars on the other ship.

"It's a pocket battleship." His mind swiftly computed. "Tall bridge tower." *Deutschland*'s was lower, squatter, and she had a single steel mast. *Graf Spee* was down. "*Admiral Scheer*."

The *Scheer* it was, commanded by Kapitän-zur-See Theodor Krancke, tall, austere, former head of the German Naval College, brilliant strategist and tactician who had supervised the preparations for the naval campaign against Norway. His orders were "to relieve pressure on German operations in the North Sea and English Channel by rapid action which would tend to upset normal dispositions of British escort forces." His first step would be to find and attack a weakly escorted convoy from Canada to Britain. But

Krancke would be wary. He had not forgotten the fate of *Scheer*'s sister ship in the Plate.

After a savage battering by fifty-foot seas in the Denmark Strait, with two men lost overboard, *Scheer* broke out into the open Atlantic. Naval Intelligence had informed Krancke of two convoys, HX83 and HX84, coming from Halifax.

At 12.40 p.m. on 5 November *Scheer*'s Arado seaplane, her "ship's parrot", returned early from its second search for the convoy HX84 – its predecessor was now too close to home waters – and observer Gallinat signalled, "Eighty-eight sea miles".

When the aircraft had been recovered, pilot Pietsch brought Krancke his chart with the position of the convoy marked. *Scheer* at once altered course to intercept, which Krancke estimated should be in about three hours, approximately 4 p.m. He wanted to attack before darkness fell, rather than shadow and attack at dawn – and risk another *Graf Spee* débacle before he could do enough damage.

At three o'clock he sighted a single ship. She appeared to be a normal freighter, but Krancke was suspicious. She might be a Q-ship, though there had been no reports of the British using them in this war so far.

She was in fact the banana boat *Mopan*, which had passed Convoy HX84 and turned down an invitation to join it. Taking off her crew and sinking her delayed Krancke an hour – an hour's grace for HX84, an hour nearer the UK and the Home Fleet. It was not until about 5 p.m. that they saw the big smoke on the horizon.

Second Radio Officer Dick Shackleton was on watch at the medium wave transmitter in *Jervis Bay*'s wireless office. The huge bulk of Hugh Williamson came tumbling in.

Right behind him was George Roe with an enemy sighting report. "Get that off on the double." Williamson sat down and tapped it out on the High Frequency set. As he was doing it there was a rumble of explosions as the *Scheer*'s first salvo fell between the fourth, fifth and sixth columns of ships.

On the bridge Fegen ordered "Full speed ahead", then a double ring on the telegraphs for maximum revs.

Jervis Bay increased speed, pulling out of the convoy and signalling to the other ships,

"Prepare to scatter."

A minute later Fegen cancelled this order and signalled, "Convoy to turn to starboard."

The Commodore repeated the signal to his ships. When *Jervis Bay* was clear of the convoy she turned to port and headed straight for the raider, putting herself between the German, now clearly identifiable as an 11-inch pocket battleship, and the merchantmen, dropping smoke floats to screen them, while ships of the convoy did the same.

Then Admiral Maltby made the signal to scatter. The enemy was keeping up a rapid fire at a range of 29,000 yards, and the third salvo caught the *Jervis Bay* amidships.

In the wireless office they were half-way through a repeat enemy sighting report on a different wavelength when the office was hit.

The bridge was badly smashed and Captain Fegen wounded. Roe came down into the wheelhouse, blood pouring from his thigh. "I've been hit. Something's hit me here." Wallis tried to help him fix a tourniquet while holding the ship on her course at the same time. Then he realized that the ship was not answering her helm. "Steering gear disabled," he reported. Dick Shackleton rushed to the bridge. "Wireless gear out of action, sir."

Fegen ordered Wallis to go aft and man the emergency steering position there. He had to jump the twelve feet from the lower bridge to the Boat Deck, as the ladder had gone, and he crawled most of the way aft on his hands and knees, sheltering behind the boats from the whining shrapnel. Fegen was on his way aft to the after docking bridge, Shackleton back to the damaged wireless office.

The ship was now being repeatedly hit, and was on fire, with her peacetime woodwork blazing. There was a big hole in the funnel, and the draft to the boilers had failed, causing the furnaces to blow back jets of flaming oil. The boiler room became a burning hell.

In spite of the blazing, broken shambles above and below decks, *Jervis Bay*'s own forward guns, old and decrepit and hopelessly outranged, were still firing at the enemy at extreme elevation. Then S2 Gun was hit and destroyed, the Transmitting Station wrecked, S1 Gun hit and its crew all killed. At P2 AB Egglestone, though wounded, kept his crew in action.

Captain Fegen reached the after control position and tried to climb up to it, but with one arm almost shot away he could not make it. He ordered Midshipman Butler, who was in the control position, to leave it and see that any loose cordite was thrown overboard to prevent the spread of fire, and to put smoke floats overboard to provide the shelter of a smokescreen. Charles Castle, who had abandoned his wrecked generating room, gave him a hand, and they got about a dozen smoke floats over. Then Butler returned to the after control position to find that it had received a direct hit and everyone there was dead. From the wheel in the after steering compartment Wallis was calling control in vain. He simply went on steering blind.

Dick Shackleton had returned to the wireless office with Hugh Williamson's life jacket. He would not be needing it. Everyone there was dead too, the office shattered by another direct hit. He took cover from the screaming shells for a minute, then made his way back towards the bridge to see if there was anything he could do there. On his way he saw the Captain and the Chief Yeoman of Signals lying dead on the deck. He saw the Captain's Coxswain, Chief PO Clark, another pensioner, and told him. Clark made his way aft and said to the wounded Roe, who was trying to con the ship from the poop, "You're in command now, sir. All the other officers are dead."

Several shells hit the ship's side and burst in the engine room, which began to flood. *Jervis Bay* fell off to port, now completely out of control. Her upperworks, from the ruined bridge to abaft the wreck of the funnel, were burning fiercely, the boats were on fire, and the whole blaze was spreading rapidly. Midshipman Butler said to Roe, "Abandon ship, sir?" It was the only possible order. "Yes," said Roe.

The word went round by messenger. Wallis could not get to his proper boat as the fires were too fierce. He saw a raft in the water quite close to the ship with several men on it, jumped and swam to it. Butler jumped overboard. Dick Shackleton made his way aft and helped stokers Beaman and Drury who were coolly organizing the launching of rafts under heavy shell fire.

John Robertson, stationed high up in the engine room, waited until the water was about thirty feet deep below him, then went up on deck. He too found that the flames made it impossible to get to a boat. He jumped and swam to a raft. Most of the rafts were on fire as well, but ceased to burn when they hit the water. AB Bains, wounded and with his own clothes on fire, was desperately trying to pull the burning clothing off another man. The wounded Egglestone kept P2 firing until it could no longer be trained. Assistant Steward Barnett stuck to his post down in the darkness of the foremost shell room after the lights had failed, trying to get the emergency lighting to work, and had to be ordered to leave. AB Bill Cooper, sight-setter at P1 Gun, stayed at his post until he realized that the whole fore part of the ship had been abandoned.

As the rafts and the one seaworthy lifeboat cleared the ship they came under heavy fire for several minutes from time-fused shell from the *Scheer*'s 5.9-inch secondary armament, then fire ceased. The *Jervis Bay* was riddled fore and aft, settling by the stern and burning furiously between the forebridge and the after control, with other fires for'ard. Men swimming in the sea struggled towards the rafts.

Leading Seaman Wood, though wounded, paddled hard to get his raft away from the ship. Young Butler saw this raft when it was a long way off, swam to it, climbed on and found that he was the only officer there. He was very cold, but having shaken himself to get some of the circulation back, took complete charge. The ship was still afloat and they could see her clearly in the light of her fires. "Shouldn't we paddle back to her, sir?" said someone. "No," said Butler, "but if you want to swim back, you can."

The AMC had been put out of action in about fifteen minutes, a swift and brutal assassination, but the *Scheer* had lingered over the coup de grace, and an hour had passed between sighting the *Jervis Bay* and breaking off to attack the rest of the convoy, which was now scattering at full speed to the north, south and west.

The raider began shelling the ships in the rear of the retreat. *Rangitiki*, which had been leading the sixth column, came in for a few salvoes, but survived.

About two hours after the enemy had ceased firing on the *Jervis Bay*, the survivors saw their battered ship, silhouetted against the fires still active on board, settle by the stern, tilt her bows into the air and sink vertically.

Engineer Robertson found that two torches which he had brought with him still worked after immersion in the sea. About an hour after the *Jervis Bay* had gone down, a ship was sighted in the distance and he started signalling in her direction.

Captain Sven Olander's 6,850-ton *Stureholm* of the Svenska Ameriko Mexiko Line, with her cargo of steel and scrap, had escaped the raider so far. When the convoy had scattered he had continued to alter course round to starboard until he was heading west-nor'-west, adjusting his speed and course as necessary to keep the smokescreen between him and the raider. This went on for four hours, until about 9 p.m., when he saw a tiny light like a hand torch away in the south-east making SOS..SOS..SOS..

The south was dangerous. The *Scheer* was down there among the fleeing sheep. About 10 p.m. aboard the 4,955-ton Reardon Smith Lines' *Fresno City* of Bideford, Devon, they saw the gunfire reflected at intervals in the sky to the northward. Parachute flares revealed the 10,042-ton CPR's *Beaverford* under attack and on fire.

Fresno City continued heading south for about an hour, then a searchlight was suddenly turned full on her from a ship on her starboard quarter. Travelling at high speed the ship opened fire when she was just abaft the beam at very short range. She could not miss. *Fresno City*'s frail merchant hull was torn by a fierce fusillade, seven shells in all, from the pocket battleship, all in rapid succession. One after the other the shells struck the engine room aft, the engine room for'ard, No. 1 Hold, No. 2 Hold, No. 2A Hold, No. 4 Hold, No. 5 Hold. The first stopped the engines completely, hatch covers were blown off, the forward hatch tarpaulins draped themselves over the crosstrees. All the compartments hit were set on fire. There was a nasty swell running but wounded men were lowered into the lifeboats and the ship was abandoned.

Sven Olander was steering for the flickering SOS, well aware that his course was taking the *Stureholm* closer all the time to the gun flashes and flares. But he held on, and about 11 p.m. he had *Jervis Bay*'s lifeboat alongside. Twenty men were rescued from it, and they told their saviour that there were rafts about. *Stureholm*'s crew then manned the empty lifeboat and in two trips rescued one officer and fifteen men. The damaged lifeboat was then abandoned, and the ship saved twenty men from a second raft by manoeuvering alongside it, which required careful seamanship. Captain Olander then set course west for Halifax.

Admiral Maltby in the *Cornish City*, which had escaped to the north, also saw the pyrotechnics in the sky, and counted about seven heavy explosions, which he thought must be tankers going up. The firing ceased about 10.30 p.m. At daylight *Cornish City* was alone. She made for the Clyde, collecting nine other ships on the way.

The other surviving ships were heading for either Canada or Britain. Twenty-one reached the UK, eleven returned safely to Halifax. Their crews well knew who they had to thank. Fegen, in deliberately steering for the enemy, knowing his own fight was hopeless, had gained time for the convoy to scatter. In sacrificing himself and his ship he had won that vital hour during which all but six ships under his protection escaped into the smoke and darkness.

It might have been seven, but for the bravery and skill of the Second Officer and fifteen men of the 11,181-ton tanker *San Demetrio*. The ship had been set on fire by shells and abandoned, but this handful of men reboarded her, put out the fires, and with all her navigation gear destroyed, brought her safely to Ireland.

The *Trewellard*, *Fresno City*, *Kenbane Head*, *Beaverford* and *Maiden* were sunk by *Scheer*'s shells, and their valuable cargoes, including steel, maize and trucks, lost. The small 2,734-ton *Vingaland*, which had straggled behind the main body of the convoy, was bombed and sunk by a long-range Focke-Wulf Condor three days later. *Fresno City*'s two lifeboats had become separated and drifted apart. Captain Lawson's boat was found by the Greek ship *Mount Taygetos* after three days in which the boat had sailed more than two hundred miles under a light jib sail, most of the time before a westerly gale.

14 The Hammer Of The AMCs

The Home Fleet, spread north and south, failed to sight the *Scheer*. On 24 November Captain George Hall's 7,448-ton cargo liner *Port Hobart* signalled just before she was sunk south-east of Bermuda that she was being attacked by a German raider, though the message did not say whether the latter was a regular warship or an auxiliary cruiser.

It was the *Scheer*, on her way south. The *Widder*, after sinking a total of ten ships in the Central Atlantic, had reached Brest on 31 October.

The small aircraft carrier *Hermes* and the old light cruiser *Dragon* were stationed between Rio de Janeiro and West Africa, in the St Helena area. The 8-inch cruisers *Cumberland* and *Newcastle* were sent to reinforce the South American Division, and the new Fleet aircraft carrier *Formidable* and the heavy cruisers *Berwick* and *Norfolk*, forming Force K, were to be sent to the Freetown area.

On 18 December the British freighter *Duquesa* of the Furness-Houlder Argentine Lines, bound from South America for Freetown, radioed,

"I am being attacked by a pocket battleship."

It was the *Scheer* again, ranging down the South Atlantic. The *Duquesa* was fat with foodstuffs, including 15,000,000 eggs and 3,500 tons of meat, but her SOS had given *Scheer*'s position to Admiral Raikes at Freetown. He at once sent the cruisers *Neptune* and *Dorsetshire* out to search for five hundred miles to the west. *Hermes* and *Dragon* and the AMC *Pretoria Castle* were ordered to rendezvous at St Helena and cover the north-east, and Force K, which was on its way to Freetown, was diverted west of the Azores. But there were too many holes in the net, and again the *Scheer* slipped through. She spent a further four months cruising in the South Atlantic and Indian Ocean, sinking another eight ships and sending home two prizes.

At 6.42 on the morning of 5 December HMS *Carnarvon Castle*, commanded by Captain H. W. M. Hardy RN, was seven hundred miles north-east of Montevideo steaming down towards the Plate at 18 knots when she sighted a ship about eight and a half miles away, the extreme limit of visibility in the morning haze.

The stranger was steaming directly away from them. The *Carnarvon Castle* increased speed and her signal flashed,

"SC (What ship?)"

There was no reply.

Hardy signalled "K (Stop immediately)."

There was still no answer from the stranger, which appeared to be a long, low freighter of under 10,000 tons painted a very dark grey or black, with two masts, one funnel, straight stem and cruiser stern. At 7.57, with the range down to about 17,000 yards, *Carnarvon Castle* fired a 6-inch warning shot, which fell some three hundred yards short.

Now the stranger responded. Two stern guns flashed, doors were raised in her sides, a big German Navy battle ensign was hoisted at her main, with a small ensign at her foremast, and she began to turn to starboard to unmask her whole starboard battery, which opened up with four-gun salvoes.

Hardy turned his big, 20,000-ton ship to port to close the gap and bring his own starboard battery of four 6-inch to bear. At least he wasn't taking on the *Scheer*. From appearances, and the weight of shell, he thought he might be chasing the *Alcantara*'s adversary.

He was right. *Thor* had been cruising the South Atlantic for nearly two months after the battle with the *Alcantara*, with the crews from her five previous captures eating up her supplies, and no further prizes from which to plunder more. Then on 26 September she made a double score. In the forenoon she attacked and sank the Norwegian whale oil tanker *Kosmos*, and just after noon overtook the British *Natia*. Captain Carr made a run for it but gave up after his ship had taken nine hits from *Thor*'s 5.9s.

Kahler now had over three hundred and fifty prisoners in his overcrowded ship. He was reluctant to release any of them into neutral hands. This was a different war, and parole meant much less than it had done in '14–18. Then on 9 November the German supply ship *Rio Grande*, which should have met *Thor* earlier but had been held up in Brazil, rendezvoused with them and took off all the passengers except four captains, including Carr, and Winter of the *Wendover*. *Rio Grande* arrived at Bordeaux on 13 December and the Allied prisoners went to POW camps in Germany.

Thor then spent three fruitless weeks on the Africa – River Plate routes, until the British AMC came out of the haze at half-past five one morning. Berlin had warned Kahler by radio that a battleship and ten cruisers were searching for him in the South Atlantic, and he had learned that the auxiliary cruisers *Queen of Bermuda* and *Carnarvon Castle* were in his area. Both AMCs had two funnels, like this one, which looked more like the Union Castle boat, well known in peacetime as the fastest ship between Southampton and Capetown. He saw her before she saw the *Thor*. It was no business of his to take on cruisers, and he ran from her. Then he saw her alter course and begin to overtake him, and he knew he would have to fight her.

Twenty minutes after the first shots had been fired the range was down to 14,000 yards, which gave *Carnarvon Castle*'s old guns a chance. Soon both ships were within range of each other. The German turned to port. *Carnarvon Castle*'s electrical fire control communications were badly shot up, making salvo firing difficult, but her gunners thought they had made hits on the enemy's stern. The raider turned to starboard, made smoke and retired behind it, then reappeared again and opened fire with her starboard battery in four-gun salvoes.

At 8.38 p.m. *Carnarvon Castle* was rapidly closing the range when two torpedoes were sighted from the bridge, their white tracks on slightly diverging courses. Hardy turned the big AMC under full helm to starboard and steered between them, and they passed harmlessly fifty yards away on either beam.

Four minutes later the range was down to 8,000 yards. *Thor*, with the British shells going over her, turned right round to bring her port battery to bear once more, and hit the *Carnarvon Castle*'s upperworks repeatedly, setting her on fire in several places. At ten minutes past nine Hardy decided to open the range and get the fires under control behind a smoke screen.

All his fire control circuits were disabled and his guns in individual control. The haze had increased, and the enemy was continually turning smoke on and off, making spotting through the splashes of her shots very difficult and hitting a matter of luck, but from *Carnarvon Castle* they saw a shell burst under the enemy's bridge at the extreme range of 14,000 yards. After that the AMCs shells were falling short, while the German 5.9s were pitching round her. The raider continued firing until the range had opened to 18,000 yards. Hardy altered course to try and keep in touch, but the enemy disappeared behind his smokescreen and the ever-increasing haze, steaming at 18 knots towards the north-east.

Thor's old guns were giving trouble with leaking recoil cylinders and barrels that would not train properly, but the *Carnarvon Castle* was in a far worse condition. It was 11.15 before she had put out all her fires. In view of her extensive damage Captain Hardy decided to steer for Montevideo. Commodore Pegram, who had succeeded Harwood in command of the South American Division at the end of August, met *Carnarvon Castle* on 6 December in the cruiser *Enterprise*, inspected her damage and ordered her into Montevideo for repair, then sent *Enterprise* north to look for her opponent, but the raider had disappeared. *Carnarvon Castle* buried her six dead and reached Montevideo at 7 p.m. on 7 December with her sick bay full of wounded. *Asturias* returned to the South American Division once more, as her relief.

The ship was too badly damaged to go into action again immediately, though there was no immediate need to dock her. The Uruguayan authorities granted her seventy-two hours to make immediate essential repairs. In contrast to the cold reception given to the *Graf Spee* a year previously when she had sought refuge from Admiral Harwood's squadron, local repair firms were eager to offer their services to the British AMC, and some of the plates cut from the pocket battleship's scuttled hulk out in the estuary were actually used to patch up *Carnarvon Castle*'s shell holes. With temporary repairs completed, *Carnarvon Castle* left for Table Bay, Cape Town. She was saluted by a special guard of honour as she passed through the harbour entrance.

Once again a German disguised raider, the same ship, had out-fought and badly damaged a British armed merchant cruiser. Both *Alcantara*'s and *Carnarvon Castle*'s actions emphasized the AMC's weaknesses – their big silhouettes, their ancient short-range guns and primitive fire-control when opposed to smaller enemy ships equipped with better guns and modern fire control systems. While *Alcantara*'s 6-inch were outranged by 2,000 yards, *Carnarvon Castle*'s were outranged by 3,000 yards, which gave her adversary twenty minutes of unopposed firing before she could get within range. *Carnarvon Castle* had received no fewer than twenty-seven hits, all her electrical and voicepipe communications had been shot away, her engine room telegraphs and telephones cut, her wireless aerials destroyed. All her boats except one were riddled, her galley completely wrecked, the main exhaust pipe from her engines extensively cut, and her forepeak flooded.

On Christmas Day, 1940, the *Scheer* and her "Commissary Department Wilhelmshaven South" – otherwise the floating larder *Duquesa* – met the *Thor* in the South Atlantic, and old friends Theodor Krancke ant Otto Kahler, now the holder of the Ritter-kreuz, met again over a fine Christmas dinner. The tanker *Nordmark* was with them too to top up the two raiders. Also on her way to the South Atlantic was Korvettenkapitän Theodore Detmers' Schiff 41, the *Kormoran*, at 8,736 tons the biggest of the disguised merchant raiders and first of a second wave of new Hilfskreutzers. *Kormoran* had broken out of the Denmark Straits on 13 December.

While the two raider captains were rounding off their Christmas dinner with some fine schnapps, the heavy cruiser *Admiral Hipper*, which had also sortied from Germany earlier in the month, was attacking troop convoy WS5A of twenty ships bound for the Middle East seven hundred miles west of Cape Finisterre. But this convoy had as Ocean Escort the cruisers *Berwick*, *Bonaventure* and *Dunedin* and the aircraft carrier *Furious*, and the *Hipper* was only able to damage one transport, the *Empire Trooper*, ironically the former German *Cap Norte*, before *Berwick* hit her and drove her off damaged.

In November the heavy AMC losses increased on the 30th when five torpedoes shattered HMS *Forfar* (ex-Canadian Pacific *Montrose*) as she was heading west to provide escort for Convoy SC14 from Sydney, Cape Breton island, and she sank with the loss of many lives, a high proportion through swallowing oil fuel in the water. Captain Hardy was on the bridge for the final plunge and went down with the ship. Admiral Forbes had proposed that the auxiliary cruisers should be withdrawn until proper anti-submarine escorts could be provided for them. The Admiralty replied that they could not be spared, but the four remaining with the Northern Patrol were taken out of the submarine danger area to work with the Halifax Escort Force, so they could escort UK-bound convoys as far as longitude 25° West, then break off to carry out two patrols in the Denmark Strait, with an interval for refuelling at Hvalfjord in Iceland, before returning to Halifax. New Ocean Boarding Vessels were to replace AMCs in the Western Patrol, their most vulnerable station.

On 19 January, 1941, the Naval Officer in Charge, Falkland Islands, at Port Stanley, received news from South Georgia Island that the 12,000-ton Norwegian whale factory ship *Ole Wegger* and the transport *Solglimt* were believed to have been sunk by a German raider a thousand miles to the east of the island. HMS *Queen of Bermuda* was ordered down to Antarctic waters to protect the rest of the whaling fleet and look for the raider and the supply ship reported to be bringing her guns and stores from Buenos Aires.

On the 20th it was confirmed that the *Ole Wegger* and *Solglimt* had been captured, together with four whale catchers, in the early morning of 14 January. On the 22nd the *Queen of Bermuda* called at Grytviken in South Georgia and was given a description of the raider, which had captured 6,000 tons of fuel, food and water from the ships taken, 150,000 barrels of whale oil and seven hundred prisoners. Local opinion thought that the captured ships would be taken to the Prince Edward, Crozet or Kerguelen Islands in the southern Indian Ocean, where the whale oil would be transferred to Japanese ships, known to have been working in these latitudes.

Later it was learned that the mother ship *Pelagos* and her seven catchers had been taken as well.

It was all the work of Kapitan-zur-See Ernst-Felix Kruder's *Pinguin*, Schiff 33, which had left Germany on 15 June, 1940, and had captured ten more ships since, taking the *Domingo de Larrinaga* in the South Atlantic at the time of the *Thor*'s fight with the *Alcantara*.

The *Queen of Bermuda* oiled and watered at Stromness in the South Orkneys and covered the whalers *Southern Empress* and *Svend Foyn* and their sixteen catchers working in an area 230 miles to the east of the South Orkneys on the southern boundary of the Scotia Sea. It was planned to replenish the AMC with fuel and water carried by the whaler *Thorshammer* when she left Grytviken and went south to the ice with her ten catchers.

Queen of Bermuda carried out a search for the raider down to the Antarctic Circle, without result. She was then ordered to destroy the elaborate whaling installations which had been built on various islands, as they could not be defended and might be of considerable use to the enemy.

The most difficult and dangerous operation was at Deception Island, in the British South Shetland Islands, which was actually the huge crater of an extinct volcano with only one part of the wall broken away to make an entrance uncomfortably narrow for the big 22,575-ton AMC even if it had been clear, and even more hazardous as it was obstructed by a large rock in the middle. She was squeezed past by fine seamanship and the handiness which had been provided in her original design for navigating the channels into Bermuda. Inside, she carried out the demolition as quickly as possible, as she would have been caught at a hopeless disadvantage in the narrow entrance had a heavily armed German raider been waiting for her outside. The fuel oil tanks were empty and had apparently not been used for some time, but the whole installation was destroyed, as well as the coal depot and its stocks. On 8 March *Queen of Bermuda* reported the job complete.

Three days after this the captured *Pelagos* let go her anchor in the Gironde, and four days later the *Solglimt* came in. The Grytvikians had been wrong about *Pinguin*'s disposal of her whaling spoils. The *Ole Wegger* and ten of the catchers were following the others to France. But the *Pinguin*'s cruise was almost over. She sailed into the Indian Ocean, where she met the raider *Komet* and was provisioned by the supply ship *Alstertori* in the Kerguelens. On 24 April she sank the British steamer *Empire Light* and on the 28th the *Clan Buchanan*, which, however, managed to send out a brief signal. The light cruiser *Leander* left Colombo, and the heavy cruisers *Cornwall* and *Hawkins* and the carrier *Eagle* of Force V put out from Mombasa on a hunt. On 7 May *Pinguin*, short of oil, shelled the small tanker *British Emperor* and tried to capture her intact, but she sank in flames, having got off the urgent "QQQQ" signal. On the morning of the 8th one of *Cornwall*'s seaplanes spotted the *Pinguin*, the cruiser intercepted, and just after half-past five in the afternoon a shell hit the raider's mines and she disintegrated.

Meanwhile ships had been going missing in the Central Atlantic. On 25 March the ex-Anchor liner *Cilicia* was on the Western Patrol when she picked up a "QQQQ" from her old firm's *Britannia III*. The surgeon in *Cilicia*, Lieutenant-Commander Tom Miller RNR, was particularly worried at the news, as his daughter Nancy was *Britannia*'s surgeon. There was no further signal, and it was concluded that the raider had sunk her.

Three anxious days passed without news, then they learned that Dr Nancy Miller's boat had been found by the Spanish steamer *Bachi* twenty-four hours after leaving the doomed *Britannia III*. At 6.25 p.m. on 28 March *Cilicia* sighted a small steamer and at 7.15 sent a boarding party on board the steamer. At 9.30 p.m. the boat was back alongside *Cilicia*, and Nancy was the first to reach the AMC's deck, to be greeted by her father. It had been her first voyage, but during the action she had, the *London Gazette* reported later, "with perfect calm attended to the wounded and dying. She continued her good work after the ship's company had taken to the boats and by her efforts saved many lives."

HMS *Voltaire* left Trinidad on 30 March, and was due to arrive at Freetown 9 April. Her predecessor, the liner of the same name, had been sunk in December, 1916, by the raider *Möwe*, and she herself was quite an old ship, 13,245 tons with a maximum speed of only 14.5 knots, having been built by Workman Clark in 1923 for Lamport & Holt's to work as a passenger and cargo liner between New York and Buenos Aires, via the West Indies, Brazil and Uruguay. She was also available for summer cruises. Sixteen guineas would buy thirteen days visiting Norwegian fjords and northern capitals or Malaga (for Granada), Palma (for Majorca) and Ceuta. The most expensive trip cost from twenty-eight guineas, and took in Casablanca, Dakar (Senegal), Bathurst (Gambia), Santa Cruz de la Palma, and Madeira. Later she served as a troopship, until taken over by the Admiralty at the end of August, 1939. She served at first in Scapa Flow as an accommodation ship for naval officers and ratings awaiting the arrival of their ships, and was a temporary home for survivors from the *Royal Oak*. Later she sailed from Scapa to North Shields on the Tyne and was fitted out as an armed merchant cruiser at Wallsend. After a short stay in Portsmouth she sailed for Malta, where she was based on contraband control duty, patrolling the Mediterranean for suspect cargo ships, then sent to Halifax to join the Escort Force on convoy duty, sometimes via Bermuda, across the North Atlantic. She had just come down to Trinidad from St John, New Brunswick, after a refit, when she was ordered to Freetown, with instructions to look for raiders on the way.

On 5 April German radio broadcast the news that a raider had sunk the *Britannia* and the British armed merchant cruiser *Voltaire*.

C-in-C America and West Indies Station ordered the Canadian AMC *Prince David* to make a search along the track of the *Voltaire* at her best possible speed. At 2 p.m. on 7 April she sighted a patch of very heavy oil covering an area of three square miles, together with charred wood, clothes and newspapers in a position half-way between the West Indies and the Cape Verde Islands. This was *Voltaire*'s estimated position on the 4th, and the wreckage was almost certainly hers. There were no survivors in the water, and it seemed likely that something like a repeat of the *Alcantara*'s and *Carnarvon Castle*'s actions had taken place – with more final results. *Voltaire* had probably been outranged and, in view of her slow speed, outmanoeuvered as well. On April she became formally overdue at Freetown.

It was indeed *Thor* again, hammer of the AMCs. The tankers *Eurofeld* and *Alsterufer* had kept her going through February and March, and Kahler had met the *Pinguin*'s ten captured whale catchers en route for France and supervised their refuelling from the *Spichern*, ex-*Krossfonn*, *Widder*'s prize, but he had made no captures himself until *Britannia* had appeared on 25 March, tried to run for it and been shelled full of holes. Kahler had had to leave her survivors in the overcrowded boats to thirst and the cruel sun, the floaters to the sharks, when he intercepted a message that an enemy ship was on her way, though he informed Berlin by radio of their plight. When a ship appeared she was the Swedish *Trollenholm* bringing coals from Newcastle to Port Said. He took off her crew and sank her.

Just after sunrise on 4 April *Thor* was steaming about nine hundred miles west of the Cape Verde Islands when her man in the barrel sighted smoke. Anxious for a capture, Kahler steered for her.

It was the *Voltaire*, though Kahler did not immediately recognize her as an auxiliary cruiser. *Thor* was flying the Greek flag when *Voltaire* sighted her, and both ships challenged each other, each fired a warning shot across the other's bows. Kahler saw that he was faced with an armed liner, unmasked his guns, and Koppen-Boehnke opened fire with salvoes outside the range of *Voltaire*'s old 6-inch. The first salvo destroyed the AMC's radio room and generator, and in four minutes her painted peacetime wood panelling was well alight.

As the range closed *Voltaire* opened fire, but with all electrical circuits gone her guns were firing individually, raggedly and at random, while *Thor*'s 5.9s were scoring hit after hit on hull and upperworks. "This time," Kahler had written in his log, "I have to finish her off."

When the range had sunk to 7,000 yards, *Voltaire* was circling at 12 knots, steering gear jammed, gulping water through the shell holes in her hull which did nothing to douse the fires racing through her decks, though some of her guns were still firing. Half an hour after the battle had begun one gun was in action forward and Captain Blackburn himself was controlling a single gun on the poop. Some of the raider's old guns had stopped when overheated training gear broke down once more, and with the range now down to 2,000 yards Kahler manoeuvered for a torpedo attack. But as he closed the AMC he could see that men were jumping into the sea from what was now a blazing wreck. Her guns finally stopped firing, and some men on the poop were even waving improvised white flags.

Kahler ceased fire and lay cautiously 4,000 yards off while his boats picked up survivors, the German boats' crews ready with rifles and machine-guns to keep off sharks. *Voltaire* sank by her stern two hours after the first shot had been fired, and Kahler, knowing that his victim had been unable to use her radio, felt free to spend five hours saving as many men as he could. With so many badly wounded then aboard, the torpedo deck had to be used as an overflow sick bay. When the final roll call was made, seventy-two men had been killed of *Voltaire*'s ship's company of 269. One seaman rescued had a copy of the book *Principles of Mercantile Law* in his back pocket.

Thor's crew had come out of the battle unscathed, but the ship had been at sea continuously for nearly eleven months and both she and her men needed servicing. When Dr. Göbbels boasted to the world on 5 April of *Thor*'s victory the day before, thus betraying her presence and position in the South Atlantic, Kahler was even more keen to be on the move for home. He steamed north-west, met the tanker *Ill* on 14 April and transferred 170 prisoners to her. On the 16th he captured his twelfth ship, the Swedish Trafikaktieb Granjesberg Oxelasund's ore carrier *Sir Ernest Cassell*. Ten days later he anchored in Cherbourg harbour to avoid a bad gale, and after some tricky navigation without the services of an Elbe pilot, made Hamburg on 30 April. Then for a change the decks ran with beer instead of salt water.

Since Christmas *Thor* had been under orders to keep her operations south of latitude 30° North. The ocean above that parallel was the province of the regular Fleet units – and the U-boats.

In the graveyard watch of 3 April a wolf pack of six U-boats attacked Convoy SC26, twenty-two ships steaming at 8 knots to the south of the Denmark Strait. The AMC *Worcestershire* was the only escort.

The order to scatter was given, but the Northern Lights were glowing, silhouetting the ships for the Germans to pick off. Ten ships were sunk, and *Worcestershire* was hit by a torpedo on the starboard side abreast the foremast, tearing a huge hole twenty-eight feet by eighteen in the side, taking great bites out of two decks, flooding the two forward holds and magazine through a ruptured bulkhead, jamming the steering gear and starting a fire in the foc'sle.

The Damage Control Party saved her. Steering was restored and the fire put out. The ship made for home, steaming slowly to avoid further damage, and after a thousand anxious miles reached Liverpool drawing forty-four feet of water for'ard and fifteen feet aft.

During the month of May, 1941, sinkings by U-boat were heavy – fifty-eight ships with a total tonnage of 325,492, over half of these in West African waters.

Salopian, which had been transferred from the Freetown to the Halifax Escort Force, escorted a slow convoy from Halifax to the western edge of the submarine danger zone and handed over to a destroyer escort from the UK during the afternoon of 12 May. She then turned west and headed back for Halifax at 15 knots.

Just before first light, about 3.30 a.m., the officer of the watch thought he saw something, possibly a submarine, on the surface, on the starboard bow. In accordance with standing orders he sounded Action Stations, increased to full speed and put the helm hard over to turn away. Almost immediately the ship was struck by two torpedoes on the starboard side, one at the position of the bulkhead between Numbers 3 and 4 Holds, one near the bow under the foc'sle.

The first torpedo was the one that counted. The shock fractured many of the pipes in the engine room, stopping the main engines. A young engineer and a fireman on watch in the distilling plant compartment immediately forward of the engine room were killed instantly. The shock also brought down all the wireless aerials, so no report could be sent out from the ship. The jet of water thrust upwards on the starboard side shattered the starboard seaboat in its davits.

Senior Engineer Bill Nisbet, who was on watch, realized that as soon as the supply of oil in the pipelines from the header tanks to the generators was exhausted they would also stop and the ship would be plunged into darkness, so he sent one of his juniors to start the emergency generator on the poop, which would also power the emergency bilge pump. As the main lights faded the emergency ones came on. Light was always a great morale booster in such emergencies. By this time the ship had been hit again on the port side at Number 5 Hold, and the subsequent flooding became too much for the emergency bilge pump to cope with.

Abandon Ship drill had been organized in two states. State One covered an emergency situation with the ship about to sink, State Two allowed for the ship being disabled but not in immediate danger of sinking – which appeared to be *Salopian*'s situation at the moment.

In accordance with State Two, therefore, the Advance Party of some deck and engineer watchkeeping officers, boarding officers, magazine crews, ammunition supply parties, cooks and stewards, pursers and paymasters, left the ship in the lifeboats at the davits, leaving behind the Retard Party, consisting of the Captain, Commander, navigator, Gunnery Control Officer and guns' crews, Damage Control Officer and his parties, Engineer Commander and two of his officers to supervise pumping, a cypher officer, wireless operator and signalman, the Doctor and one sick-berth rating. The Retard Party were to fight the ship as long as possible, leaving eventually in two spare boats in cradles on Number 3 and 5 Hatches and the Carley floats.

The operation worked very smoothly. The Advance Party left in good order and condition without any accidents in lowering the boats, taking with them the emergency supplies of blankets, food and water which were kept in handy lockers on the upper deck. They hauled off and lay clear of the ship, awaiting events.

Soon after they had left, the U-boat surfaced, presumably to finish off *Salopian* with shell fire and conserve her stock of torpedoes, in the belief that the whole crew had abandoned ship. But *Salopian* was using Q-ship tactics. Her guns' crews had remained closed up and immediately went into action, firing a dozen rounds of 6-inch at the submarine, which dived at once. To sink the ship she would now be forced to use up more of her valuable torpedoes – if *Salopian*'s shells had not inflicted any significant damage.

Captain Alleyne realized this and knew that the submarine would not go away until she *had* sunk his ship. He therefore gave orders to hoist out the two spare boats ready for final abandonment.

Lieutenant-Commander Peate was in charge of hoisting out the spare boat on Number 3 Hatch. He had about forty men on a tackle putting the boat out over the starboard side against a slight port list when another torpedo hit the ship aft on the starboard side abreast Number 5 Hold. This caused the ship to heel slightly to starboard and made their job much easier. An old three-badge AB left the fall and ambled over to the ship's side where he saluted in the general direction of the U-boat and said, "Thank you, Fritz, just what we wanted."

While this was being done the U-boat came in at periscope depth and took a good look. She was so close that the 6-inch guns could not be depressed enough to have any chance of hitting her with a shell under water, and she was in the wrong spot for a depth-charge, which, with *Salopian* stopped, would have gone off right under her own stern.

As soon as the two spare boats were in the water, Peate, who was still on board, went up to the emergency generator on the poop to make sure that there was no-one still standing by it in the deck-house, then took a walk round the ship. On the way he met the Captain and the Commander, who were doing the same. They told him to go down to the port motor boat, which had come back alongside, then they themselves went down into the forward spare boat.

When Peate got to the boat ladder he was hailed from the boat and asked to pass down five two-gallon tins of petrol which were lying on deck. They swung him a davit lifeline, which he rove through the handles of the five tins, tying an overhand knot in the end of it. He tried to lift this whole collection over the guard rail but the full tins were much too heavy for him and he had to reeve them back along the rope and pass them down one by one. It all seemed to take an eternity, but he was glad of the extra petrol when he went down and took charge of the boat.

At no time did there seem to be any sense of danger or urgency among *Salopian*'s ship's company. During the abandonment of the ship quite a number of men who were not busy went back to their cabins and picked up valuables and treasured possessions. Peate found time to go to his quarters at the last moment to collect all his pipes, tobacco and watches, and picked up a carton of cigarettes which he saw lying on the deck. Engineer-Sub-Lieutenant Bert Poolman decided to go below to retrieve a silver inscribed salver which had been presented to him on board on his silver wedding anniversary. Once there he decided to change into his best uniform, which he "didn't want to give to the fishes". His absence on deck was noted and an anxious colleague hurried below to find him.

"It's all right," he said casually, "she won't go just yet." He climbed down into his boat clutching the precious salver.

With the wireless down, no message had been sent out, but after the boats had got away a signal "AMC torpedoed" giving the position was transmitted on the old Board of Trade emergency set in the motor boat, which was reputed to have a daylight range of fifty miles. Men on the Carley floats were all transferred to lifeboats, and all the boats gathered together about a quarter of a mile astern of the ship, which did not seem to be sinking. The buoyancy drums in her holds were doing their best to keep her afloat.

The men in the boats saw the U-boat's periscope cutting through the water close by them. then there was an explosion in *Salopian* abreast Number 5 Hold where another torpedo struck her. Still she floated upright on an even keel and at very little more than her normal loaded draught, a tribute to her ballasting and buoyancy. "The old ship just rocked but still sat there like a duck," Bill Nisbet remembered in later years. A short time afterwards another torpedo hit her on the port side amidships. This one broke her in half. Both halves stood on end and disappeared together in less than a minute. As soon as she had gone down, the U-boat surfaced, then, much to the relief of the men in the boats, made off.

For the rest of that day they simply waited, wondering whether their feeble signal had been picked up. Peate noticed that the rating who was the ship's barber was in his boat. He asked him if he had brought the tools of his trade. The barber said that he had, and produced the little attaché case he kept them in. He also pulled out a roll containing £60 in notes, the proceeds from hair cutting. "Harry" Champion, the ship's Master-at-Arms, compiled a complete nominal role of the ship's company from memory. When the boats congregated together for the night he called the roll, and it was then that they discovered that they had lost three men, the engineer and stoker who had been working close to where the first torpedo had struck, and the bosun's mate of the watch, who had been in the wheelhouse, then started round the ship piping Action Stations, and must have been washed overboard by the column of water descending after that first explosion.

During daylight hours on the following day, 14 May, the boats stretched out on a north–south line at visibility distance to make a better target for any searchers. The men were rationed to half a biscuit, an inch cube of corned beef and two half-measures of the small white water dipper per day. Sub-Lieutenant Poolman's silver salver came in handy, as the back of it was used for cutting up the bully beef. The boats collected together again at dusk to ride out another night.

Next morning, the 15th, Alleyne despatched Peate in the motor boat to steer south as far as his fuel would allow in the hope of intercepting the fast convoy which they knew was on its way from Halifax.

Just as he was losing sight of the boats astern Peate sighted a destroyer right ahead. She had also seen them, and soon picked them up, then carried on to rescue the rest of the survivors. They learned that their "AMC torpedoed" SOS had been picked up by the Commodore of the convoy which they had lately escorted. He realized which AMC she must be and relayed the message to C-in-C, Western Approaches at Liverpool. Cypher Officer on duty there was Second Officer Wren Sheila Isherwood, niece by marriage of Sub-Lieutenant Poolman of *Salopian*. Anxiously she waited for news of survivors, though she would be unable to tell the family anything. Destroyers were sent to make an anti-submarine sweep in the area of the attack and look for *Salopian*'s boats. HMS *Icarus*, her fuel running low, was on the last leg of her final broad sweep when she sighted them. She took the *Salopian* survivors to Reykjavik in Iceland, and by the time she got there was down to 12 knots to conserve fuel. On their first day in *Icarus*, *Salopian*'s barber set up shop and gave every survivor a free haircut.

As they were approaching the quay in Reykjavik Captain Alleyne told Peate to go over to where the *Salopian* hands were fallen in ready to disembark and tell them that when they got alongside he wanted them "to march off smartly and not shuffle off like a flock of sheep". As Peate walked across the deck he wondered what to say. He called them to attention and said, "Men, although we are all very sorry to have lost our ship, we still have the best part of her with us. It will only take another eighteen months to build another ship, but it has taken eighteen years to build the youngest men among you." Later Sub-Lieutenant Poolman travelled down to London in the train with a young survivor from HMS *Hood*, sunk by the great battleship *Bismarck* on 24 May, and realized his own good luck in being alive. The

Bismarck herself had been sunk, but he thought what might have happened if she had got among the ships of the convoys – which could have included *Salopian* on her next trip from Halifax. He arrived home in Bath on the first night of the Baedekker blitz on that gracious city. He survived that too and later the threat from a Japanese raider when in the boom defence ship *Devon City* in the Indian Ocean.

15 Ships And Seafoxes

The U-boats were winning in the spring and early summer of 1941, but there were now enough corvettes, sloops and ex-US Navy destroyers and coastguard cutters to relieve some of the vulnerable AMCs on escort work. In August they stopped working with the Sierra Leone convoys, although C-in-C, South Atlantic, kept some for patrol. In October AMCs were withdrawn from the Halifax Escort Force.

As they were taken out of service most of them were turned into troopships, but other AMCs were refitted and rearmed for patrol duties in the South Atlantic, some with catapults to operate aircraft.

HMS *Canton* and *Pretoria Castle*, built in 1938 and 1939 respectively, and among the newest ships in the AMC fleet, were refitted in the summer of 1941 and each was equipped with a catapult and crane and two Fairey Seafox seaplanes. Each Ship's Flight also included two pilots, two observers and some eight maintenance ratings under an air artificer, all from the Fleet Air Arm.

Pretoria Castle's flight was at first looked upon sideways by the rest of the ship's company because their beautiful swimming pool was converted into a sunken hangar for stowing the second aircraft, the other being kept on the catapult. Petty Officer Pilot Doug Elliott had previously been in the cruiser *Nigeria*, and immediately found the ex-luxury liner's accommodation a great change for the better. For a petty officer to have a large ship-side cabin (with a scuttle), hot and cold running water, and capacious wardrobe, was unheard of, and any destroyer captain would gladly have swapped cabins with him. The officers' quarters were, of course, even better, and some of the senior ones had suites. "When one looks back, of course," wrote Oscar Baker, then a young petty officer observer in *Pretoria Castle*," one realizes that we were a sitting duck on a floating petrol can, but life on board compared to the rigours of a Fleet Aircraft Carrier was very pleasant indeed."

Other AMCs were to be equipped with aircraft during refit, including the South American Station stalwarts *Alcantara*, *Asturias*, *Carnarvon Castle* and *Queen of Bermuda*, but they could not all be spared at the same time. The first to get the goodies was *Asturias*, which arrived at Newport News, Virginia, US of A, on 4 July, 1941.

Meanwhile there were more convoys to look after, raiders to hunt, with or without aircraft. In September, 1941, *Queen of Bermuda*, due for her refit at Newport News, was diverted to escort a special convoy from Durban homewards. The convoy comprised the Union Castle liner *Durban Castle*, with the King of Greece on board, the Canadian Pacific liner *Duchess of Bedford*, the Polish *Sobieski* and the Dutch *Nieuw Zeeland*. It was to split up at St Helena, whence *Durban Castle* was to speed home escorted by *Queen of Bermuda*.

An hour before the convoy left Cape Town the German-biased radio in Portuguese East Africa announced, "The details of this convoy are known, including the presence of the King of the Hellenes. Neither the *Durban Castle* nor the auxiliary cruiser *Queen of Bermuda* will reach port."

Added anxiety was caused by the state of the *Queen*'s engines. It was three months since Captain Peachey had reported them to be in a precarious if not dangerous condition, but she was so valuable in use that all she had had was some local treatment by her own engineers.

The convoy was seen safely to St Helena, and *Queen of Bermuda* and *Durban Castle* steamed on at the overworked AMC's best speed. *The Queen* was bursting her rivets to keep up with the faster, fitter new motor ship, load indicators on the danger mark, apoplectic oil pressures, reduced vacuum and "every worst bogey known to the engineer", Peachey reported. Maximum horsepower, which would normally yield a speed of 20½ knots, only produced revolutions for 18½, and a constant advance of 16 knots over the ground was a fine effort in the circumstances.

But when dawn came on 15 September *Durban Castle* was nowhere to be seen. Radio silence had to be maintained for security, but it was felt that something would have been heard if the King had been torpedoed during the night. There was great anxiety until the liner was sighted hull-down on the port quarter. The Commodore in *Durban Castle* had decided that conditions were so overcast and dark that he stopped zigzagging before dawn and ordered a steady course, which was applied when the ship was on a port leg instead of on the main course. The *Queen* being on the reverse zigzag at the time, there was a good distance between them by the time it was light enough to see. The voyage then proceeded to a rendezvous in the North Atlantic, where destroyers took over the escort.

Queen of Bermuda called at Trinidad for bunkers and after the strenuous efforts that had been necessary to maintain the ordered speed, it was frustrating to meet long delays in getting ashore for refuelling. The tired ship had sustained maximum revs for 5,000 miles during the *Durban Castle* convoy, 15,000 miles in all since Captain Peachey had given his warning about the state of the engines at Freetown. Boiler tubes had burst, been plugged, closed off and repaired on passage without reduction in speed, the difficulties having been accentuated by having one complete boiler unit out of action for several months, and oil pumps which frequently broke down.

In late October British cruisers were keeping a watch on a convoy of six Vichy French merchant ships from Indo-China heading round the Cape of Good Hope into the South Atlantic, escorted by the sloop *D'Iberville*. On 1 November the heavy cruiser *Devonshire*, the old ex-Northern Patrol light cruiser *Colombo* and the AMCs *Carnarvon Castle* and *Carthage* were designated Force F, to carry out Operation Bellringer, the task of intercepting the convoy. On 2 November the convoy was still in the Indian Ocean, 500 miles from the South African coast between Durban and Port Elizabeth. The *Devonshire* had shadowed it for twelve hours, but the convoy commander in the sloop would not follow her instructions to shepherd the merchantmen into Port Elizabeth. The Senior Officer of Force F, in *Devonshire*, therefore ordered boarding to be started as soon as *Carnarvon Castle* had joined the other ships of Force F, and weather permitting.

The French ships were intercepted and the merchantmen (*Bangkok, Compiègne, Cap Padaran, Cap Vanella, Cap Tourque* and *Commandant Dorise*) were boarded. Some of them attempted to scuttle themselves, but were caught in time. There was no violence, only passive resistance, and the boarding parties had to take over the sailing of the ships. *Cap Padaran*'s engines were sabotaged, and *Carthage* had to tow her into Port Elizabeth. *Commandant Dorise*'s steering gear was blown up, but the boarding party rigged hand steering. *Carnarvon Castle*, which had dealt with the *Compiègne*, reported that she carried 260 tons of leather, 65 tons of wax, 420 tons of graphite, 400 tons of rice, 145 tons of bark extract, 110 tons of ricine oil grain and 75 tons of mica, all meant for Marseilles, with 300 tons of coffee, 797 tons of tin, and 530 tins of food for Dakar, as well as general cargo.

Devonshire's sister ship *Dorsetshire* had been searching for raiders in the southern oceans for the best part of four months. Later in November she joined the *Canton*, which had only recently arrived in the area, and *Dunedin*, to look for a raider reported in the South Atlantic.

It was *Devonshire*'s aircraft which spotted a suspicious vessel north-east of Ascension Island, and on 22 November the cruiser came up with the ship, which was refuelling a submarine, the *U126*. The ship was Bernhard Rogge's *Atlantis*, Schiff 16, the first of the disguised raiders to leave Germany, to which the time-expired vessel was trying to return, though the Staff kept ordering her to suckle thirsty U-boats – she had only just finished refuelling *U68* south of St Helena. She had been away from the Fatherland for the best part of two years, wandering the South Atlantic, Indian and Pacific Oceans like the Flying Dutchman, sinking nineteen ships and sending home three prizes, occupying hunting forces from Iceland to the Tuamotus. She cast off the U-boat's lines, cut the fuel hose and tried to make a run for it, but Captain Oliver kept out of range of those notorious 5.9s and systematically pounded her to pieces with his 8-inch shells until her forward magazine blew up and she sank.

Oliver steamed off in a hurry. He had his Walrus to recover, and there were several U-boats in the area. He was too quick for the waiting *U126*, which surfaced when he had gone and picked up as many of *Atlantis'* survivors as she could pack into her narrow hull and on her wave-washed casing, towing the rest in six boats towards Brazil. After three days of this misery he met the supply ship *Python* and transferred the passengers. But on 30 November *Python* was refuelling the submarines *U68* and *UA** south-west of St Helena when Captain Agar's *Dorsetshire* caught them. The U-boats scrambled clear, *UA* dived and fired five torpedoes at *Dorsetshire*, which missed. *Python* was scuttled, leaving the two submarines to pick up the *Atlantis* and *Python* men. The *U124* and *U129* were ordered by Dönitz to meet them and relieve some of the congestion. *U129* showed up but Jochen Mohr's *U124* was delayed when she sighted the *Dunedin* on patrol alone and sank her with heavy loss of life. *Canton's* Seafox Flight spent several very harrowing days flying three-and-a-half to four-and-a-half-hour sorties searching unsuccessfully for survivors from the old British cruiser, which had been in earlier days such a pillar of the Northern Patrol. Seventy-two survivors were rescued eventually, after suffering terribly from exposure and sharks, by the American merchantman *Nishmaha*.

During a long refit in Newport News dockyard *Asturias'* ancient 6-inch guns were removed and replaced by the more modern 6-inch of HMS *Delhi*, which was at Boston being refitted as an anti-aircraft cruiser. *Asturias* also received a modern fire-control system and an aircraft catapult. Her old Second Class accommodation and her mainmast were removed to make room for an aircraft hangar. She was also given an RDF (radar) system. This consisted of a very primitive set installed in the pantry of the old Winter Garden or Moorish Lounge on the Boat Deck. A hard tug on what resembled a mangle wheel moved a steel rod, to which it was connected without any gearing, which turned the aerial, mounted on the funnel.

* Built in Germany as the Turkish *Batiray*

Alcantara, Carnarvon Castle and *Queen of Bermuda* arrived at Newport News in December, 1941, for refitting, which included the fitting of aircraft catapults. *Alcantara* was given better guns, and she too lost her mainmast. A gantry was fitted to her one remaining funnel to take the radio aerial. Considerable alterations were carried out in the *Queen of Bermuda*. She was fitted with a catapult aft, a deckhouse hangar at the after end of the Promenade Deck, and a crane on the starboard quarter for recovering aircraft, of which she was to carry three. Her anti-aircraft armament was slightly improved, although it was not brought up to its proper strength until later. Her beautifully balanced appearance, with the three symmetrically spaced funnels, was spoiled when the after funnel, which was a dummy, and mainmast were removed to give the high-angle guns a better field of fire.

The rearmed and refurbished AMCs from C-in-C, South Atlantic's Command returned to Southern waters early in 1942, at a time when the victorious Japanese were still radiating their power over the Pacific and East Indies and were in Burma and the Indian Ocean.

On 5 April Japanese carriers sent seventy-five aircraft to attack the harbour and airfield at Colombo. Among the ships in the harbour was the 11,198 ton ex-Alfred Holt AMC *Hector*. She took four direct hits by 500-and 250-pound delayed-action fused bombs forward of the engine casing. Numbers 1, 2 and 3 Holds were flooded, and her midships section gutted by fire. She was written off as a constructive total loss, but later salvaged and returned to service as a merchantman.

It seemed possible that the AMCs in the South Atlantic might soon have the ships of the junior Axis partner to deal with. The value of their reconnaissance aircraft thereby doubled in value.

The Fairey Seafox seaplane, with which they were equipped, had strong associations with the South Atlantic, having made itself famous in the Battle of the River Plate when one of the cruiser *Ajax*'s Seafoxes had spotted for the guns of Admiral Harwood's squadron and flown on reconnaissance every day afterwards until its observer was able to signal that *Graf Spee* had scuttled herself.

The Seafox had been designed from the start to operate from cruiser catapults, and had been in Royal Navy service since 1937. As built it was a two-seater of orthodox classic biplane configuration, with two unusual features in the combinations of metal monocoque fuselage with fabric-covered wings, and the fitting of an enclosed cockpit canopy for the observer, the pilot being given an open cockpit to facilitate catapult launching drill. Fitted with a 395-horsepower Napier Rapier Mark VI engine, the Seafox cruised at 106 mph, with a top speed of 124 mph, had a range of 440 miles and endurance of 4½ hours, and climbed to 5,000 feet in something over ten minutes, reaching its ceiling at 11,000 feet. The engine of one of *Canton*'s Seafoxes had come from *Maia*, the upper, seaplane unit of the pre-war Mayo flying boat/seaplane combination. One Vickers gas-operated machine-gun was carried in the rear cockpit, and there were racks for light bombs below the mainplanes.

Seafox sorties from *Canton* were sometimes ad hoc, but often planned on the previous day. The Navigator's Assistant normally plotted out the area to be searched, and the actual tracks to be flown were then decided either by the Navigator or the Captain or, if a routine search were ordered, by the observer flying on it. Search shapes varied but were usually a form of "step aside" diverging search, or a search parallel to the ship's track on first one side of it at, say, twenty miles starboard of track, then to port of track.

When a "first light" sortie was planned, the observer would be called an hour and a half before take-off. After an early breakfast he would go to the bridge for final instructions from the Captain.

Canton's catapult, an old cordite-propelled installation, was sited starboard-to-port on the after well deck. The trolley on the catapult, normally placed roughly amidships to facilitate manning the aircraft, would be wound out to the end of the extension to starboard, and the aircraft launched. David Pennick, one of *Canton*'s observers, had been told to face aft for the launch, with the safety belt across his front, as being less sick-making, but he soon learned that his stomach muscles got a lot less sore with the belt across his back, grasping hand-holds for'ard, and it was easy to tuck the head down far enough to avoid a broken neck. The Seafox's speed at the end of the catapult was about 55 knots, so, given a knot or two for side wind component, it left the ship marginally above stalling speed. There were a few stomach-quaking plunges but somehow the 395 horsepower of the little Napier engines always dragged them into the air.

Pretoria Castle's catapult directing officer was an RNR man who had done a short course in HMS *Pegasus* on catapult and aircraft recovery procedures, and until the Flight's two pilots, Sub-Lieutenant Barry Edgar and Petty Officer Elliott, persuaded him otherwise, would stick strictly to the routine laid down of firing the catapult exactly three seconds after the pilot had given the thumbs-up sign that he was ready to be launched. The result was quite often that the aircraft was fired off pointing either straight down at the sea or up into the sky. After a time and several exciting launches, the directing officer got used to holding off the launch until the ship was approximately level. This was not easy to master, as the catapult in an AMC was very high above the waterline and the ship more often than not rolling badly. The first time *Asturias* flew off an aircraft, with a noisy audience filling every vantage point, the pilot put his thumb up in response to some remark from the crowd, and the directing officer fired the catapult. Frantically the pilot got up revs. The Seafox slid off the end of the catapult and just cleared the water, to loud cheers from the crowd.

For recovery of the aircraft the Seafox alighted in the smooth "slick" made by the ship for the purpose, and taxied underneath the jib of the crane. Hooking on was done by the observer standing roughly over the pilot's cockpit, taking a strap out of a socket in the centre section of the top wing and engaging the Thomas Grab, a special hook lowered from the ponder ball of the main purchase of the crane. Pennick's best time for hooking on was fifteen seconds, his worst, in a rather nasty lop, about eighty-five seconds, plus two stitches in his scalp where the Grab struck him a glancing but fairly fierce blow. He was getting quite wet, but only found he was gashed when he wiped what he thought was spray off his face and forehead and found it was red. Aircraft were frequently damaged and quite often capsized.

Pretoria Castle's catapult and crane were also rather ancient affairs, which had been removed from *Warspite* when the battleship was given more modern equipment on refit. Their crane was of the non-compensating type, which made recovery operations in the almost permanent swell of the South Atlantic hazardous at times. A compensating crane would automatically take up the slack in the wire when the aircraft rose on a swell, and pay it out when it fell, but in *Pretoria Castle* the crane operator, on orders from the directing officer, had to pick the moment when the wire had the weight for a snatch recovery.

Being a diesel-engined ship, *Pretoria Castle*, familiarly known as *PC*, was able to do long patrols without refuelling, and her refrigeration and cargo spaces enabled her to be well stocked up with stores. Patrols were of forty-two days' duration, and on these the main enemy was boredom. *PC*'s normal run would begin with a fast convoy to the vicinity of the Cape of Good Hope, followed by forty-two days' patrol, then Freetown for five days' storing and refuelling, before another forty-two day patrol, ten days' relaxation in Cape Town, and back to Belfast for a de-coke and some leave, before starting the whole cycle again.

Though boredom did set in during the long patrols, with the large deck spaces available the ship's company were able to enjoy many organized activities, including deck hockey, and other deck sports, skeet shooting, loader competitions, .22 rifle shooting, and of course Uckers (Bingo). There was also an excellent cinema, with the luxury of two projectors, which did away with the usual "Just one moment while the operator changes the reel." The NAAFI was always well stocked up with goodies, and there was a good "gopher" (fizzy drink) Bar, which also dispensed icecream. These were American luxuries fitted as a matter of course at Newport News. Amateur theatricals and variety shows by the ship's company also filled in many a dull moment.

In spite of these unusual benefits, life was not a pleasure cruise for *PC*. On 26 April, 1942, Doug Elliott, with Sub-Lieutenant Gordon-Smith as observer, was launched at 6.45 on a morning patrol, with orders for return at 9.15 a.m. It was a routine operation, with the Seafox departing on the ship's starboard quarter and sweeping on patrol right round the ship from beam to beam, well ahead. Gordon-Smith was told that so far as was known there were no ships in the area, but they were to return immediately to report any suspicious vessel sighted.

These patrols were normally of about two and a half hours duration, and the Seafox was on the last leg of this one when, at 8.43 a.m. they sighted an unknown steamer some way off. Gordon-Smith ordered Elliott to approach within half a mile. Circling round before coming in for a closer view, Gordon-Smith challenged her with his Aldis lamp. The stranger replied with flag signals, making the identification letters GSLD. The Seafox's crew had no means of decoding them or checking the identity of the ship, as they were not permitted to break radio silence. They flew low over and around her, making a close inspection at close range. She appeared to be a vessel of about 5,000 tons, with one funnel, two slightly raked masts, samson posts on the for'ard side of the mainmast, one derrick hoisted aft, but no structure on the well decks. She carried a merchantman's normal defensive armament, but apparently no anti-aircraft guns. Some of the crew on deck waved at them, and they could see none of the signs that would indicate that she was other than an innocent merchant ship. There seemed to be no places for hidden guns, no dummy masts or funnel, and no suspicious marks on the sides which could have been made by a U-boat rubbing alongside when refuelling. The only unusual features were roundels painted on the hatch covers.

By this time the Seafox's fuel was running low, so Elliott told his observer that they would have to return to the ship, and Gordon-Smith gave him a course to steer. At 9.10 a.m. they turned back for PC, forty miles distant.

During the time of sighting the strange ship and of their investigation a succession of squalls had moved through the area and the wind had freshened, which put them slightly out on their Estimated Time of Arrival, and also affected their dead reckoning navigation. Neither aircraft nor ship had radar or direction-finding gear, and W/T silence was in force.

When *Pretoria Castle* failed to sight the Seafox by 9 a.m. as expected, she broke radio silence and called up the aircraft, and Gordon-Smith said they expected to be back at 9.40, but that time came and it was still nowhere to be seen.

The Seafox had reached its ETA, but there was no sign of PC, so they flew up-wind looking for her, and sighted her about ten miles ahead after about ten minutes. The aircraft's main fuel tank was by this time almost empty and Elliott changed over to the reserve tank, which should have given him about thirty minutes more flying time.

After about two minutes his engine cut dead. He had to force-land into a choppy sea with a heavy swell. As they came down Gordon-Smith signalled, "SOS 270° 5 miles". The Seafox touched down on the rough water and fractured its starboard float struts.

The ship was closing, but the distance was nearer twelve miles than five.

Pretoria Castle came up with the damaged aircraft, but in the choppy sea repeated attempts to recover it failed. It was not until just after 12 noon that it was hoisted inboard, in a sorry state, and Gordon-Smith could report the unknown ship. The identification letters GSLD which she had given belonged to the SS *Anglo Canadian*, but this vessel was not on *Pretoria Castle*'s shipping plot, and it was decided to investigate further.

The suspect's estimated mean line of approach was roughly parallel to *Pretoria Castle*'s own course, and to get well ahead she held on at 16 knots until 1.15 in the afternoon, before turning to intercept. It was anticipated that the quarry would be in sight by 5 o'clock, but by 5.30 she had not been sighted, and *Pretoria Castle* turned to cross the stranger's probable track. At 5.45 she signalled the authorities to ask if the *Anglo Canadian* was in the area, to be told that the latter had arrived in Bombay on 19 April. Further air reconnaissance was impossible, as *PC*'s second Seafox was also unserviceable, and although the ship searched until well after dark nothing was seen of the suspicious vesel, which it was assumed could have been an enemy supply ship. The air search was a frustrating operation, which might have had a better result if so much time had not been lost recovering the Seafox. The origin of the forced landing was investigated and was thought to have been an airlock forming in the refuelling pipe during the final states of refuelling, causing fuel to spout out of the fuelling hole in the aircraft, so that the fitter wrongly assumed the tanks to be full.

Such incidents were part of the game. In fact Doug Elliott experienced another forced landing, in more dangerous circumstances. *PC* was on a fast convoy run escorting the CPR *Empress of Asia*, which was packed with troops for the Middle East. Elliott had been launched, with Sub-Lieutenant Hunt as his observer, and had been flying for about ten minutes out to the patrol point of departure when his engine cut out.

The observer did not have time to get off a distress call before they landed in a roughish sea, damaging one of the floats, which filled with water causing the Seafox to capsize and sink, although before it went under Elliott had the time and presence of mind to recover the Verey pistol, which he secured to himself by knotting his scarf through the trigger guard, and to stuff some cartridges into the pockets of his flying suit.

They had no inflatable dinghy, only the old-fashioned canvas covered "Mae West" lifebelts, which they had to inflate themselves by blowing. They floated in the choppy sea, thinking over their situation. There was little cause for optimism. *PC* and *Empress of Asia* were steaming at speed directly away from them, and did not know they had ditched. *PC*'s other Seafox was unserviceable for flying, and with his charge loaded with troops it was unreasonable to expect the Captain to take the risk of turning the other ships back on track for them when they failed to arrive back on ETA at the end of their patrol time. If he did take the risk it would be highly unlikely that he would find two small specks in the ocean, without the assistance of an aircraft in the search. In the sea conditions prevailing, they were not likely to survive very long, particularly as this was a shark area.

They had been in the water for several hours when Elliott saw what appeared to be a spot in the sky a long way away. Hunt could not see it and was sceptical, but Elliott was convinced that it was an aircraft, hauled up the Verey pistol, loaded it with one of the now damp cartridges, and fired it straight up into the air. Instead of flaring like a normal cartridge it gave off much more smoke, which hung in the air, so Elliott immediately fired two more. The speck drew nearer and turned into the familiar shape of a Seafox.

As soon as it had become obvious that they were overdue, *PC* Flight's other pilot, Sub-Lieutenant Stevent, had speeded up work on the unserviceable aircraft and got it serviceable enough to fly in a search which the Captain decided to lay on with both ships and aircraft. The crew of the Seafox were on the final leg of their search pattern and about to return to the ship when they saw the smoke and conned the ship to the rescue. The helpless airmen had never seen such a marvellous sight as *Empress of Asia* when her three funnels hove into view.

16 Tail O' The Bank

The U-boat offensive in the Atlantic, renewed with even greater determination in the New Year of 1942, reached a peak of intensity in August, when grim battles of attrition were fought between convoys and wolf packs. HMS *Audacity*, the first of the auxiliary carriers to see service with the Royal Navy, had been sunk by a U-boat on 21 December, 1941, after just two round trips to Gibraltar, a fortnight after Japan bombed Pearl Harbor. Five more of these ships had been converted for the RN in American yards, but the first one, HMS *Archer*, was back in the USA with engine trouble, HMS *Avenger* and *Biter* were in Britain for time-consuming modifications and were booked for Torch, the Allied invasion of North Africa, in the autumn, and HMS *Dasher* was about to leave New York for Britain. HMS *Activity*, a British conversion, was to be used for pilot training.

On 18 August *Cheshire* was on passage from Freetown to the United Kingdom when she was hit by a torpedo on the port side of the bow. A hole forty feet by thirty was smashed in the plates, and the starboard side plating perforated in many places. All the structure below the middle deck was distorted. The sea rushed in to fill the forepeak and Number 1 Hold immediately and leak into

Number 2 Hold. The ship's fighting efficiency was seriously impaired, and A Gun could not be trained, but main and auxiliary machinery was undamaged. There were no further attacks – probably because the U-boat had used up all her tinfish – and *Cheshire* continued her voyage home at 8 knots. Repairs and a refit kept her out of action for three months.

Queen of Bermuda, back in service after her big winter refit at Newport News, was soon in dock again. As she was leaving Halifax with a big convoy she backed on to a reef, and her stern was so badly damaged that she could not be steamed. She was towed down the coast to New York, and repaired at the Brooklyn Navy Yard, and at the same time refitted so that she could combine trooping with her cruiser duties. It was an American-type conversion. 2,000 troops were accommodated on one deck only in "standee" berths, and ate in a cafeteria.

When the work was done she escorted a big convoy to Northern Ireland and another one to Iceland with troops. The *Queen* then returned to her old parish of the South Atlantic.

She was searching for a Japanese raider off the South African coast in the dark when she met a strange ship. She signalled the stranger, requesting recognition signals, and was answered with gunfire. The *Queen Bee* returned the fire, and a fierce action began. Both ships sent urgent radio calls for support, both were ordered at once to cease fire. The "enemy" was an American naval tanker from California, but no harm had been done, and the nearest thing to a hit was a shell passing between the *Queen*'s two funnels.

Asturias tracked the Vichy French merchantman *Mendoza* all the way up the South American coast from Montevideo, then pounced and arrested her when she left the three-mile limit off Brazil to cross the Atlantic, and was rushed back to join the Falkland Islands Defence Force to stop a Japanese task force reported heading for the Falklands. At Port Stanley she was given an extra dummy funnel, and steamed up and down between The Plate and Tierra del Fuego with the dummy either up or down and other alterations to her profile, all spare hands on deck in khaki greatcoats – to fool Axis agents that troopships were bringing reinforcements to the Falklands. But the Japanese never came.

Twelve more AMCs were taken out of service in 1942. *Antenor, Ascania, California, Cathay, Circassia, Derbyshire* and *Dunnottar*

Castle became troopship, *Aurania* emerged from her second conversion as the repair ship *Artifex*, *Ausonia* was also turned into a
repair ship, and the Australian *Manoora* into an infantry landing
ship. After conversion to a submarine depot ship, *Montclare* was
bought by the Admiralty and became flagship of the Fleet Train
(Supply) in the Pacific. Most of the remaining twenty-three AMCs
in commission were switched to other duties in 1943.

Cheshire had a memorable last commission as an AMC. Repairs
and refit complete, she sailed on 22 December, 1942, from the Tail
o' the Bank at Greenock in the Clyde in perfect weather to meet
sixteen big liners in battleship grey packed to capacity with troops
bound for North Africa via the Cape of Good Hope, with *Cheshire*
and two small corvettes as their only escorts. The fine weather held
until they rounded the Cape, then they hit the heavy rollers of the
Indian Ocean, but *Cheshire* was ordered back to Montevideo to
pick up a floating dock and see it towed safely to Freetown. The
dock was not ready. *Cheshire* sailed out again, past the rusty,
forlorn wreck of the *Graf Spee*, steered north to enjoy carnival in
Rio, then back to the Plate for the dock. Tugs towed the two
sections, with *Cheshire* in attendance. There were three days of
good progress, then a stiff gale sprang up and the dock sprang a
leak. *Cheshire* left it at Bahia and headed for home across an
Atlantic full of U-boats. *Cheshire* had been twice torpedoed, twice
survived. Those 30,000 oil drums might not save her a third time.

She was trailed by a U-boat in the Western Approaches, but a
Liberator destroyed it. Next day at dusk they heard the sound of
depth-charges and an aircraft from an escort carrier appeared
flashing "Out of control. Ditching". *Cheshire* flashed: "Ditch as
close to my port bow as possible". The first cutter was manned on
the double, and by the time the pilot had circled again and cut his
engine the boat was in the water and pulling hard for the spot off
the port bow where the pilot made a perfect three-point landing
with hardly a splash. *Cheshire* presented a perfect lee, and the boat
had the three men out of the water, returned to the ship and
hooked on just seventeen minutes after the plane had appeared.
Two days later they were in Greenock, and *Cheshire* was paid off
to become a trooper. For a long time in those southern seas the ship
in her grey disguise had been almost the spacious, gracious liner
again.

Queen of Bermuda's last voyage under the White Ensign was as Ocean Escort to the convoy carrying the last Australian troops back from the Middle East to Fremantle, carrying troops herself. She could not compete for speed with the *Queen Mary*, but tried so hard that the other ships gave her a silk ensign. She dodged two U-boats on her way home to be fitted out as a troopship to carry 4,500 men.

Alcantara had returned to Britain after her refit at Newport News, and in March, 1942, joined a big troop convoy going to the occupation of Madagascar. At Freetown *Alcantara* was detached and resumed her old South Atlantic patrol work, with some escorting of convoys to Cape Town and Durban, and trips as radar screen for the *Queen Mary* and *Queen Elizabeth* bringing troops south.

The 7,160-ton Liberty ship *Clymer* of the American Mail Line was a few hundred miles from Ascension Island on 30 May, 1942, carrying mixed cargo and twenty-four aircraft from Portland, Orgeon, to Cape Town, when her main shaft and thrust block bearings split and she broke down. She sent out an SOS. Ascension had an airstrip but no aircraft available at the time for escort. The C-in-C, South Atlantic, was short of ships, but eventually sent *Alcantara*.

The *Clymer* drifted alone for two hundred miles. At 8 p.m. on 6 June a torpedo hit her on the port side between boiler and engine rooms, followed by another further forward, and *Clymer* reported a U-boat attack. Some of her men panicked and took off in the boats, but her gunners remained behind, and at 8 a.m. next morning she was still afloat. A British aircraft flew over her and signalled that help was on its way, and *Alcantara* poured on the power to get there, keeping double lookouts for U-boats.

But the *Clymer* had not been hit by a U-boat. The attack had been made by the disguised raider *Michel*'s special motor boat *Esau*, a 37-foot, 11½-ton, 42½-knot craft armed with two torpedo tubes and a 20-millimetre gun.

The *Alcantara* arrived at four o'clock that afternoon and found the tough Liberty ship still seaworthy. The AMC got her towing hawser out, but *Clymer*'s load of wooden railway sleepers and deck cargo of tractors for Iran made her an almost impossible tow. Meanwhile Leutnant von Schack had taken *Esau* back to the

Michel to be congratulated by von Ruckteschell, who stayed well over the horizon.

Alcantara struggled on with her Herculean labour for a week, casting off the tow at night and leaving the scene, while Washington, London and Freetown argued about what to do with the *Clymer* and her cargo. Eventually it was decided to sink her. But her buoyant cargo made that difficult. *Alcantara* blew holes in her side with shell fire to allow the timber to float out, but this was a very slow process. Attempts to sink her by aircraft bombing failed too. Finally depth-charges dropped right beneath her broke her keel and when the *Alcantara* cleared off, *Clymer* was bottom-up and too low in the water to register as an echo on RDF. Some weeks later a ship reported an obstruction to navigation in the area. The sleepers were still holding the *Clymer* up. *Alcantara* went on to search for blockade runners off the Cape, escorted a floating dock from Trinidad to Freetown, and was finally paid off as an AMC on 30 June, 1943, to become a troopship.

The escort carriers, converted merchantmen, were the new auxiliaries, and there was a new development, the Merchant Aircraft Carriers or MAC Ships, cargo-carrying grainers or tankers with a flight deck and three or four Swordfish aircraft with rockets or depth-charges. Forty-six escort carriers were commissioned into the Royal Navy in World War 2, five converted in British yards, the remainder in the USA.

The AMC *Pretoria Castle* was converted into an aircraft carrier and became Trials and Deck Landing Training Carrier for the "Woolworth carriers'" new pilots. On *PC*'s return to the Tail o' the Bank to pay off before her second conversion, it was decided to lower her seaplane over the side and taxi it ashore to the local seaplane base. During the run something holed one of the floats. As the pilot and observer had their "rabbits" in the aircraft, a mad race ensued to reach the beach before the holed float filled with water. They just made it.

Asturias remained on armed duty in the South Atlantic. In July, 1943, she went to Bahia to escort the floating dock which *Cheshire* had brought up from Montevideo across to Dakar. She started from Bahia with the two sections of the dock and five frigates and corvettes just before midnight on 24 July and had reached a point 400 miles from her destination when the track of a torpedo was sighted heading for her. The alarm rattlers were sounded, the wheel swung hard-a-starboard, and the torpedo narrowly missed the bows. Less than a minute later a second torpedo hit the ship just abaft the forward bulkhead of the boiler room on the port side, killing three firemen and greasers and the engineer on watch in the engine room, and tearing a hole twenty-three feet by twenty, through which the sea poured, flooding the boiler room, engine room, auxiliary machinery room, galley and deep oil fuel tanks. The ship listed to port, lost all lighting and power. In four minutes there were thirty feet of water in the engine room. *Asturias* was stopped and helpless; the dock and its other escorts carried on.

The bulkheads held. The frigates *Exe* and *Moyala* turned back with portable pumps which got rid of some of the water in *Asturias*, frequently choking on tea leaves, flour and peas in the flooded stores. The Admiral's quarters fitted in the ship was used to store Brazilian bottled beer, and "All hands to Admiral's quarters for ham sandwiches and beer" was piped. A big ocean-going tug arrived but struggled to cope with the big ship and the 10,000 tons of water inside her. *Asturias* rigged a huge sail, made from deck awnings sewn together, on the fore-topmast forward stay to help keep the ship's head on course. At last, on 1 August *Asturias* reached Freetown, and lay there for eighteen months, infested with rats, cockroaches and white ants, and was finally towed home early in 1945, too late for any more war service but useful for the emigrant service to Australia.

Canton returned to Britain from South Atlantic duty in July, 1942, was refitted, and she, *Corfu* and *Cilicia* were equipped with American Kingfisher seaplanes, which had twice the range (908 miles) of the old Seafoxes and 50 mph more speed (152 mph cruising, 171 maximum).

Corfu, as she was finally fitted out, was one of the best equipped of all AMCs, with nine 6-inch guns, two twin 4-inch anti-aircraft guns, two 2-pounder guns and nineteen 20-millimetre Oerlikons, two Kingfisher seaplanes and catapult, air and surface warning radar, and a high-angle director-control-tower fitted with gunnery control radar. It was all a distinct advance on Emergency Equipment. *Corfu* spent from 3 March, 1943, to 7 December, 1943, and *Cilicia* from 6 January, 1943, to 4 January, 1944, on duty in the South Atlantic.

Canton arrived in the Indian Ocean in February, 1943, to join the Eastern Fleet, first at Kilindini in East Africa, where it had been forced to retreat by the Japanese, and later at Colombo, where it returned in September, 1943. Also serving with the Eastern Fleet were the AMCs *Alaunia*, *Bulolo*, *Carthage*, *Chitral*, *Kanimbla*, *Rajputana*, *Ranchi*, *Ranpura* and *Worcestershire*, until one by one they left to become troopers. They followed a mostly unspectacular routine of convoy escort between Bombay and Aden or Socotra across the Arabian Sea, with occasional raider hunts and odd jobs like *Chitral*'s urgent trip to Durban to lift dockyard machinery across to Diego Suarez. On 30 September *Rajputana* rescued survivors from the British merchantman *Banffshire*, sunk by a U-boat in the Indian Ocean. In January, 1944, *Canton* joined the cruisers *Newcastle*, *Kenya* and *Suffolk*, the escort carrier HMS *Battler*, the frigate *Bann* and the destroyer *Nepal* for Operation Thwart, mounted to intercept a blockade runner reported to be making for Europe from Japan. The ships, *Battler*'s Swordfish and three Catalina flying boats made wide sweeps to the south and southeast from Mauritius but Thwart was thwarted of any results. This was *Canton*'s last operation as an AMC, and all the remaining armed merchant cruisers were also paid off in 1944, most of them to become troopships, with the *Monowai* and the Canadian AMCs *Prince David*, *Prince Henry* and *Prince Robert* being turned into infantry landing ships.

In the early part of the war some small merchant ships were fitted with concealed guns and classed as Special Service Vessels. For a time they operated as decoy or Q-ships, with the aim of trapping U-boats as in World War 1, altering their appearance with dummy funnels, derricks, deckhouses, deck cargoes, and changing their names from time to time. But the arming of ordinary merchant ships kept the U-boats down, and the decoy ships had no success. Four of them then served as AMCs in the Pacific, looking for German disguised raiders, but none came their way.

There were ten of these ships, *Antoine/Orchy*, *Brutus/City of Durban*, *Chatsgrove*, *Cape Sable/Cyprus*, *Edgehill*, *Fidelity*, *Lambridge/Botlea*, *Looe*, *Maunder/King Gruffyd*, and *Prunella*. They were armed according to size with from four to nine 4-inch guns, two to four 21-inch torpedo tubes, and depth-charges. *King Gruffyd* had seven 4-inch guns and four torpedo tubes, *City of*

Durban eight, later nine, 4-inch guns, one 12-pounder AA and two 2-pounder AA guns. *Fidelity* as originally armed had three 4-inch guns, two 75-millimetre, one 37mm, three 25mm and one 20mm AA. *Edgehill* and *Prunella* were sunk early on, and all the others, except *Fidelity*, taken out of service in 1941. *Fidelity* had her armament increased on the lines of the German disguised merchant raiders to include four 4-inch guns, four torpedo tubes, two aircraft and a motor torpedo boat. She was returned to Special Service but was unsuccessful and was eventually sunk by a U-boat.

"Most definitely," writes an ex-World War 2 armed merchant cruiser officer, "the AMCs were but token men of war and certainly recognised as such by all who sailed in them. Later there were some reasonable conversions but even they were not popular. The handicaps of bulk and slow speed made them particularly vulnerable."

"Token men of war" they undoubtedly were. Vulnerable they were. "Suicide ships" they have been called. Yet they were a solid part of the fabric of naval warfare, to which they made a very positive contribution.

In the First World War HMS *Carmania* destroyed *Cap Trafalgar* before she could begin her career, and though badly damaged lived to continue service. The first *Alcantara*, of 1916, was lost but her interception destroyed the *Greif*, again before she could attack Allied shipping; the second *Alcantara* made the aggressive *Thor* retreat, though at great cost to herself. *Rawalpindi*, like a true cruiser, gave her Admiral warning of the enemy before succumbing to odds which would have crushed much greater resistance than she could put up, and in fighting doggedly to the finish she was a source of inspiration at a time when the British public needed an example of courage and self-sacrifice. *Jervis Bay* needs no apologia. Against such overwhelming strength her defeat as a ship was inevitable. But she saved her convoy, and that was a victory.

The loss of ship after British ship to enemy submarine torpedoes was also inevitable, for the AMCs were perfect targets. But against these losses must be set all that the AMCs achieved in carrying out the blockade. Their success can be counted in vessels intercepted, ships boarded in dangerous seas, disguised enemies identified and captured, guilty neutrals apprehended.

The addition of aircraft to an auxiliary cruiser greatly improved her potential as a fighting ship. This was proved positively as early as 1917 by the raider *Wolf* and her *Wölfchen*. This small, frail floatplane helped *Wolf* slip the blockade and saved her from discovery, as well as spotting for victims. In the Royal Navy in the First World War landplanes were flown successfully from platforms on cruisers, and HMS *Yarmouth*'s Sopwith shot down a Zeppelin, but the auxiliary cruisers were poor relations and were never given the new weapon which might have made blockade and raider hunting easier and the U-boats' job harder.

The British Admiralty intended to remedy this mistake in the Second World War, but lacked the means. There were grave shortages of both aircraft and catapults for boosting off. What catapults could be begged (usually from battleships or regular cruisers refitting) were used to equip the Fighter Catapult and Catapult Aircraft Merchant ships to fight the Focke Wulf Condor menace, which in the event turned out to have been overestimated, and the regular cruisers got the aircraft. The AMCs were the Cinderellas again, when just one old Seafox or Swordfish on floats might have saved *Rawalpindi*, or given *Jervis Bay* more warning. *Scheer* with her "ship's parrot" Arado seaplane had it all on her side. Pet aircraft might well have saved some of the AMCs butchered by submarine. U-boat skippers did not like the presence of aircraft, and a puffin in flight was enough to keep some of them down out of harm's way. The fitting of some AMCs with aircraft and catapults came very late in the day. HMS *Corfu*, in her final version, was impressive, with her two aircraft and her gunnery control radar.

As the Commonwealth shrank, the traditional role of the cruiser in guarding the old Empire sea routes withered. No merchant ships were stiffened after the Second World War, either to carry guns or aircraft. Hawker Siddeley Aviation, later part of British Aerospace, consistently advocated making provision in merchant ships for the operation of their V/STOL Harriers, which could take off and land on small platforms, and developed schemes for the use of container ships as light carriers, but the Navy, slow to adopt the Harrier anyway, ignored them.

On 2 April, 1982, Argentine forces invaded the Falklands. Britain, her surface fleet in the process of run-down after the 1981 White Paper *The Way Forward*, was faced with the challenge of mounting a major amphibious assault 8,000 miles away from the

UK, in the worst weather, with the nearest base over 3,000 miles to the north on Ascension Island.

If she was short of warships, with no substitutes in the merchant fleet, there was an even greater lack of ships to make up the massive support force needed. As never before, the Merchant Navy was called on for help, with previous experience this time restricted to practice in using car/passenger ferries to move troops to Europe, and the reserving of two BP tankers as escort oilers.

Over fifty ships were in the end requisitioned or chartered, out-numbering the warships involved. The golden days of the great liners were long gone, and there were only nine large liners left under the British flag. The P & O's 44,807-ton *Canberra* was snatched from a Mediterranean cruise and in seven days converted into a troopship which took the 3,000 men of 3 Para and the Royal Marine Commandos south to Falkland Sound. She lived dangerously through the first landing, suffered the first air attack and saw *Ardent* sunk close by. The educational cruise ship *Uganda* disembarked her schoolchildren at Naples and at Gib became a 1,000-bed hospital ship in sixty-five hours. The great 67,140-ton *Queen Elizabeth* 2 was swiftly modified to move the 5th Infantry Brigade of Scots and Welsh Guards. Helicopter platforms were built over the strongpoints of swimming pools with stiffening steel rushed from Wales and the Midlands. Thirteen other ships had heli-pads fitted. Ro-Ro ferries transported troops, ammunition, tanks, bridges. Sealink's *St Edmund* had her bow doors welded up against the savage weather of the South Atlantic.

Fifteen merchant tankers supplemented fourteen RFA oilers and were modified for refuelling at sea. The 5-crew diving and surface oil-rig support ship *Stena Seaspread*, which could hold her position within 3 metres in force 9 winds, was hauled out of the North Sea Thistle Alpha field and with her sister *Stena Inspector* sent south with the contents of a Portsmouth heavy machine shop as a repair ship. She repaired eleven ships battle-damaged by rocket or bomb, including HMS *Glamorgan*, whose five hundred survivors she also fed aboard. Seven vessels, from 5,000 to 12,000 tons, were requisitioned as store ships. They lifted missiles, ammunition, fork lifts, trucks, garage equipment, cargo lighters and mountains of military stores. *Strathmere*, commandeered in the Indian Ocean, was even armed – with two old Oerlikons.

The cable ship *Iris* became a despatch vessel, carrying essential stores, mail and personnel between Ascension Island and the Task Force. The new ocean-going tug *Wimpey Seahorse* saw service as a mooring vessel. With enemy mines to clear, the little offshore RN minesweepers were inadequate for the trip and the weather, and the two available 650-ton *Hunt* class sweepers could not make it without a mother ship, normally HMS *Abdiel*, again not up to the job. RMS *St Helena*. 3,150 tons, much modified, became the mother. Meanwhile five sturdy deep-sea trawlers which could stay with heavy seas for sixty days were quickly fitted with sweeping gear as the 16th Minesweeping Squadron. Most ships needed copious modifications – extra store rooms, cabins, lavatories (often Portakabins and Portaloos) for many extra men, RAS gear, control equipment for helicopters, even new transverse bulkheads for safety in emergency load conditions (designed on Ship Department's computer in Bath), UHF and satellite communications gear, and some experimental reverse osmosis desalination plant for extra fresh water. None of this was in reserve; all had to be scrambled together in a hurry.

Then there were the aircraft ferries, all converted container ships. The Task Force's two carriers, HMS *Hermes* and *Invincible*, had to anticipate losses of 10–15% of aircraft. These the ferries would have to replace, or the whole operation could be threatened. So it was that the first major unplanned conversion of the STUFT (Ships Taken Up From Trade) fleet was the 15,000-ton container ship *Atlantic Conveyor*, about to return to trade from reserve.

In Devonport Dockyard the part of the upper, container deck which was to serve as the landing area was strenghtened to take landing Harriers and heavy-duty Chinook helicopters. Huge 15-ton panels were made at one end of the Dockyard and brought two miles to the ship. Containers were stacked round the sides of the open container deck to protect the aircraft from the sea. UHF and satcom were fitted, helicopter and V/STOL control gear, a 5-ton liquid oxygen tank, accommodation for 122 extra men, more life rafts, new ladders, extra hatches, and her stern doors were modified to unload in an open anchorage. She sailed in eleven days. From Ascension she carried a mix of twenty-five Harriers and helicopters.

There was no thought of using the unarmed *Atlantic Conveyor* to *operate* her aircraft, though one Harrier was kept at standby, but when she reached Falklands waters Task Force Harriers began using her as a third carrier. On 25 May, Argentine's national day, enemy aircraft made a series of attacks. Bombs from four Skyhawks sank HMS *Coventry*, and two Super Etendards sortied with two of Argentine's last remaining Exocets, looking for a carrier or the *Canberra*. The ship they found was the *Atlantic Conveyor*, loaded with Chinook choppers and fuel for San Carlos. One Exocet hit the *Conveyor*, killing twelve of her crew, including Captain Ian North, the bearded lookalike to Captain Birdseye of the TV commercial, and sinking the ship.

Following *Atlantic Conveyor*, her sister ship the *Atlantic Causeway* carried the re-formed RN 825 Squadron of Sea King and Wessex 5 Commando helicopters to the fight. This was a famous squadron, which had attacked *Scharnhorst* and *Gneisenau* in the Second World War and flown Swordfish on Russian convoy runs from the escort carrier HMS *Vindex*, a converted merchantman. ("What we need down there," reflected her old Senior Pilot in 1982, "is another *Vindex*.") The smaller *Contender Bezant*, 11,445 tons, was fitted with a hangar aft of her forward bridge, and a flight deck over her after hatch covers. Largest of this breed was the *Astronomer*, 27,867 tons, which had a hangar for'ard with a plated roof, and facilities for repairing and servicing helicopters. She had a token armament of two Second World War Oerlikon 20mm cannon.

From the Falkland aircraft ferries have come some interesting new developments in armed merchantmen. On 3 March, 1984, it was announced that Harland & Wolff of Belfast had won a £30 million contract to convert the *Contender Bezant* into an "aircraft training vessel" for the Royal Navy. She was also to replace the RFA *Engadine*, which had been one of the first ships to land a Harrier on her heli-pad. This was followed by the conversion of the *Astronomer* into the RFA *Reliant*, a Helicopter Support Ship, at Cammell Laird's.

Astronomer needed little structural modification, merely enough to allow the fitting of a standard prefabricated helicopter deck to the cargo hold covers. All the rest of the extra equipment is based on quickly fitted containers – hangar and aircraft control facilities, operating systems for lightweight defence missiles, accommodation and domestic facilities (including freshwater production and sewage plants) for extra personnel, fuel supply, support stores and various storage tanks. In this way a commercial container ship can be quickly and cheaply converted into a warship – in this case to operate five Sea King helicopters and service other aircraft, but other options are available.

A container ship can be similarly fitted, within as little as forty-eight hours, with containerized units covering her conversion to a Harrier light aircraft carrier, including containerized runway and skijump, or a helicopter assault ship – both with containerized missile defence systems.

A wide range of general cargo merchant ships could also be fitted with various containerized weapon systems, including Lightweight Seawolf (for defence against aerial targets including sea-skimming missiles like Exocet), Lightweight Sea Dart (air defence or surface-to-surface), Sea Eagle SL (advanced anti-ship system), Ikara long-range missile system for anti-submarine homing torpedoes, gun and electro-optical fire control, electronic countermeasures and decoy systems. Containerized facilities for a Harrier or helicopter could also be fitted.

The role of the Royal Navy under NATO is based on the defence of North Atlantic convoys. Merchant ships armed swiftly and cheaply with a variety of these containerized weapon systems should be able to defend a convoy effectively against attack, freeing regular warships for more flexible use, or be valuable as independent warships themselves in an active seek and destroy role. Such vessels could be the most effective armed merchant cruisers ever commissioned.

Index

Willis, Chief Steward, 73
Wilson, Captain A.K., 6, 7, 8, 9, 10
Wilson, Thomas, 39, 44
Wimpey Seahorse, 212
Winand, Captain Joseph, 119, 120
Winter, Captain, 175
Wirth, Korvettenkapitän Julius, 22, 23, 24, 25, 26, 27, 28, 29–30
Wolf, 65, 75–6, 156, 210
Wölfchen seaplanes, 65, 156, 210
Wolfe, 141, 143–4
Wood, Leading Seaman, 170
Woodward, Captain Walter, 92–3
Worcestershire, 120, 130, 132, 183–4, 208

Workman Clark, 180
World War I: AMCs engaged in, 13–93, 209
World War II: AMCs engaged in, 98–209
Worth, Leading Seaman Alf, 71, 72
Wyniatt, PO Pyndar, 124
Wynter, Captain, 148

Yarmouth, 210
Yarrowdale, 66, 69–70, 73, 75; renamed *Leopard, q.v.*
Young, Captain, 53, 54, 55, 56, 59, 61

Zimmermann, Arthur, 80